3 40

W9-BUZ-030

THE
SOCIAL & POLITICAL IDEAS
OF SOME ENGLISH THINKERS
OF THE AUGUSTAN AGE
A.D. 1650–1750

THE
SOCIAL & POLITICAL IDEAS
OF SOME ENGLISH THINKERS
OF THE AUGUSTAN AGE
A.D. 1650-1750

A SERIES OF LECTURES DELIVERED AT
KING'S COLLEGE UNIVERSITY OF LONDON
DURING THE SESSION 1927-28

EDITED BY
F. J. C. HEARNSHAW M.A. LL.D.
FELLOW OF KING'S COLLEGE AND PROFESSOR OF MEDIÆVAL
HISTORY IN THE UNIVERSITY OF LONDON

NEW YORK
BARNES & NOBLE, INC.

First published 1923
Reprinted 1950 by special arrangement with
GEORGE G. HARRAP & CO., LTD.
39-41 Parker Street, Kingsway, London, W.C. 2

G 647

PREFACE

THE term "Augustan Age," as applied to literature, denotes, of course, primarily the period 31 B.C. to A.D. 14, during which Cæsar Augustus ruled as *princeps* over the Roman world. It was the period within which Virgil and Horace, Propertius and Tibullus, Ovid and Livy, flourished and wrote. The common characteristics of the widely varying works of these eminent men were, on the one hand, an unprecedented perfection of form, but, on the other hand, a certain decline from the originality and vigour of the less polished writings of their predecessors. The age was self-conscious and critical rather than spontaneous and creative.

These same features—external splendour, internal decadence—have marked other periods in the history of other countries, and in particular the reign of Louis XIV in French history, together with the age which in English history saw the fall of the Stuarts and the accession of the Hanoverians. Hence to these periods too the name "Augustan" has been appropriately applied. In England the outstanding figure in the literary world of the first half of the Augustan Age was Dryden; that of the second half was Pope. It is not, of course, possible to assign precise date-limits to an era so vague and indefinite as one distinguished by the form and content of its literary masterpieces. For the purposes of the present volume, however, the rather wide extremes of A.D. 1650 and A.D. 1750 are taken. During this century the strenuous animosities of Roundheads and Cavaliers died down into the petty bickerings of Whigs and Tories; while the ferocious fanaticisms of Puritans and Papists subsided into the polite argumentations of rationalistic Latitudinarians with the almost indistinguishable Deistic rationalists. Simultaneously with this fall in controversial temperature occurred a marked rise in literary lucidity. The majestic and magnificent confusion of Milton's prose was reduced to the ordered beauty of Dryden's musical periods; the rugged

5

eloquence of Hobbes was subdued to the smooth monotony of Locke; the incoherent outpourings of Cromwell's dæmonic oratory were refined to the golden glory of Bolingbroke's brilliant verbiage.

The Augustan Age in English history, therefore, was not marked by any large output of original ideas, social or political. Hence the term " great," which figured in the titles of the preceding three volumes of this series, has been deliberately omitted from the title of this volume. It is true that one of the thinkers here treated, viz., John Locke, was indubitably great : his philosophy marked a distinct stage in the development of European thought. But a single swallow does not make a summer ; and, further, in political and social theory Locke owed too much to such predecessors as Hooker and Hobbes to rank as a pioneer. Apart from Locke, the thinkers dealt with in this volume were, as compared with those treated in the earlier volumes, small fry. They were concerned rather with party problems than with eternal principles ; they wrote concerning the controversies of the fleeting moment rather than concerning the questions common to all mankind at all times.

The party politics of this Augustan Age were, nevertheless, peculiarly interesting. The century under review was the period in which Whiggism and Toryism took shape, and beneath the surface of the disputatious details respecting which the champions of these two systems brawled there lay implicit fundamental differences of social and political philosophy. Whiggism stood for progress, movement, novelty, adventure, freedom, the future ; Toryism stood for order, stability, tradition, security, authority, the past. The Whigs were the party that supported Parliament, Nonconformity, commerce, industry, the moneyed interest, an active and aggressive foreign policy ; the Tories were the party that supported the Crown, the Established Church, agriculture, rural life, the landed interest, an isolated England defended from " the envy of less happier lands " by a strong and loyal navy. There was no ' middle party '; and so long as politics are determined by principle and not by interest there can be no ' middle party.' All who are not sheep are goats ; and both sheep and goats have their indispensable uses. Of the writers treated in this book Halifax alone tried to be a ' trimmer '; the completeness of his failure

6

PREFACE

will be evident to all who study Professor Reed's sympathetic sketch. Of the rest, Locke, Hoadly, and Defoe were Whigs; Filmer, Swift, and Bolingbroke were Tories.

Filmer in point of time stands rather apart from his fellows. He died in 1653, and he wrote his *Patriarcha* some eleven years earlier. This best-known book of his, however, was not published until 1680, when it played a prominent part in the Exclusion Bill controversy, and to its confutation Locke devoted the first section of his great treatise on *Civil Government.* All our other thinkers were contemporaries: the last to be born was Bolingbroke (A.D. 1678); the first to die was Halifax (A.D. 1695). For the seventeen years between these two dates the whole band of them were simultaneously militant here on earth. Whence it follows that the studies included in this volume have the peculiar feature that they all treat of the same series of events; they all display their subjects against the same historic background; they all reveal the same social and political phenomena from different points of view. It is hoped that this conspectus will conduce to a more complete and comprehensive understanding of the complex age under survey than would any other method of study.

Perhaps I may mention in closing that the next series of lectures projected will deal with some notable French thinkers —*e.g.,* Montesquieu, Voltaire, Rousseau—of the Age of Reason.

F. J. C. HEARNSHAW

King's College
University of London
May 1928

CONTENTS

PAGE

I. INTRODUCTORY : THE AUGUSTAN AGE   11
By G. N. CLARK, M.A., Fellow of Oriel College, Oxford.

II. SIR ROBERT FILMER   27
By J. W. ALLEN, M.A., late Professor of History at Bedford College, London.

III. GEORGE SAVILE, MARQUIS OF HALIFAX   47
By A. W. REED, M.A., D.Lit., Professor of English at King's College, London.

IV. JOHN LOCKE   69
By C. H. DRIVER, M.A., Assistant Lecturer in History at King's College, London.

V. JACOBITES AND NON-JURORS   97
By H. BROXAP, M.A.

VI. BENJAMIN HOADLY, BISHOP OF BANGOR   112
By the Rev. NORMAN SYKES, M.A., D.Phil., Lecturer in History at King's College, London.

VII. DANIEL DEFOE   157
By Miss A. E. LEVETT, M.A., Reader in Economic History at King's College, London.

VIII. JONATHAN SWIFT   189
By G. B. HARRISON, M.A., Lecturer in English at King's College, London.

IX. HENRY ST JOHN, VISCOUNT BOLINGBROKE   210
By the EDITOR.

9

THE SOCIAL AND POLITICAL IDEAS OF SOME ENGLISH THINKERS OF THE AUGUSTAN AGE

I

INTRODUCTORY

THE AUGUSTAN AGE

THE course to which the present lecture serves as an introduction is to deal with the social and political ideas of some English thinkers who wrote in a period of which the end was nearly two hundred years ago, and the length about what we commonly reckon as three generations. It begins just before the Restoration of King Charles II. It covers the twenty-five years of intrigue and excitement through which he dexterously kept his crown. It takes in the reign of Charles's brother James II, who was ousted by his son-in-law William of Orange and his daughter, who became Queen Mary. After the time of these successful revolutionists it leads us through the glorious reign of Mary's younger sister Queen Anne, in which domestic politics still revolved round the chances of plots and counterplots, into the more comfortable days of the Georges, when counter-revolution ceased to be a serious possibility, when fallen ministers retired to the country instead of fleeing to the Continent, and the United Kingdom settled down to become powerful and rich without the Stuart dynasty and all it had meant. What the Stuarts had meant to themselves and to contemporaries, and what were the other ideas which political writers opposed to theirs or tried to reconcile with them : these are the subjects with which we shall be occupied. The political events, Parliamentary divisions, movements of troops and fleets, State trials, impeachments, executions, were in the background of the social and political ideas. They were present to the minds of these authors as they sat writing; so much so that most of their works were pamphlets or books of no great length, written without delay and without too much consideration, consciously intended to have a practical effect, to uphold or to destroy some existing political fact. But even the most practical of them express something more than the men of action could have put into words : they supply a commentary without which the meaning of the events could not be seized.

There is, to be sure, but little in the commentary about the first of our events, the Restoration. During the preceding twenty years of civil war and constitutional experiment there had been an abundance, indeed an excess, of speculative writing of every kind. The theorists had been so bold and vociferous that the average man was wearied, and Charles II, who, with all his cleverness, had much in common with the average man, came back to deliver him not only from the rule of the saints, but also from their arguments. His restoration did more than end an heroic age in English politics and action : it ended also the heroic age of English political thought. It did not come about as the result of propaganda or literary persuasion. It was neither heralded nor, for the time being, justified, nor even opposed by any writer of even secondary weight. The days of the great controversialists seemed to be over. Thomas Hobbes was nearing eighty years of age, a harmless pensioner of Charles, a bear to be baited by the wits of the Court, writing little about the State and uncertain whether the King would permit him to publish even that little. Monarchy had no need of theorists now, for it had no longer any fear of the theorists of liberty. For them it was a time of humiliation. Selden, Lilburne, Winstanley, had not survived to see it. James Harrington was imprisoned, to be liberated only when he had lost his reason. One only, the greatest of them all, remained the man he had been, and his judgment on the new era may be read in the words of his Samson :

> But what more oft, in nations grown corrupt,
> And by their vices brought to servitude,
> Than to love bondage more than liberty—
> Bondage with ease than strenuous liberty—
> And to despise, or envy, or suspect
> Whom God hath of His special favour raised
> As their deliverer ?

Nevertheless, although the wars were ended, although one side was down and the other triumphant, the history of the succeeding years was a continuation of the past, and its quarrels, less bloody, but scarcely less passionate, turned on the same differences of principle which had led to the Civil War. We know now that fallen institutions can no more be restored than dilapidated buildings. The restorers of Charles II believed their somewhat modified structure to be the old monarchy, much as the Gothic revivalists believed their reconstructed buildings to be mediæval. Some of the more odious and some of the more cumbrous institutions were indeed not revived, but it was not anticipated that there would still be radical criticisms of the working of monarchy and a formidable opposition to the Court. As the long reign of Charles wore on these dangers came in sight. The historic party divisions arose upon which the political development of the country was woven throughout the eighteenth and nineteenth centuries. The English became a nation of Whigs and Tories. Those names have signified different things at different times, but they had a real continuity and a real affinity with the old differences of Roundheads and Cavaliers. So much was this the case that our period was first and foremost a sequel to the last, a sequel in which, under changed conditions and in a new environment, the fortunes of the earlier drama were reversed, and the heirs of the conquerors were gradually dispossessed by those whom the Restoration had overthrown. The dominance of party was reflected in political thought. Of the writers with whom we shall be concerned almost every one took a hand in party politics. The only one who lay under the reproach of not being a robust party man was the 'trimmer' Halifax, and Bolingbroke, who wrote against the spirit of party, was the most violent partisan of all.

It is partly for this reason, their closeness to current political controversy, that few of them hold a high place among writers on the fundamental problems of political obligation. The only one who can seriously be called a philosopher is John Locke. Locke's position in the history of thought is very eminent. Covering in his voluminous works a great range of subjects, both speculative and practical, he almost always succeeded in hitting exactly that level of reasonableness and moderation which satisfied the minds of his readers. He was on the side of toleration and liberty, but he never soared high in their praises like Milton. He was against the sovereignty of the State, and he believed in the responsibility of rulers to their subjects ; but he was so far from being a subversive thinker that he made the maintenance of property the first end of civil government. He had the knack of writing as though his general principles, far from being the elaborate products of centuries of disputation, were simply what occurred to him when he applied his orderly mind to the subject without prepossessions. It is seldom that he indicates his relation to earlier writers on theoretical matters. He happens in one place to tell us that, shortly before his death and after all his important works were written, he has never read the one political book we should have thought him most likely to read, Algernon Sydney's posthumous *Discourses concerning Government.* By the same chance we know that he was acquainted with the works of a now forgotten country baronet, whose marble tombstone, in a Buckinghamshire village church, is surmounted by an angel holding a tablet inscribed with the presumptuous words " HOBBES REFUTED." But the ancestry of Locke's ideas is hard to trace. He set them out as though they were quite natural and straightforward. His own generation and the next for the most part accepted them at his valuation, so that they became a sort of orthodoxy with the dominant Whig party, and for many years met with little criticism of any importance from outside it. Locke's influence produced a calm in the region, formerly so stormy, of the philosophical theory of the State.

The area of disturbance was the problem of the relations between the State and the Church or Churches. Like the old Puritan revolution, the new party warfare had some of its greatest causes in religious strife. The Restoration had brought back not only the Stuart monarchy, but also the Established Church, and against his better judgment the great Lord Chancellor Clarendon had allowed that Church to become once more intolerant. Charles and James had deserted it by becoming Roman Catholics, so that, until the Protestant succession was finally made certain at the death of Queen Anne, the history of parties was inextricably involved in the three-cornered contests and shifting combinations of Anglicans, Romanists, and

Protestant Dissenters. Our period exactly coincides with that of the Vicar of Bray. He and his less flexible fellows were directly affected by every political change, and did what they could to control the course of events. We find therefore that the authors we are considering are not only party men, but also men much taken up with ecclesiastical affairs. Swift was a dean and Hoadly a bishop. The Non-Jurors were perhaps more religious and certainly more clerical. Even the layman Locke wrote about natural theology. Between them they made many important steps in the long process of reconciling the ideals of free Churches and a free State.

It is not within the scope of this introductory lecture to examine their opinions in detail. What we must now consider are preliminary questions which will give us our bearings for beginning that task, and first we must ask what new influences came in from outside to aid in the working out of these old conflicts, to modify the problems and lead to new solutions, new compromises, new problems. Political life, of course, never stands still; but, besides having to adapt itself to this variable subject-matter, political thought has also independent sources of variation of its own. Not only are the problems different, but men bring to them different minds, and we must see what were the tendencies extraneous to English politics which at that time acted on political ideas. There is one such force which had been very active in the earlier phases of English political thought, and was soon to be so again, but which in this period deserves little attention. That is the infection of ideas imported from foreign countries. In the sixteenth century it had been a great dynamic influence. The Continental Reformation had started an upheaval of ideas, and all through the earlier seventeenth century the political writers of England were stimulated, whether in the way of sympathy or the way of opposition, by the writings of the protagonists in those great debates. That was now ended. The time of the last Stuarts was one of the periods in which England had least to learn from abroad. History had made of her what she still remains, an exceptional country. There was nothing else like her ecclesiastical polity or her embryonic constitutional monarchy. Only one other country which was at all important to her shared to some extent her exceptional position, the Dutch republic; but, although political thought was not inactive in Holland at this time, it was so much concerned with conditions peculiar to Holland, or at least unknown to England, that its influence here amounted to comparatively little. It cannot, indeed, be denied that Dutch freedom powerfully assisted English freedom in thought as in action. Just as Dutch armies intervened more than once against the Stuarts, so Dutch ideas and institutions helped to mould the opinions of Englishmen who went there, like Sir William Temple as ambassadors, or like Locke himself as political refugees. But it is hard to trace any close or detailed coincidences, borrowings, or reactions between the political authors of the two nations. The Dutch influence, though strong, was not particularised, but broad and atmospheric.

Elsewhere on the Continent political thought had got into a stage in which it had little to teach. Most of our authors belong to the period in which Europe was dominated by the armies and the policy of Louis XIV, and in which the intellectual ascendancy of France even surpassed her political hegemony. Monarchy on the French model was making headway everywhere save in the few exceptional countries, of which only England and Holland were prosperous and energetic. As monarchy progressed it overshadowed political thought, and until the last phase of Louis's reign the general upshot in France and the countries which imitated France was the completion of the theory of despotism. In Louis's closing years his defeats and his tyrannical oppressions provoked a movement of liberalism; but it was not such as to have any message for the island neighbour where more thoroughgoing doctrines of freedom had been known for long before. It is true that one of its classical books, the *Télémaque* of Fénelon, had, at a later date if not immediately, a large circulation in England; but it may be presumed that it was esteemed here mainly for that quality of harmless high-mindedness which made it in the reign of Queen Victoria the favourite of young ladies' schools. The broad truth is that in political thought at that time England gave and did not take. The name of Locke stood higher abroad than the name of any foreign political writer stood at home. Even Bolingbroke, who lived long in exile in France, and in some directions owed much to French thought, influenced Continental writers more than he was influenced by them.

Great changes in thought were, however, in progress, in which the English, the Dutch, and the French alike had their shares, which had their centre far from politics, but profoundly changed the methods by which political problems were approached. They were changes in the general conduct of thought so fundamental that, however remote their origin, they could not leave politics untouched. It is a familiar truth that the history of political thought is a department of the history of thought in general, and that it is constantly liable to invasion from the neighbouring departments. This very period affords, for instance, some among many instances of the adaptation of theological ideas to the interpreting of politics. To take another example, in the generation previous to our own, after the discoveries of Darwin, political thought, like almost every other activity of the human mind, came under the rule of conceptions taken from biology. Biology seemed to have become what theology had been in the Middle Ages, the queen of the sciences; and it would scarcely be an exaggeration to say that in every age there is one science which lords it over the rest. What biology was to the nineteenth century, mathematics were to the seventeenth. Mathematical studies were in a state of conquering vitality : it was the age of Descartes, of Pascal, of Huygens, of Newton. As one discovery succeeded another, and all were observed to form a coherent system, men came to think that the clearness and certainty of mathematical reasoning were the typical qualities of reasoning as such. It became the aim of every systematic thinker to use methods and obtain results like those of the mathematicians—indeed, if possible, to make his own subject into a department of mathematics. Thus the great philosopher Spinoza, a contemporary of the earlier among the English thinkers we are considering, besides going deeply into geometrical and physical problems, wrote his *Ethics* in a series of propositions mathematically demonstrated. One of the literary curiosities of the period is a work published in 1699 by John Craig, a Scotsman who was a friend of Newton and became a canon of Salisbury, called *Theologiæ Christianæ Principia Mathematica*. Even literary curiosities are evidence of the tendencies of the time, and we find the same endeavour after something like mathematical forms among the best scientific intellects of the England of Charles II. Among the memorable occurrences of his reign was the final foundation of the Royal Society, the same great Royal Society which we still reckon as one of our most impressive institutions. Its earliest members, according to their first historian, were resolved to express their reasonings about 'natural philosophy,' as the natural sciences were then called, without "amplifications, digressions, and swellings of style: to return back to the primitive purity, and shortness, when men delivered so many *things* almost in an equal number of *words*"; so that the society "exacted from all their members a close, naked, natural, way of speaking; positive expressions; clear senses; a native easiness; bringing all things as near the Mathematical plainness as they can."

While the scientists, for their own immediate purposes, used this economy of means in the construction of prose, they were taking much the same direction in which the literary men, the artists in prose and verse, were proceeding independently.[1] Simplicity, precision, and ease are the characteristics of the best writers of that time both in England and in other countries. Among the many things that were changing in the time of Charles II, one was English prose. Sir Thomas Browne, a master in the older manner, was still writing with the "amplifications, digressions, and swellings of style" reprehended by the Royal Society of which he was not a member; but he had formed his manner, elaborate and leisurely, full of colour and conceits, in the distant days of Charles I. He belongs to the generation of Milton, and the contemporaries of the great scientists were almost as much reformers of the art of writing as the scientists themselves. Halifax and Temple have their place in the movement, and with Swift, who began as Temple's *protégé*, it is virtually complete. Marvellous as is his faculty of using it, we can still say without absurdity that Swift's language is our own. The earlier instrument strikes us as archaic, the later as modern. Swift, at any rate, can do with words most of the things that modern writers want to do; but they no longer want to do what Milton and Sir Thomas Browne could

---

[1] Unless we are to accept the interesting suggestion made at the time by Fontenelle, that "*l'ordre, la netteté, la précision, l'exactitude qui règnent dans les bons livres depuis un certain temps*" had their origin in the *esprit géometrique*, and, in particular, in the example of one great man, who is presumably Pascal. *Œuvres* (1818), vol. i, p. 34.

achieve, nor even what was done by the earlier masters of pointed brevity, like Hobbes or his master Bacon. What had been powerful adjuncts of reasoning seemed now to be super-fluous ornaments and pedantries. It was an episode of an almost universal revolution in the arts : the crowded canvases and exuberant sculpture of the baroque were becoming dis-tasteful to the creators of the polished neatness which we call rococo. Nowhere is the change more clearly seen than in English poetry. There, as in prose, Milton closed a period : the verse which corresponds to the prose of Swift and Addison is that of Pope. The European movement of which Pope was the English representative had in it much that was French in origin and spirit ; there is no need to mention how the poetry and drama of France had served as models to English writers ever since Charles and his courtiers had come back from an exile which had taken them to, among other places, the French centres of politeness. It had also its more distant classical ancestry, and there is much in its smooth and accomplished elegance that calls to mind the poetry of the Roman principate, the period of Virgil, of Ovid, above all of Horace. In English poetry it has long been called the Augustan Age. Nowadays we do not think of it, like those who gave it that name, as the best age of poetry ; but we may still call it the age of the greatest purity and refinement, the pre-eminently classical period. In English prose it well merits the same title ; and those who planned this course of lectures have had the happy notion that it is equally so in the history of English thought.

For the revolution was more than a revolution in style. The men who speak a new language have new things to say, and English thinkers altered their attitude of mind as much as their technique. A name which serves as a link between scien-tific and political studies is that of a wonderfully gifted man who was one of the early Fellows of the Royal Society, Sir William Petty. Petty wrote about what he called " political arithmetic." He worked at the figures of population and trade and suchlike matters, and he deserves to be called the inventor of the application of statistics to public affairs. In his time the invention was still rudimentary, but the steady process had begun by which the quantitative method has become one of the foundations of the sciences and arts of government. What

19

is more, Petty's work, like that of most of the greatest inventors, came at the time when the world was ready for it. Other workers were in various countries engaged on similar researches: Dutchmen were busy at the actuarial calculations on which life insurance was based; Frenchmen were soon to investigate the relation between their system of taxes and the taxable resources of their country. Political economy did not claim as yet the rank of a science, but everyday economic controversies more and more assumed a methodical and systematic form. They were dominated by calculations about the ' balance of trade,' and in the last years of the seventeenth century the British Government made careful arrangements for providing the figures by which this balance could be ascertained. The paradoxes of one age are the platitudes of the next, and it is hard for us to understand that this was the sign of a fundamentally new point of view. In general terms we are aware that in earlier times, when theology and moral philosophy had been the dominant studies, economic questions were supposed to turn on considerations which could not be expressed in figures : some of us, indeed, are for reviving some of the forgotten economic truths that were reached by those methods. We know, too, that the later seventeenth century saw an increase and improvement in the available information about trade and industry, and a clearer statement of the organic relation between one economic fact and another. But it is hard for us to see how novel was the application of arithmetic to the wealth of nations. It is no more than an extension of the idea of a tradesman's balance-sheet, and we think nothing more natural than to regard a nation as one great trading unit. We must remind ourselves that there were times when even the balance-sheet was a new discovery. It is itself a humble product of the scientific spirit, the use in the small world of a ' business ' of the tremendous idea of ordering by quantification. A daring modern writer has said that the invention in the late Middle Ages of the system of book-keeping by double entry was the first manifestation of the spirit of Galileo and Newton. It was that spirit which prompted the first compilers of economic statistics.

Turning back to the other departments of political thought with which we are concerned in these lectures, we find the same desire to arrive at certainty by means of theorems at least superficially resembling those of mathematics. The idea of equilibrium was taken over from mechanics into many spheres. Earlier writers, like Harrington, had enunciated the doctrine of the balance of property. The belief that constitutions should work by checks and balances was cherished by theorists of the seventeenth and eighteenth centuries. Even the lawless confusion of international relations was reduced to a deceptive appearance of order by the plausible doctrine of the balance of power, the European equilibrium. Although these theories had little in them that was truly scientific, they stood for more than a mere borrowing of the scientists' vocabulary. Beneath them lay a serious if misguided attempt to explain by weighing and measuring, by adding and subtracting.

This influence of scientific upon political thought may be illustrated in another way. It may be seen in the growth of the notion of a science of politics, and, if the necessary information were at hand, the outlines of that growth could probably be most conveniently traced by following the history of the name 'political science.' Unfortunately, so far as I know, that history is still to seek. Our lexicographers do not seem to have investigated the rise of the phrase, and there does not seem to be any good collection of examples. In the absence of such a collection I should guess that both the name and the idea were beginning to pass into currency in the time with which we are dealing. The earliest example of the name that I can find is in one of our authors—in that author where perhaps one would have looked for it last. It occurs in *Gulliver's Travels*, in the chapter of cutting satire where Gulliver explains the civilisation of Europe to the King of Brobdingnag. The King has formed a low opinion of some European institutions, but Gulliver ironically excuses him and his people thus : " I take this defect among them to have risen from their ignorance, they not having hitherto reduced politics to a science as the more acute wits of Europe have done." This sentence was published fifteen years earlier than the essay in which David Hume contended " that politics may be reduced to a science." It implies that such an idea was in the air, and, in spite of its contemptuous twist, it indicates that a real attempt was being made to handle political questions scientifically. It would indeed be an anachronism to suppose that either Swift or Hume

21

had in mind what we understand by ' political science.' What they meant by ' politics ' was the art of government, and our nearest word for it is ' statecraft ' or ' statesmanship.' Nor did ' science ' mean quite the same then as it means now. The prevailing idea of science was, however, in some ways the same as it is to-day. Then as now it meant something impartial, general, systematic. Science has no purpose except to find out the truth; its truths are to apply to many facts, and not merely to some facts arbitrarily selected to support them. It is something wrought by reason, and in this sense a political science was growing up not only in name, but also in reality.

One of the clearest expressions of this tendency is to be found in an author whom I have already had occasion to name more than once—one of the writers of the time who are not to be discussed in detail in these lectures, Sir William Temple. Temple made a considerable figure in the history of England under Charles II, and among his literary works one of the best is the shrewd little essay on the origin and nature of government, in which he anticipates the doctrine, famous afterward in other hands, that the forms of government are largely determined by climate. His little book on the United Provinces had the same sort of reputation in his time as Lord Bryce's *American Commonwealth* has had in ours. It was the standard example of a study of a foreign constitution. In the preface to it he gives the reason why he thought such historical and descriptive works would be valuable : " I believe it will be found, at one time or other, by all who shall try, That whilst Human Nature continues what it is, The same Orders in State, the same Discipline in Armies, The same Reverence for things Sacred, And Respect of Civil Institutions, The same Virtues and Dispositions of Princes and Magistrates, deriv'd by Interest, or Imitation, into the Customs and Humours of the Peoples, will ever have the same Effects upon the Strength and Greatness of all Governments, and upon the Honour and Authority of those that Rule, as well as the Happiness and Safety of those that obey." The study of politics is to proceed from the assumption that the same cause will always produce the same effect, the fundamental assumption of science.

The point of view from which this passage was written coincides with that of the modern study of 'comparative politics,' and it was a point of view not peculiar to Temple, but shared more or less completely by his contemporaries in general. There was about that time a widespread desire to collect and classify and compare the scattered materials of knowledge, and one of its manifestations was the publication of a large number of books which resembled Temple's in their scope and method. These theoretical and descriptive works may seem remote from the world of wire-pulling and place-hunting in which writers like Defoe and Halifax made their careers. The symptoms of the penetration of political thought by the scientific spirit may seem to have merely an antiquarian interest. For the purpose of explaining what these writers were really driving at, they may seem to be no more relevant than illustrations of the changes in the social manners and customs of the period. The lecturers who are to analyse and discuss these writers one by one will indeed be occupied mainly with the reactions of their minds to actual questions of civil and ecclesiastical polity, or to questions of principle which arose from such concrete matters as the change of a dynasty, the force of an oath, the appointment of a bishop, a minister's electioneering pledge to the Dissenters, or a discredited intriguer's hopes from an heir apparent. At present, however, we must not go beyond the task of an introduction, a preliminary reconnaissance of the area. We must endeavour to see whether there is a broad outline by which all these details can be charted. For that purpose it is not irrelevant to consider the surrounding tracts of literature and events : it would not even be irrelevant, if we had the time for it, to consider changes of social manners and customs. No writer, however cloistered or academic, can avoid being affected by the world about him, least of all a writer like those with whom we are dealing, for these were, almost all of them, versatile men, men of wide interests, who thought and wrote about many other things besides political things. Thus there can be seen in their political works a real contrast between the state of the atmosphere at the beginning and at the end of the period. It had changed *pari passu* with the change of ideas in general ; and, in spite of all their controversies and oppositions, these men were affected by one general movement which dominated all that age. If I may be permitted to use an old-fashioned simile, they may be compared with the steersmen of ships, some tacking against the wind, some running before it, some outdistancing others, some trying to avert collisions, others cheerfully putting on sail to engage and board. Each absorbed in watching the rest, they are unaware that all together are being steadily borne out of their courses by an unseen current of the ocean. All of them are unaware of it, unless one or another takes his bearings by the stars. The current was the age-long and world-wide movement to which an eminent historian gave the name of the rise and progress of the spirit of rationalism.

When these writers are taken individually one would hardly expect to find that they were all in sympathy with this trend of the times; and I should not care to predict that the Jacobites and Non-Jurors will turn out to have infused much of this spirit into their impossible loyalties. Perhaps they were standing out against the spirit of the age as well as against the supplanters of the Stuarts. For the others, however, the evidence is surprisingly clear. Sir Robert Filmer is the one who would be regarded as the least rational and the most reactionary among them; yet he has his modest place among the advocates of reasonableness, for he took a hand in destroying the blind and cruel belief in witchcraft. The latitudinarianism of Hoadly is closely akin to Locke's individualist, utilitarian rationalism—indeed, Hoadly's politics are simply Locke's—and though Bolingbroke is in many things the antithesis of Locke, it would be hard to say which is the better representative of the age then opening, which has long ago been nicknamed the age of reason. Swift himself, the supreme artist in his own *genre*, was as fierce an enemy of the irrational as Pope; and Daniel Defoe, another master of imagination, wrote on the whole duty of man in a commercial country in a way that anticipated Mr Pancks.

Much more was happening along with this; but it was primarily in this change of thought that the change from the England of Charles II to the England of George II was accomplished. The former was full of loyalists and fanatics, with civil war close behind them and religious intolerance both behind and before; but it was an age of great men and brave ideals. Parties still seemed to be auxiliaries in the contention of hell and heaven. It is to that age that we turn for inspiration rather than to the unromantic days of Hoadly the sceptical bishop, of Swift the sceptical dean, of a Church party led by Bolingbroke the atheist. Politics had come down to the same level as religion : there were no longer any political ideas for which men were willing to die, nor even any for which they would kill with or without due process of law. Yet we are not likely to underrate the gain. We know that two great things had been established in the life of England to which we still must steadfastly adhere—religious tolerance and political moderation. They did not come, as is too easily imagined, only because men were morally exhausted, or because they sank into scepticism and indifference. Scepticism and indifference were there, with open cynicism and contempt of public spirit. One side of the age is summarised in Pope's famous lines :

> For forms of government let fools contest ;
> Whate'er is best administer'd is best ;

or in that pleasing poem by George Bubb Dodington, Baron Melcombe, which begins :

> Love thy country, wish it well,
> Not with too intense a care ;
> 'Tis enough that, when it fell,
> Thou its ruin didst not share.

But that mood was transient. Before the death of Boling-broke, which came as late as the year 1751, there were men alive who had in them the germs of new gospels and new philo-sophies. In France a prominent lawyer, the President Mon-tesquieu, had published his profound and learned comparative study of laws, and Jean-Jacques Rousseau had written an essay that had won an academic prize. There was an Irish student of the Middle Temple who was soon to begin his literary life as the parodist of Bolingbroke, and to end it long after as the assailant of Tom Paine, who wrote *The Age of Reason*: his name was Edmund Burke. They and others like them were to sweep away many of the negations of their predecessors and to herald an age in which new faiths were born and old faiths awakened, in which once more there were to be depths and heights. There are two crowded centuries between us and the *Patriot King*. But the successors of our authors did not reverse their con-clusions. They took from them an inheritance to which they added many new acquisitions, not without losing something and endangering more of the original property, but still using it as the capital of their ventures, and retaining much of it through all their ups and downs.

That which they kept, that which is permanent so far as the gains of political thought and experience can be lasting, is, as I have said, the inestimable treasure of tolerance and moderation. These are no residuum left by the negative and destructive force of reason, but a product of creative and constructive effort. The positive labour of knowing and understanding political life, the application of science to these affairs, builds up the conception of a common work which men must undertake because they form a real community, and in which they cannot succeed unless they will abstain from narrow-minded and short-sighted assertions of rights. Real toleration is created by respect, and not by indifference; it comes not from inattentiveness, but from an exertion of the mind. Real moderation is like it—not weakness, but strength controlled in the service of an end worth gaining. Neither can be preserved without vigilance and exertion. For both, the disinterested search for truth is the most certain guarantee, and we may sum up in a sentence the best in the political ideas of this old period by saying that in it reason was advancing toward a strenuous liberty.

G. N. CLARK

BIBLIOGRAPHY

Cambridge Modern History: vol. v, " The Age of Louis XIV " (1908); vol. vi, " The Eighteenth Century " (1909).
HALLAM, H.: *Introduction to the Literature of Europe*. New edition, 1872.
LEADAM, I. S.: *Political History of England*, 1702–60. 1909.
LECKY, W. E. H.: *History of England in the Eighteenth Century*, vol. i. 1878.
LODGE, R.: *Political History of England*, 1660–1702. 1910.
MACAULAY, LORD: *History of England*. Edited by C. H. Firth. 1913.
STANHOPE, LORD: *The Reign of Queen Anne until the Peace of Utrecht*. 1870.
WARD, A. W.: *Great Britain and Hanover*. 1899.

II

SIR ROBERT FILMER

SIR ROBERT FILMER has, I fear, no connexion with anything Augustan; and the only visible excuse for his appearance in the present series is that he was not included in the last. But he was a thinker well worth considering, and, in my opinion, has never received his due. He fought for a losing cause, and suffered the fate of the vanquished. Even on his own side of the great controversy there were few who agreed with him. His thought was so far from being typical of the Royalist thought of his time that he was to a great extent isolated.

Not only was he rather lonely among defenders of the Royalist cause, few of whom believed, in any sense, in absolute monarchy or wished to see it established in England, but he was, above all else, a critic of conceptions that after his death became more and more generally current and received the stamp of Parliamentary approval. His writings were, probably, not much read in his own day; and, under Charles II, they were read chiefly in connexion with the controversy over the Exclusion Bill. That means that he was misunderstood even by his friends. A little later still he seems to have been almost forgotten, or was remembered only by the caricature presented in Locke's essay. That first of Locke's essays on *Civil Government* was, in truth, a shameful piece of party journalism. Either Locke had failed to understand Filmer, or he misrepresented him deliberately. One may prefer for him either horn of that dilemma; but there is really no alternative. I doubt whether Locke had even read Filmer's writings. He had read the *Patriarcha* and, I suspect, nothing else. That is no kind of an excuse for Locke. To write about Filmer when you have only read the *Patriarcha* is, from my point of view, mere dishonesty. In any case, if you want to understand Filmer's thought it is no manner of use to read Locke.

27

Sir Robert was born some time in the fifteen-nineties, and he died in 1653. He was a Kentish squire of studious and retiring habits, and was knighted under Charles I, whether compulsorily or not I do not know. At the time the Civil War began he was, no doubt, too elderly for active service; but his loyalty earned him some loss of property and a short imprisonment. The earliest of his writings was the *Patriarcha*. It seems to have been written quite early in the Civil War, and Filmer never published it, and did not even complete it. It was not published till 1680. It was certainly not prudence that prevented Sir Robert from publishing it, for later he published other writings at much more dangerous moments. He probably thought it not worth publishing and, if so, was not very far wrong. It reads like the writing of a man who has been moved by a crisis in public affairs to put his ideas on paper and has failed to get his thought clear. Anyhow, the *Patriarcha* is quite certainly the thinnest and most confused of all Filmer's writings, and the least revealing and therefore the least important.

In 1648 Filmer published a far more mature and complete statement of his views in a treatise entitled *The Anarchy of a Limited and Mixed Monarchy*. It was written specifically as an answer to the *Treatise of Monarchy* of Philip Hunton, one of the best of the writings that had so far been produced on the other side. In the same year appeared a booklet called *The Necessity of the Absolute Power of all Kings*. This is little more than a sheaf of extracts from Richard Knolles' translation of Bodin's *Republic*. It must be regarded as a compilation rather than as a writing of Filmer. But his publication of these extracts may fairly be taken to mean that they expressed his own views, so far as they went.

Then, in 1652, was published Filmer's *Observations upon Aristotle's Politiques touching Forms of Government*; and with this was bound up a separate essay, entitled *Directions for Obedience to Governours in Dangerous and Doubtful Times*. Lastly, in the same year, 1652, appeared the *Observations concerning the Originall of Government*, which consists of criticisms of certain propositions of Hobbes, of Milton, and of Grotius. A work called *The Freeholder's Grand Inquest* has also been attributed to Filmer, but is certainly not his.

All these writings were published anonymously. By far the most important of them, for an understanding of Filmer's position, are the *Anarchy* and the *Observations upon Aristotle*. Next in importance to these is the *Directions*; and when you have read these three you may read the *Patriarcha*. The *Necessity* merely tells us how far Filmer agreed with Bodin; and his criticism of Hobbes, Milton, and Grotius added little to what he had said already.

Filmer repeated himself a good deal. But it has to be remembered that, in considering the relative place and importance of particular propositions in a man's system of ideas, repetition is, perhaps usually, significant.

In 1642 and in the years that followed it was of no use whatever to go on repeating that God had commanded obedience to any and every form of actually constituted public authority and had forbidden active resistance in all cases. That proposition had served England well throughout the sixteenth century, and was still generally held to be undeniable in 1642. The assertion was still being made; but it was being made by the writers on both sides. For it was now claimed that sovereignty in England lay with Parliament; and it was claimed that in case of dispute among the " Estates " in Parliament the right of final decision lay with the Houses, or even with the House of Commons alone. There had developed a strong tendency to see the King as merely the head of an executive, with, in addition, a veto on legislative measures proposed by the Houses. Writers on the Parliament side habitually denied that they were rebels; and St Paul's words about obedience to the Higher Powers left their withers unwrung. Both sides agreed that every soul should be subject to the Higher Powers: the question was which or what, in England, is the Higher Power. Filmer to some extent argued from Scripture; but he did not argue from the Epistle to the Romans.

In face of these assertions, and of the theories that lay behind them, Filmer went to the root of the matter. He tried to show that the King in England must be regarded as the sole sovereign, and therefore as an absolute monarch. He asserted that an absolute or, as he preferred to call it, an arbitrary power must needs exist somewhere in every society that is governed by law. But he went much farther. He maintained that

29

sovereignty could not exist at all in any other form than monarchy, except by legal fiction. Most fundamental of all was his assertion that the fictitious sovereignty of any group, or of such a body as the English Parliament, was necessarily devoid of moral authority.

Here we come upon a conception which is absolutely essential in the structure of Filmer's thought. It is implied everywhere in his writings, but so axiomatic was it to him that he nowhere gave it clear expression. Government, he declared, is the exercise of a moral power, which is sovereignty.[1] Always, and quite definitely, he conceived of political authority as a right to demand obedience as a positive duty. There might be limits to that right, and in fact Filmer recognised that there were limits. He laid down quite distinctly that commands of the Sovereign contrary to the express law of God are never to be obeyed.[2] But, whatever limits there may be, within those limits real authority consists in an absolute right to command on one side and an absolute duty of obedience on the other. That, of course, had been the ordinary way of thinking throughout the sixteenth century. Neither Filmer nor anyone else denied that the " people," or rather any large body of people, possessed coercive force, and could confer it. But Filmer was convinced that, in the long run, no organisation of force could give peace and order to society in the absence of a sense of moral obligation to obey. No ordered and stable society could be founded on a general and rather vague and inaccurate sense of common interests, backed by an organisation of force. Unless men recognised the duty of obedience to government as normally absolute, and the duty of refraining from active resistance and rebellion as quite absolute, the stresses arising from conflicts of interest within society must, sooner or later, snap the bonds of union and produce anarchy. Rightly or wrongly, so Filmer believed ; and so had believed most English people up almost to his time.

It was with these conceptions and convictions that Filmer's thinking started ; and only by reference to them are his writings intelligible. In those writings he set before himself two main objects. It seemed to him that his adversaries of the camp opposite were, though all unwittingly, destroying the basis on

[1] *Anarchy* (1648), p. 17.   [2] *Directions* (1652), p. 50.

which alone society could rest securely. He had, first of all, to show that that was so. And, secondly, he had to find reasons for believing that the moral authority he thought of as necessary for its welfare did actually exist in society.

Naturally Filmer was far more nearly successful with the first of these tasks than he was with the second. He is far stronger as a destructive critic than as a constructive thinker. But destructive criticism is as necessary and, in a sense, as valuable as the attempts at construction which it must needs precede and accompany. Filmer's criticism of current contentions issued logically in a mere negation. On the other hand, his positive conclusion happened to be an unpopular one. These facts go far to account for his isolation in his own time, and for the neglect or contempt of him later.

Filmer's criticism of the theories maintained by his adversaries was intended to clear the ground for his own construction, and must be dealt with first. In his actual writings criticism of other people's views and exposition of his own are rather confusingly mixed. Disentanglement, however, is not difficult. It must be remembered that Filmer was criticising specific assertions, and that, dialectically at least, he had a right to deal with them in the form in which they were made. As he wrote with practical purpose, that was, indeed, the practical course to pursue.

What exactly was he attacking? Time and space forbid me to attempt to answer this question except in a very summary, incomplete, and therefore highly unsatisfactory manner. It was, in 1648, being loudly asserted that man is born free; that he is free by nature; that no man has a right to give commands to another unless by his consent. It was asserted that, originally, men were under no obligation to obedience to any authority but that of God; or even that they were under no obligation of any sort unless to themselves. Consequently, it was declared, all human authority is created by the act of man, even though God sanctions it and commands obedience to it. " By the natural law," Hooker had written, " the lawful power of making laws to command whole politic societies of men, belongeth so properly to the same entire societies, that for any prince or potentate . . . to exercise the same of himself, and not either by express commission immediately and personally received from God or else from authority derived at the first from their consent upon whose persons they impose laws, it is no better than mere tyranny." [1]   Political authority is vested ultimately in the people as a whole, and the people may establish government in any form it pleases, confer sovereignty on anyone it chooses, and limit the authority so conferred. The sovereign people delegates its own natural authority, and all actual political authority is derived from such a delegation. It was, also, freely asserted that political society originated in contracts, one or more than one, and that kings and other legal sovereigns held authority under such a contract, and forfeited if they broke it.   Hunton declared that " the consent and fundamental contract of a nation of men " was the root of all sovereignty.   All these propositions were old, but they did not become fashionable in England before the Civil War.   It was the system of ideas thus very roughly indicated that was attacked by Filmer.

Up against these assertions Filmer, it may be said, began by pointing out that, unless in some mystical sense, man is certainly not born free.   There is no living thing less free than a new-born baby.   He went on to point out that it was universally recognised that parents have a natural right to control their children.   Law recognised this, and every one agreed about it.   But, " if it be allowed that the acts of parents bind the children, then farewell the doctrine of the natural freedom of mankind." [2]   It will be said, of course, that this natural subjection lasts no longer than childhood.   When, then, Filmer inquired, does it cease?   When the child ' comes of age '?   But coming of age is a merely legal fact and " in nature t ere is no nonage." [3]   Coming of age has meant different th.ngs in different places and times.   Without pressing the point farther, we are at least bound to say that man is born into a condition of natural subjection.   He is not born free ; he is born a subject.

It follows that it is simply untrue to say that man is naturally under no obligation to obedience to anyone.   But, further, we know that, so far from men being originally free, all human societies were originally under a patriarchal government that was certainly not set up by themselves.   This we learn from

[1] *Ecclesiastical Polity*, Book I, ch. x.   [2] *Anarchy*, p. 10.   [3] *Ibid.*, p. 10.

the Scriptures, and unless we disbelieve the Scriptures we cannot deny it. Filmer was very insistent on this point, as he had a right to be, since his opponents did not deny his assertion. He complains that people do not sufficiently consider the statements and the implications of the Scriptures as to the earliest human societies, and that they refer by preference to Aristotle and other heathen writers who, necessarily, knew nothing about the matter. The contention may seem absurd to us, but it was not absurd in Filmer.

"Men are naturally willing," Sir Robert remarked, "to be persuaded that all sovereignty flows from the consent of the people."[1] Yet, he added, "there are many and great difficulties in the point never yet determined."[2] To begin with, what is meant by this phrase 'the people'? What people? A natural right to freedom must exist universally if it exist at all, and if a natural sovereignty be inherent in the people, where can it lie but in the whole people of the world? Particular communities, in that case, could only derive authority from a grant by the whole population of the world.[3] No one will maintain that such a grant was ever made. What must be meant is that sovereignty belongs by nature to the people of each particular country. But what is a country? There are no distinct countries till there are governments; and we are speaking of a hypothetical time before governments existed. "Nature hath not distinguished the habitable world into kingdoms nor determined what part of a 'people' shall belong to one kingdom and what to another."[4] Talk about 'countries' can only mean that, originally, every localised community had a right to set up for itself and establish a government. But, if that be so, when and how did that right cease to exist? Natural rights, surely, do not cease to exist. "And so," it appears, "every petty company hath a right to make a kingdom by itself; and not only every city but every village and every family; nay and every particular man a liberty to choose himself to be his own king if he please."[5] Such a theory leads straight to anarchy. But if such a right existed originally

---

[1] *Observations* (1652), p. 40. It is always the *Observations upon Aristotle* that is thus referred to here.
[2] *Observations*, p. 41.   [3] *Anarchy*, p. 8.   [4] *Ibid.*, p. 9.
[5] *Ibid.*, p. 9.

C

and naturally, no momentary agreement could conceivably nullify it. Natural liberty is a morass from which no escape is possible.

Again, Filmer asked, what is this authority that resides in a mere multitude, and how comes it to exist? Is there any reason for supposing that any sort of authority but that of brute force resides in a multitude? We know that God forbids men to kill each other, or even to kill themselves. But a right to kill is involved in a right to set up government. *Nervus potestatis politicæ præcipuus et summus est supplicium capitale.*[1] Melanchthon's view on this point is precisely Filmer's. How can any number of people confer a right that not one of them has? We know of no grant of such a right being made by God to any people. What we do know is that God established first patriarchal government and then kings.

Let us, however, suppose that a people is somehow possessed of a right to set up coercive government and delegate its authority. How is this actually to be done? Assuredly no complete people ever actually met to establish a government. " It cannot truly be said that ever the whole people or the major part or indeed any considerable part of the whole people of any nation ever assembled to any such purpose." [2] How could a people be assembled in any form or sense unless government existed already? [3] In the absence of a lawful summons, how could the absent conceivably be bound? Those who maintain, Filmer insisted, that governmental authority is derived from delegation or consent are bound to show how this consent can be given or this delegation made. Since every man is originally free, it would seem that consent must be universal before anything could rightfully be done. If it be asserted that this need not be so, then those who make that assertion are bound to show what constitutes a sufficient consent.[4] It cannot, in fact, Filmer declared, be shown that any people has such a right as is postulated; but it can be shown that if it did possess such a right it could not practically exercise it. After all, what is a people? " It is a body in continual alteration and change; it never continues one minute

---

[1] Melanchthon, *Philosophiæ Moralis Epitomes.* The quotation is mine, not Filmer's.
[2] *Anarchy,* p. 10.   [3] *Ibid.,* p. 10.   [4] *Observations,* p. 41.

the same." [1] " Mankind is like the sea, ever ebbing or
flowing ; every minute one is born, another dies ; those that
are the people this minute are not the people the next minute ;
in every instant and point of time there is a variation." [2] If
there be such a thing as a natural right to freedom, even
infants must possess it, at least potentially, " not to speak
of women, who by birth have as much natural freedom as
any other." [3] By hypothesis, " these ought not to lose their
liberty without their own consent." When and how was it
given? Exactly similar reasoning, Filmer pointed out, applies
to the notion that political society originated in formal contracts. How could such contracts be made binding or be made
at all ? " To imagine such pactions and contracts between
Kings and people as cannot be proved ever to have been made,
or can ever be described or fancied . . . is a boldness to be
wondered at." [4]

It is said, however, that authority was conferred not by an
act literally of the whole people, but by the act of a majority,
and that this is sufficient. No such thing, Filmer declared,
ever really happened ; and if it did happen, why should it be
held sufficient?

Will it be said that some relatively small group of people
came to an agreement and took action thereupon, and that the
mass consented tacitly to what was done? Consented, that is,
by silence. Silence may, in a sense, give consent ; and it may
well be an enforced consent that is so given. Any violent
group might conceivably obtain for its doings consent of that
sort. Must that be held sufficient? If a group may act for
the people, what follows but that any group may do so? If
this be the contention " a wide gap is thereby opened for any
multitude whatsoever that is able to call themselves, or whom-
soever they please, the people." [5] The remark was not without
a certain prophetic quality.

But even supposing that an actual majority of the people
took action, how could their action conceivably bind the
minority? It is unimaginable that a natural right to freedom
should be destroyed by a majority vote. " The major part
never binds, but where men at first agree to be so bound or

---

[1] *Observations,* p. 40.   [2] *Anarchy,* p. 10.   [3] *Ibid.,* p. 10.
[4] *Directions,* p. 45.   [5] *Observations,* p. 40.

where a higher power so commands." [1] In actual law the decision of a majority is often binding, but this is simply the result of the command of a sovereign. No reason can be given why anyone, in the absence of positive law, should ever consider himself to be bound by the decision of a majority.

It has, in fact, Filmer pointed out, to be assumed that originally it was unanimously agreed that the decision of a majority should bind every one. "This first agreement cannot possibly be proved either how or by whom it could be made; yet it must necessarily be believed or supposed, because otherwise there could be no lawful government at all." [2] And that, he concluded, is precisely the case. There can be no such thing as a popular government holding real authority by consent or delegation. "If it be imagined that the people were ever but once free from subjection by nature, it will prove a mere impossibility to introduce any kind of government whatsoever, without apparent wrong to a multitude of people." [3]

In his *Observations concerning the Originall of Government* Filmer suggested an objection to the theoretic construction of his adversaries, still more radical than those I have summarised. It is the consent of each individual that authorises the sovereign. Let us grant to our believers in the sovereignty of the people all the universal agreements and unanimous contracts they require: what reason is there that any one of us should hold himself bound by them? A man's consent to be governed in some particular fashion is to be taken, they say, as having been given. Granting that it has been given, why should it not be withdrawn? Why should not a man change his mind "and say he will resume his natural right . . . and be restored unto his natural liberty and consequently take what he please and do what he list: who can say that such a man doth more than by right he may do?" [4] Filmer did not positively assert that this was the case: he left it to his opponents to answer the question if they could.

Sir Robert might have been content to stop here and leave his opponents to simmer. But he was, evidently, anxious to make his criticism exhaustive, and to deal with every question

---

[1] *Anarchy*, p. 9.   [2] *Observations*, p. 39.   [3] *Anarchy*, p. 11.
[4] *Observations concerning the Originall of Government*, Part III.

they raised. He pointed out that the conception of sovereignty as vested in the 'people' is practically bound up with
systems of representative government and of government by
majorities. And here he found two absurdities. Radically
absurd, to begin with, he asserted, is the notion of government
by majority. " The power of a major part is grounded upon
a supposition that they are the strongest part." [1] But this
appearance of actual power is illusory. A majority is a thing
" uncertain and changeable "; [2] it " expires in the very act
itself of voting ": [3] it is, or it may be, a mere thing of
a moment. What is called the will of a majority " is not
the whole and entire will of every particular person in the
assembly, but that part only of his will which accidentally falls
out to concur with the will of the greater part." [4] Filmer put
this awkwardly. He meant that a majority vote on any particular point does not imply any profound agreement or even
agreement on any point but the one voted upon. Whatever
government by majorities may be, Filmer emphatically declared that it is not government by the people. It would
not be that, he says, if the minority consisted of one man
only.

Not only so but, Filmer declared, there is really no such
thing as 'representative' government. He gave more reasons
for this assertion than ever did Rousseau. Government is
representative only by legal fiction. The representative of a
people should, ideally, be chosen by the whole people : but no
actual representative is really elected even by the people of any
one district. Actually so-called representatives are chosen by
mere minorities of electors in a number of separate constituencies.[5] The act of a majority of the miscellaneous crowd
thus got together is ridiculously styled an act proceeding from
the will of the people. The majority is conceived of as expressing a single will, as though it, or 'the people,' were a
single person. Thus, Sir Robert remarks, do democracies try
to look like monarchies ! [6] The disguise is miserably thin.
The palpable fictions involved disappear as soon as you look
at representative bodies in action. Their proceedings resolve
themselves into a struggle of " parties or factions . . . fighting

[1] *Observations*, p. 42.   [2] *Ibid.*, p. 23.   [3] *Ibid.*, p. 42.
[4] *Ibid.*, p. 42.   [5] *Ibid.*, pp. 37, 40.   [6] *Ibid.*, p. 17.

and scratching." [1] They are compelled to do their work through committees, which represent the representatives. The result is government by log-rolling. "One man for himself and his friend may rule in one business and another for himself and his friend may prevail in another cause." [2] All this is " the next degree to anarchy."

These ridiculous arrangements, Sir Robert observed, are called 'liberty.' It is a misuse of the word, and ambiguous at that. If liberty means permission to do as you please, there is no more liberty in a democracy than under any other form of government. The only liberty that attaches to a 'popular' system of government, as such, is the liberty of taking a minute and indefinite part in legislation, coupled with the possibility of taking a somewhat larger part as a 'representative' and doing a little log-rolling on your own account. "If the common people look for any other liberty, either of their persons or their purses, they are pitifully deceived." [3]

As to a mixed constitution or a limited monarchy, in which sovereignty is supposed to be divided, Filmer, following Bodin very closely, declared that the thing is inconceivable. The suggestion of such a thing was, he says, never made till the day before yesterday, and the thing itself exists nowhere.[4] How can limitation be imposed on sovereignty? "The power that limits must be above that power which is limited." [5] If the power of a monarch be restrained by law those that made that law have the sovereignty. If the sovereign be conceived as bound by the law of the land, then there is no legislative power, and consequently no sovereignty. Continually and with emphasis Filmer repeated the assertion that sovereignty consists essentially in power to make law. "A law in general is the command of a superior power." [6] "To govern is to give a law to others," [7] and "to be governed is nothing else but to be obedient and subject to the will of another; it is the will in man that governs." [8] "There never was nor never can be any people governed without a power of making laws, and every power of making laws must be arbitrary, for to make a law according to law is contradiction." [9] "They that say

[1] *Observations*, p. 16.   [2] *Ibid.*, p. 37.   [3] *Ibid.*, p. 39.
[4] *Anarchy*, p. 2.   [5] *Ibid.*, p. 7.   [6] *Patriarcha*, p. 101.
[7] *Anarchy*, p. 5.   [8] *Observations*, p. 15.   [9] *Anarchy*, Preface.

the Law governs the kingdom, may as well say that the Carpenter's rule builds the house and not the carpenter: for the law is but the rule or instrument of the ruler."[1]   The very existence of law implies the existence of a legally unlimited authority.   " There can be no laws without a Supreme power to command or make them. . . . That which giveth the very being to a King is the power to make Laws."[2]   Forms of government, Filmer declared, can only rationally be distinguished by reference to the seat of legislative power.   " It is the difference only of the authors of the laws . . . that alters the form of government, that is, whether one man or more than one make the laws."[3]   Like Bodin, he concluded that any attempt to limit or divide sovereignty leads straight to civil war.   " We do but flatter ourselves, if we hope ever to be governed without an Arbitrary power."[4]

It was said that, in England, sovereignty lay with Parliament in the full sense.   Filmer went a little out of his way to argue elaborately that, if that were so, England was not a monarchy.   He took great pains to show that Hunton's " mixed monarchy " was not a monarchy at all.   This was not a mere wrangle about the use of terms.   Hunton would have been shocked and pained by being told that he was a republican and wanted to destroy the English monarchy; and Filmer meant him to be shocked and pained.   He undertook to prove that Hunton and his friends left to the monarch in England little more than a " vain title."   Nor was Filmer's argument about the use of terms entirely wasted.   What he was asserting was that the essential question at issue was, Who or what has power to make law?

Granting, however, that sovereignty is legally vested in a full Parliament, Filmer argued that such a sovereignty is a mere legal fiction.   King, Lords, and Commons make up a single sovereign when they are in technical agreement.   When they are not there is none.   Filmer pointed out that the legal relations between the " Estates " were in many respects undetermined.   If disagreement as to these matters arises among them, what is to happen?   There is no judge, and you reach a deadlock.   What sort of sovereignty is this?   The sovereign

---

[1] *Patriarcha*, p. 89.
[2] *Ibid.*, pp. 99–100.
[3] *Anarchy*, Preface.
[4] *Ibid.*, first words of Preface.

cannot govern directly, has no real will, exists only intermittently, comes into formal existence only when summoned by some one who is not sovereign, and, even when sitting, has to come to so-called agreement by majority votes before there can be any act of sovereignty. And the whole monstrosity rests on a fiction of representation, and not even consistently on that, since, as Filmer pointed out, the Lords represented nobody !

Altogether absurd, declared Sir Robert, was the claim of a right to depose the King for breach of an entirely imaginary contract, on the ground of a sovereignty of the people which has and can have no substantial existence. If it be not possible to proceed against the monarch by way of law, how can it be right to do so by way of force?[1] But, in any case, if a question arises as to whether the presumed contract has been broken, who is to judge? " By no law of any nation can a contract be thought broken except that first a lawful trial be had by the ordinary judge."[2] The accusing party to the contract is supposed to be something called ' the people.' If the people is to be judge in its own cause, that simply means that it may depose the King whenever it chooses to do so. " So farewell limited monarchy, nay farewell all government, if there be no judge."[3]

In his *Treatise of Monarchy* Hunton had faced this difficulty, and Filmer rejoined to his solution. The subject, Hunton had declared, is bound to obey as long as the King's irregular proceedings are of small moment and do not tend to the subversion of public liberty. If, however, the King's action tend to destroy public liberty and subvert the Constitution, redress is first to be sought by petition, and, that failing, by active resistance. In such a case, he says, " the fundamental laws of that monarchy must judge and pronounce the sentence in every man's conscience, and every man . . . must follow the evidence of truth in his own soul, to oppose, or not oppose."[4] Appeal, he obscurely suggested, may be made to the "conscience of mankind."

" These," commented Sir Robert, " are but fig leaves to cover the nakedness of our author's limited monarchy."[5] If the monarch be bound by law no breach of law on his part can

---

[1] *Necessity* (1648), p. 12. [2] *Patriarcha*, p. 72. [3] *Anarchy*, p. 20.
[4] *A Treatise of Monarchy* (1643), Part I, 7, p. 18. [5] *Anarchy*, p. 20.

possibly be of small moment, and every such breach must tend to subvert the Constitution. Hunton's confused language can only mean that every man has a right in every case to decide for himself whether or not to rebel. Talk about the conscience of mankind is practically meaningless, and talk about fundamental laws begs the question. " I would very gladly know of him what a fundamental law is, or have but any one law named me that . . . is a fundamental law of the monarchy."[1] He cannot mean the Common Law: it would be too absurd to pretend that that is unalterable. And how, in any case, can laws, fundamental or not, pronounce a sentence, even in conscience? Hunton is merely claiming for every man a right to rebel whenever he thinks he ought to. " I also," concludes Sir Robert triumphantly, " appeal to the conscience of all mankind, whether the end of this be not utter confusion and anarchy."[2]

So far Filmer was meeting the enemy on his own ground, destructively and effectively. There follows, in the logical order, an argument to show that pure absolute monarchy is practically the best of all forms of government. This may be very briefly summarised. There is hardly anything in it that had not been repeated over and over again for the last hundred years. The mere fact, Filmer says, that monarchy was established by God for the Chosen People, raises a presumption that it is best. But on this ancient argument, repeated in England ever since Henry VIII's time, he laid little stress. Government, he says, exists for the sake of good life, and that means chiefly two things: godliness and peace.[3] We find that neither has ever been for long secured except under monarchy. People talk of Venice and of the Low Countries as examples of successful republican states. But how do they stand in respect of godliness? In Venice there is no religion, and in the Netherlands all sorts of religions.[4] As to peace, " the mischief of sedition necessarily waits upon all popularity."[5] As to tyranny, the worst of kings is restrained by fear, and for his own sake will desire to maintain justice and order. But in a democracy men think of themselves or of their party, and not of the public.[6] A mob fears nothing.

[1] *Anarchy*, p. 21.   [2] *Ibid.*, p. 22.   [3] *Observations*, p. 17.
[4] *Ibid.*, p. 18.   [5] *Patriarcha*, p. 65.   [6] *Ibid.*, p. 69.

" There is no tyranny to be compared to the tyranny of a multitude." [1]   In the words of Bodin's translator : " A pure absolute monarchy is the most sure Commonweal and without comparison the best of all." [2]

Filmer's case was complete as I have stated it.   He was not logically bound to go any farther.   He had pointed out that the assertions made by his adversaries rested on groundless assumptions and manifest fictions ; and that what little was known about the origin of politic society contradicted their assumptions flatly.   He charged them with evading the questions their assertions bound them to answer and with refusing to face consequences.   It seemed to him, no doubt, that he had conclusively proved that no theory of government under contracts or of an ultimate popular sovereignty provided any basis for the establishment of real authority.   Government must needs, he was sure, rest on a sense of a duty of obedience. All that the people, in any sense, could, by any sort of agreement, confer was an indefinite amount of actual coercive power.   It is useless to talk of pacts and contracts.   An inexplicit pact could bind nobody ; an explicit contract could result only in the disabling of government.   If the sovereign be a mere delegate of the people, then government rests on force and fear, and no society can stand long on such a foundation.   If men believe that they have themselves created sovereignty, they will not obey ; nor is there any imperative reason why they should.   Government can rest securely only on a sense of absolute obligation ; and the fundamental question that must be answered is the question whether any such thing exists.   Filmer charged his opponents with either evading the question or adopting theories that logically destroyed the moral authority of government and the foundations of ordered society.

He might, conceivably, have been content with a merely negative conclusion.   He might have concluded that there is, strictly speaking, no such thing as political obligation; or that it exists only to the extent to which each individual, in his own conscience, happens to recognise it.   He would, of course, have fully admitted that, under natural law, a man is bound to do the best he can for his fellow-subjects.   That, however, of

[1] *Patriarcha*, p. 70.   [2] *Necessity*, p. 15.

itself does not bind him to acquiesce in the decisions of a majority or to refrain in all cases from active resistance. Every man for himself must be the judge of the needs of society and every man, so far as natural law goes, is free to act on his judgment. He has always a right to make forcible resistance to any act of the sovereign that he judges to be detrimental to general welfare. That right cannot conceivably be taken from him by majority votes or by anything less than a divine grant of a right to demand his obedience as a duty. The question is, has such a grant been made? If it has not been made, then no such right exists, and we are all on the road to anarchy. Filmer might have affirmed that that was actually the hopeless case.

It would, I imagine, have seemed to him nothing less than blasphemy to say so. To him the existence of real authority was absolutely necessary for the welfare of humanity, and he believed, with Hooker, that " those things without which the world cannot well continue have necessary being in the world." [1] He was sure that the necessary divine grant must have been made. He believed that it was made to kings and to nobody else. He asserted that no right or duty can be created out of a supposition or a sense of need; that no majority can impose on a man an obligation that did not previously exist; that unless God has granted authority to demand obedience there is no such authority in the world; and, finally, that such a divine grant has been made to kings only. These propositions, taken together as they must be, constitute what may properly be called the theory of the divine right of kings. That hackneyed and ambiguous phrase has been used far too freely, and often with singularly little consideration. But it may, accurately enough, be used of Filmer's theory. In England he was, I think, by far the best exponent of it; and I am not sure that, in England, he was not the first. I cannot reckon James I as a rival. King James, it seems to me, had expressed no theory at all. What he had expressed was a mere unexplained sense of divinity in kings; which is a quite different matter.

When Filmer came to construction, it must be admitted that he became, to say the least of it, unconvincing. That is

---

[1] *Ecclesiastical Polity*, Book III, ch. iv.

a phenomenon by no means peculiar to Filmer's case. His argument to show that real authority actually exists in the world is so confused and so evidently futile that it is hardly worth pausing long over. He embarked on a difficult proof that existing kings had acquired a divinely given absolute sovereignty from the patriarchs of the Old Testament. The notion that the earliest form of government was that of the father of a family, and that monarchy had developed from this, was, of course, very widely held long before Filmer wrote. It is worth while to point out that a writer calling himself Arnisæus had published, at Frankfort in 1612, a book which anticipates Filmer's so-called " patriarchal theory " in the completest manner.[1]

Filmer and Arnisæus both maintained that kings had inherited or acquired authority given by God to the patriarchs. The fashion in which they had done so remained obscure, but, whatever exactly had happened, God had sanctioned the change over to monarchy, and sovereignty had been handed on continuously. *Qui succedit in locum succedit in jus*, says Arnisæus. Filmer explained that the original grant of sovereignty involved power of alienation,[2] and argued lengthily that a usurper's right becomes good in process of time, because successful usurpation must be taken as an act of God.[3] He agreed with Arnisæus that there is no reason to believe that divine sanction was ever given to any form of government but monarchy. But the divine grant of authority was continued to all those persons who, by whatever means, became the representatives of the original patriarchs. " The paternal power cannot be lost : it may be either transferred or usurped, but never lost or ceaseth." [4]

Sir Robert, unfortunately, got himself into a sad muddle between the rights of fatherhood conceived as natural and patriarchal sovereignty conceived as heritable. He committed himself to the rash assertion that in every community there must always be some one person who has a right to be king as the nearest in blood to Adam. Locke, of course, saw in all this a fine opportunity for amusing his readers and at the same time misleading them. His criticism of Filmer turns almost

---

[1] *De Autoritate Principum.*
[3] *Ibid.*, p. 46 *et seq.*

[2] *Directions,* p. 46.
[4] *Ibid.*, p. 46.

entirely on what is nothing but an historical argument gone wrong. He insisted effectively on the obvious and indulged in cheap ridicule. He pointed out that the sovereign rights of fatherhood as such could not really have been inherited. If Adam were sovereign as father, what happened when he died? Did his sovereignty descend to all his sons as soon as they became fathers? If it descended to one only, what became of the sovereignty of fatherhood? I may remark that all that Locke had to say on the point had been said long before, in a book written by a certain Edward Gee and published in 1648.[1] And it was all really irrelevant to Filmer's main contentions.

What Filmer had been trying to find was a basis for belief in a moral authority in government and a duty of obedience. He contended that none can be found, unless we are prepared to suppose that God has specially conferred a right to demand obedience as a duty. He contended that history shows that this actually happened, and that we must suppose that the right originally given to the patriarchs continued in kings. We cannot assume more than that, because the evidence does not suggest that God ever conferred authority upon any group or any ' people.' Besides, he argued, not only is there no evidence to show that God ever did this, but we can see for ourselves that it would have been an absurd thing to do. We cannot show precisely how kings acquired the rights of the patriarchs, and perhaps they all originally did so by usurpation. But unless we suppose that God sanctioned the transfer of authority to usurpers, and even to elected monarchs, all governments are left without moral authority. Locke's criticisms simply do not touch the contention.

My business is merely to try to explain what Filmer thought. I desire to refrain from comment. But I claim that Filmer was a thinker of uncommon power, and even of uncommon originality. It is true that almost everything he said had been said many times before. But he was, at least, original enough to differ from almost every one of his own time in England; and he was original also in that he really tried to answer fundamental questions. As a political thinker he was, in my opinion, far more profound and far more original than was Locke. I may remark that it seems to me nothing less than absurd to speak

[1] *The Divine Right and Original of Civil Magistrates from God.*

of his view of things as "the patriarchal theory," and dismiss it at that. That is to perpetuate the egregious mistake of Locke. What is called his patriarchal theory was, in fact, no more than an argument from history. It was, I admit, a shockingly bad one; but it was not in the least essential to his system of ideas. Even his belief that real authority existed in no other form than monarchy is unessential. What is essential in his thought is, first, the assertion that society needs absolutely a general recognition of a moral authority in government that is hardly limited and in every case precludes rebellion; and, secondly, the assertion that unless such authority is conceived as divinely sanctioned no basis can be found for it at all. Filmer uncompromisingly raised the old question as to why any man should consider himself bound to submit to government. What is the nature of political obligation, and what, if any, are its limits? His answer, admittedly, was unsatisfactory, and even, in detail, extravagant. But if anyone supposes that we, nowadays, are in possession of an answer much more satisfactory, I should very much like to know what that answer is.

J. W. Allen

BIBLIOGRAPHY

Filmer, Sir R.: *The Anarchy of a Limited and Mixed Monarchy.* 1648.
   Observations upon Aristotle's Politiques. 1652.
   Directions for Obedience to Governours. 1652.
   Observations concerning the Originall of Government upon Mr Hobs [sic] *Leviathan*, etc. 1652.
   The Necessity of the Absolute Power of all Kings (1648), republished as *The Power of Kings.* 1680.
   Patriarcha. 1680.
Bohun, E.: *A Defence of Sir R. Filmer.* 1684.

III

GEORGE SAVILE, MARQUIS OF HALIFAX

THE period of sixty-two years covered by the life of George Savile, Marquis of Halifax (1633–95), has an importance in the political and constitutional history of Great Britain that is fundamental. In that history Halifax played a part that won from Macaulay the just verdict that among the statesmen of his day he was in genius the first. His genius, it is true, was of a kind that makes no appeal to the common sentiments of most readers of history. One is not predisposed to admire the man who asserted the political virtues of a ' trimmer.' Yet it was to Halifax more than to any other single statesman that the Revolution owed the constitutional qualities that won for it the admiration of Burke.

The Saviles were a Yorkshire family of Lupset, Thornhill, and Wakefield, accustomed to take a responsible part in the administrative life of their shire. They were wealthy, and by marriage were well connected. The great-grandmother of Halifax was a daughter of the Earl of Shrewsbury ; his grandmother was a sister of the great Earl of Strafford ; his mother, Anne Coventry, was the daughter of the Lord Keeper and sister of Lady Shaftesbury. His father, Sir William, of Thornhill, was an unswerving Royalist who held a command in the Civil War, and for a time occupied Leeds and Wakefield. Appointed Governor of Sheffield, he died there six months before the battle of Marston Moor.[1] His son, then a boy of eleven, was probably present when his mother, in spite of the delicate state of her health, resisted the surrender of Sheffield Castle after the battle. To this courageous mother the boy was indebted for the wise control of his education. He appears to have studied abroad in Paris and Geneva.

He married before the Restoration, and settled at Rufford, in Nottinghamshire, on a beautiful wooded property formerly

---

[1] His will has a bequest of £50 to his faithful friend John Selden.

the demesne of a Cistercian abbey. Four years later his political life began with his election to represent Pontefract on the Convention, but he was not active in the Parliament that followed. The family was fortunate in that it had not been impoverished by the war. Savile was a wealthy man, and at no time in his life did he expose himself to the suspicion of using his political position for unworthy ends. It was one of the difficulties of the French Court that in their English intrigues they had to acknowledge him incapable of corruption, and it may have been this quality of integrity as well as his known capacity for business that led to his nomination by the Commons in 1668 to act as a commissioner to inquire into the scandals of the financial administration of the Navy. It is significant that Charles raised him to the peerage on his appointment as a commissioner, a fact which lends support to Macaulay's suggestion that rank had attractions for him.

A little later he built for himself a house at the north corner of King Street in the new *piazza* now known as St James's Square, and there from 1673 he lived when in town, " within a stone's throw of the embassies and half the political grandees." It was not, however, until Clarendon had fallen, the Cabal had been dissolved, and Danby's ministry had come to its end that he was admitted to the administration. In 1678 Temple's plan for the creation of a council of thirty representative men of wealth and position was adopted, and Charles reluctantly acquiesced in Temple's demand that Halifax should be included. His keen, witty, and searching criticism of the ministerial policies of the Cabal and Danby's administration had made him a power in the Lords to be respected, though to the King anything but a *persona grata*. The council of thirty was both too large and too small. It was too large both for the transaction of confidential business and for expedition; it was too small for deliberation. An inner council was formed, of which Halifax was a member, and by his wit and suavity Charles was captivated. It is from this point that the political life of Halifax must be followed. Hitherto he had been an observer and critic; now he was a responsible minister.

The situation that had developed in the eighteen years that had passed since Charles was crowned was one that might well have troubled a political thinker. It is characteristic of

Halifax that he always viewed even the most desperate political situation, as it were from a distance or an eminence, without perturbation. The country was distracted and excited. Its political life was embittered by religious persecution. Dissent had become a political force. In 1672 there are said to have been twelve thousand Quakers released from prison, but the year that witnessed their release witnessed also the closing of the Exchequer, and the nation was coming to know that Charles had bargained with the Catholic Louis XIV to make him independent of Parliament. The country was as vehement, therefore, in its distrust of Catholics as it had been in the days before the Armada. Yet the Duke of York, on the passing of the Test Act, had declared himself a Roman Catholic, and he was heir to the throne. The question of the succession was therefore at stake, and Shaftesbury, the most unscrupulous political leader of the time, made capital with the Commons by abetting the egregious fabrications of the Popish Plots. The excitement of the populace seems to have affected the Bench, and innocent Catholics were condemned to execution. In the Commons, where Anti-Catholic feeling ran high, Shaftesbury secured the passing of the Exclusion Bill. He was playing for high stakes as a king-maker, backing the handsome and popular illegitimate son of the King, the Duke of Monmouth; but Halifax defeated him in the Lords by persistent debating power, and the Bill was thrown out by 63 votes to 60.[1] To the professional party man, therefore, it appeared that Halifax was a Tory; yet he followed up his triumph by attempting to secure conditions for the Constitution that would have deprived James of a veto as King on any Act of Parliament, of all power of negotiating with a foreign Government and of controlling civil or military appointments. Shaftesbury meanwhile had secured the impeachment and execution of the aged Lord Stafford for alleged complicity in the Popish Plots. Against this iniquitous act Halifax protested without success. The depths to which in their support of Titus Oates Shaftesbury and the Whigs had descended were their ruin. Popular excitement subsided, the elections showed that public clamour was not a true

---

[1] " He was too hard for Shaftesbury, answering him each time he spoke, sixteen timea in all."

D

indication of the nation's mind.   Shaftesbury fled to Holland,
where he died.   A Tory reaction followed.   The Rye House
Plot to murder Charles and James on the way to Newmarket
led to a vindictive and retaliatory attack on the Whigs, and
there followed the execution of Lord Russell and Algernon
Sidney.   And just as Halifax had resisted the condemnation
of the Catholic Lord Stafford, so he defended Russell and
Sidney.   It was not the least of his virtues that he refused to
identify the welfare of the country as a whole with the success
of either the Whig party or the Tory.   Whenever popular
discontent became riotous and unrestrained he was a firm
champion of constitutional order, but when liberty was endangered he was a Whig.   In his championship of liberty he
anticipated Burke, when in the Tory reaction at the end of
the reign of Charles he championed the cause of the New
England Colonies.[1]

During the last two years of Charles's reign his energies,
hitherto directed to checking the Whig excesses, were
absorbed in combating the growing power of James.   This
influence was directed obstinately and persistently toward
Catholicism and the French alliance.   Its success would have
involved the loss of national independence, the suppres-
sion of Parliamentary power, and the absorption of Great
Britain in a scheme of things to which the good sense of
the country was opposed.   Could anything be done by a
reconciliation of Monmouth with the King ?   Monmouth
would, at least, make Protestantism safe, and thus keep alive
the spirit of the Triple Alliance.   Under wiser control than
Shaftesbury's he might save the situation.   It was in his
favour that he was popular.   Halifax found his hiding-place
after the Rye House Plot, and arranged a meeting with the
King ; but the influence of James was too strong for him.   So
determined, however, was his opposition to this influence
that he at last prevailed on Charles to sign a letter inviting
Monmouth to return to Court while at the same time he
circulated his famous pamphlet, *The Character of a Trimmer*.

---

[1] A note by Halifax on this point has interest : " Upon occasion of Gov^t to be
settled in New England ; I arguing for the liberty of the people hee [Jeffreys] replyed
whosoever capitulateth, rebelleth.   This at the Cabinet Councell." (Foxcroft, vol. i,
p. 428.)

By the middle of January 1685 he was able to write to Monmouth that in order to avert the possibility of a counter-plot Charles would send James to Scotland; but the King died a few days later, and was succeeded by his brother. Halifax, who was attached to Charles personally, embodied his impressions of his personality in his *Character of King Charles II*, a singularly dispassionate estimate if the political circumstances are considered in which it was composed.

It is clear from what has been said of the last years of Charles's reign that the problem uppermost in the mind of Halifax had been that of the succession. He stood firm both for hereditary and constitutional principles. Unless the bastard Monmouth could be legitimately interposed, James must succeed, and in the succession of James he acquiesced. For a time he remained on the council, but, although he was assured that " all the past is forgotten except the service you did me in the debate on the Exclusion Bill," he had not the King's confidence; and when he refused to countenance the repeal of the Test Act and of the Habeas Corpus Act his name was removed from the council. It was while James was attempting in the interests of Catholicism to bribe Nonconformity that Halifax published his *Letter to a Dissenter*, and when the King tried to win the Church's support he attacked his bribe in a second pamphlet, *The Anatomy of an Equivalent*.

During James's reign, nevertheless, he steadily opposed the idea of a revolution. William of Orange had sent Dykvelt to organise English opposition in his wife's interests, but Halifax steadily repelled his overtures. In standing for a strictly constitutional development he opposed not only the Francophile policy of James, but also the risk of sacrificing the independence of England by too close an association with the Francophobe policy of William. In 1688 he visited the Seven Bishops in the Tower—a gesture that cannot have been misunderstood by the King—yet when William landed Halifax was a member of the small commission sent by James to interview him. In spite of William's insistence on full publicity Halifax and Burnet exchanged significant words :

" Are the invaders desirous of getting the King into their hands? " asked Halifax.

" No," was the reply.

" But what if he has a mind to go away ? "

" Nothing so much is to be wished."

When the embassy returned to report James had fled the capital, and his representatives found themselves left, as it were, in the air. That the dispatch of the commissioners had been a feint to enable the King to save time and send his wife and infant son to France is clear from his words to Barillon :

> You know the temper of my troops. None but the Irish will stand by me. A Parliament would impose on me conditions which I could not endure. I should be forced to undo all that I had done for the Catholics, and to break with the King of France. As soon, therefore, as the Queen and my child are safe, I will leave England and take refuge in Ireland, in Scotland, or with your master.

During the absence of the King Halifax presided over the council for the defence of London. He had worked for an honourable compromise and failed. When James returned Halifax joined William at Windsor, and presided there at the consultation of peers. Throughout the subsequent deliberations, and in the convention that grew out of them, he acted as chairman or Speaker of the Lords. His influence during the interregnum was paramount. The Commons decided that James had broken the original contract between king and people, had abdicated the government, and that the throne was vacant. In other words, the Whigs triumphed in the Commons. Halifax championed their views in the Lords, and it was mainly due to his debating power that the proposals of Sancroft, the Tories, and the Bishops for the establishment of a regency were defeated. So long as there had been any chance of saving James without sacrificing the Constitution Halifax had been a Tory. He was now leading the Whig cause, and it was he who in the Banqueting Hall at Whitehall solemnly requested William and Mary to accept the crown. " The revolution, so far as it can be said to bear the character of any single mind, assuredly bears the character of the large yet cautious mind of Halifax." [1]

For two years he took an active part in the Whig administration under William and Mary, but once more found himself inevitably forced into opposition. " The Commons acted

[1] Macaulay.

slowly, as if the whole world were only Westminster." He was impatient with those persons of rank who looked for office merely because they had been serviceable in bringing about the Revolution. " Rome was saved by geese," he remarked, " but I do not remember that these geese were made consuls." Nor did he escape from the excesses and injustices of party politics that he had always condemned. He was examined by the committee appointed to inquire into the responsibility for the deaths of Russell and Sidney, and it ought not to have been necessary for Tillotson to have to testify that Lord Russell had in his last speeches commended Halifax's humanity and kindness. He withdrew from office, but not from active interest in affairs. In his retirement he found pleasure in writing, and it is to these last years that we may assign his *Maxims of State*, his *Political, Moral, and Miscellaneous Thoughts and Reflections*, and his *Rough Draught of a New Model at Sea*.

In his later days he lived at Acton, and when questions arose in the Lords on which the prevalent feeling excited his opposition he spoke and voted. Thus he opposed in 1693 the renewal of the censorship of the Press in a signed protest which declared that the signatories " could not think it for the public interest to submit all learning and true information to the arbitrary will and pleasure of a mercenary and perhaps ignorant licenser."

He died in 1695, within a month of the death of Queen Mary, and within a few days of the death of Dorothy Osborne, " the most accomplished, the most enlightened, and the most estimable of the statesmen," if we may use the words of Macaulay, " who were formed in the corrupt and licentious Whitehall of the Restoration." He was buried in the chapel of Henry VII. His two sons were dead, and his title soon became extinct, but his daughter married Philip Stanhope, third Earl of Chesterfield.

II

When Sir Walter Raleigh wrote his penetrating introduction to the edition of the " Complete Works " he regretted that as a writer Halifax was neglected :

53

English literature is very rich; only a very rich literature could have afforded to neglect so distinguished a writer. But it is not rich in practical wisdom; and the neglect of Halifax is a thing to be regretted and amended.

The works of Halifax are "crammed with lessons drawn directly from his experience" of the practical business of public life, and no one has done more to rescue them from neglect than their admirer and editor, Raleigh. They are the reflections of a political thinker, and it is in this light mainly that they must be considered; but his *Advice to a Daughter* or, as he also described it, *The Lady's New Year's Gift*, stands in a place apart. As this daughter became the mother of Philip Dormer, Earl of Chesterfield, one may play with the thought that the *Letters to his Son*, though better known than the *Advice to a Daughter*, owe their inspiration to Halifax.

The charge that Halifax was without religion lends a special interest to the chapter on "Religion" with which the *Advice* opens. It is as a Latitudinarian that he writes, and though he mentions neither Papists nor Dissenters he has them in mind. He denounces the "loud answers and devout convulsions" of the zealots. "Religion," to him, "is a cheerful thing. Nothing unpleasant belongs to it, though the spiritual cooks have done their unskilful part to give an ill relish to it."

The young lady is advised how to deal with the husband whom it may fall to her lot to have to manage, be he choleric, sullen, covetous, close-fisted, or given to wine. Even the incompetent man is included: "If your husband shall resolve to be an Ass, take care that he may be your Ass."

From the husband to the home is an obvious step. That children, he warns his daughter, are not naturally grateful is not a defect in their good nature so much as "a shortness of thought in them." Their first thoughts have in them "no small mixture of mutiny." This is natural, and a parent's anger only increases it. Evenness of temper, quietness, ease and regularity in the conduct of household business, are virtues highly esteemed by servants in their mistress. Obedience naturally follows. The "empty, airy thing that sails up and down the house to no kind of purpose" he dismisses as the *insignificant* housewife.

"It is now time," he goes on, "to lead you out of your

House into the *World* "—a dangerous step, where virtue must be supported by prudence. A gallery of feminine types exhibited as a warning includes *the good-humoured woman, the complaisant woman, the girl of fifty*. A perpetual watch must be kept even upon the eyes, for the extravagances of the age and the " too great Licence of ill Men " have made reserve and caution necessary. Vanity and affectation are the prevailing faults of the women of the day. Vanity he wittily describes as the sin, and affectation the punishment. As for the *Jolly Ladies* who affect endless diversion, they end by making themselves *cheap*, than which there cannot, he concludes, " be an unkinder word bestowed upon their sex." As a picture of Restoration manners, the *Advice* is invaluable; of all homilies it is the least dull; without it Restoration comedy would be without its best commentary.

The political writings of Halifax have the interesting characteristic that it is not easy to identify without external assistance the occasion for which they were written. His power lay in his capacity to extract from the most complex and disturbed situations principles of action that have abiding validity. It is upon this genius for generalising, this quality of philosophical serenity, that their value rests as political writings. They exhibit no acrimony; there is in them nothing inflammatory, nothing personal. They were nevertheless occasional tracts inspired by particular situations, and are best understood by taking into account the circumstances in which they first appeared. As an example of this occasional character we may take his *Cautions offered to the Consideration of those who are to chuse Members to serve for the Ensuing Parliament*. References in the pamphlet to the Triennial Bill and Place Bill enable us to place it very precisely. The Lords had defeated the latter Bill, and on March 14, 1693, the King had vetoed the former, only, however, to relent and give it his royal assent in December 1694. To this assent Halifax refers in his *Cautions*, but as he died within a month we must assume that it is his last political pamphlet, written within the last weeks of his life in anticipation of a general election to which he attached great importance, but which he did not live to see. It is interesting that his last words as a Parliamentary constitutionalist were addressed to electors. He urges them to see to it that it is an election and not a fight, and that it is free from influence as well as force; for influence is only a degree of force.

Active times breed knaves and busybodies; candidates, therefore, who are unquiet in their natures must give more than ordinary proofs of their integrity. "It would be ingratitude in some men to turn honest when they owe all they have to their knavery." "Great drinkers are less fit to serve in Parliament than is apprehended." "Nothing is more frail than a Man too far engaged in wet Popularity." If a man have a small estate and a numerous family, it is not a recommending circumstance for his election. "Avoid the man of tinsel-wit who shines only among those who cannot judge "; and equally avoid "True Heart of Oak Ignorance." "There is an abuse which daily increaseth, of sending such to Parliament, as are scarce old enough to be sent to the University." "If the House of Commons is a School it must be for men of riper age."

Nor are superfine gentlemen to be chosen, "carpet-knights, men whose heads may be said to be only appurtenances to their perukes." Men who are law-breakers cannot change their nature out of respect to their country. They must be excluded. Prodigals and hoarders alike are men unfit to trust with the guardianship of public money. The interest of a country is best placed in the hands of such as have some share—*i.e.*, considerable estate—in it. *Outliers*, as Halifax calls carpet-baggers, should be considered trespassers. "Lawyers, by the same reason that they may be useful, may be also very dangerous." They are generally men who hope to be advanced. He puts in a powerful caveat against men tied to a party. Such a man can hardly be a free agent. Even in times of peace a party exercises martial law. "The man that quitteth, if they had their will, would be hanged for a deserter." "Nothing is more evident than that the Good of the Nation hath been sacrificed to the Animosities of the several contending Parties." "It is pretty sure that while these opposite sets of angry Men are playing at Football . . . they will do more hurt than their pretended zeal for the nation will ever make amends for." Military officers are out of their element when they are misplaced in the House of

Commons; nor should any man be admitted who holds a place in the public service. He is dependent on the Government. Above all let the electors think twice before voting for a man who voted against the Triennial Bill. And if in conclusion it be asked whom, then, one must choose: " My Answer must be *Choose Englishmen*; and when I have said that, to deal honestly, I will not undertake to say that they are easy to be found."

There is a sting in the words " choose Englishmen." Halifax had not debated with himself the question of the succession without hesitating long in his choice of evils. Under James the danger was French domination, with William it lay in Dutch influence; and the Dutch were our maritime rivals. William disliked the Triennial Bill. Would he attempt to influence the new election? It seems that Halifax distrusted him.

Ten years earlier in his *Character of a Trimmer* he had disclosed one of the motives of his political conduct:

> Our Trimmer is far from Idolatry in other things, in one thing only he cometh near it, his Country is in some degree his Idol; he doth not worship the Sun, because it is not peculiar to us, it rambles about the world, and is less kind to us than to others; but for the Earth of *England*, tho' perhaps inferior to that of many places abroad, to him there is a Divinity in it, and he would rather dye, than see a spire of *English* Grass trampled down by a Foreign Trespasser: He thinketh there are a great many of his mind, for all plants are apt to taste of the Soyl in which they grow, and we that grow here, have a root that produceth in us a Stalk of English Juice, which is not to be changed by grafting or foreign infusion.

Another example of the importance or interest of recognising the occasions which led Halifax to enunciate his views may be cited. There were in his opinion three forms of government, to one of which England must be subjected: Absolute Monarchy, a Commonwealth, a Mixed Monarchy. He refused to close his eyes to the smooth efficiency of the unlimited power of the French absolutism. He saw and admired it. Government, nevertheless, he argued, being a means to an end—viz., that mankind should live in some competent state of freedom—he found it unnatural to have the end (freedom) destroyed by the means (government). But England, he states, cannot subsist under a despotic power. Our being would be destroyed by it. For we are a very little spot on the map of the world, and make a great figure only by *trade*, which is the creation of liberty. Destroy this and the other perishes. Measured by acres, we are a poor, inconsiderable people. Our situation, humour, trade, good laws, and excellent Constitution exalt us above our natural bounds. For us, then, there is no mean between being a " Free Nation and No Nation."

He is not prepared to say that another revolution might not turn England into a commonwealth, but he thinks it highly improbable. He allows that abstract considerations suggest that a commonwealth best serves the interest of a nation, and he holds interest to be an unfailing criterion in human actions; but only if it is recognised. He denies that mankind as he knows it is capable of discerning its own true interests. It is incapable of responding to the vision of a commonwealth. Moreover, in England he finds a general dislike to the idea; the national humour is against it, the herd is opposed to it. A commonwealth, he concludes, is not fit for us, because we are not fit for a commonwealth. A mixed, bounded, or limited monarchy, therefore, is the form of government most likely to prevail and continue in England, provided that it always retains the means to restrain the exercise of despotic power.

These general considerations upon the nature of the Government most fitting for England are found where one would least expect them. Like the *Cautions*, they were written in the last year of Halifax's life in a short pamphlet entitled *A Rough Draught of a New Model at Sea*. The French war had virtually closed the Mediterranean to English and Dutch merchantmen. In February 1693 the Smyrna fleet of four hundred left under convoy; but such was the incompetence—some said treachery—of the English admirals, or the efficiency of the French, that the fleet was taken or dispersed. There was great excitement on the Exchange and in Parliament, inquiries were instituted, and the Admiralty was placed under a new commission. Naval efficiency became the problem of the day; and the burning question was from what sort of men the officers of the fleet were to be recruited—gentlemen or tarpaulins?

Halifax opens his discussion with a striking sentence :

> It may now be said to England, *Martha, Martha*, thou art busy about many things, but one thing is necessary. To the Question, What shall we do to be saved in the World? there is no other Answer but this, Look to your Moate.

That all officers should be tarpaulins he cannot allow; it would be in reality too great a tendency to a commonwealth. Similarly, that all officers should be gentlemen would be to open the way to the abuse of arbitrary power. For the Navy he holds to be of so great importance that he can call it " nothing less than the *Life* and *Soul* of our Government."

There remains the solution by mixture; a mixture in the Navy of gentlemen and tarpaulins, as there is in the constitution of the Government a mixture of power and liberty. But he exacts a stern condition. The gentlemen shall not be capable of bearing office at sea except they be tarpaulins too; that is to say, except they are so trained up by a continued habit of living at sea that they may have a right to be admitted " free Denizens of Wapping."

It was probably during the two or three years of freedom from administrative responsibility enjoyed by Halifax at the close of his life that he put together the collections of apophthegms and opinions entitled *Political, Moral, and Miscellaneous Thoughts and Reflections*. These, though disjected aphorisms, throw light on his teaching, as well as on the temper of his mind. Thus his attack on the loose use by party politicians of the specious term ' fundamentals ' leads him to the statement:

> A Constitution cannot make itself; somebody made it, not at once but at several times. It is alterable; and by that draweth to Perfection; and without suiting itself to differing Times and Circumstances it could not live. Its life is prolonged by changing seasonably the several Parts of it at several times.

The prerogative of the King, he continues, is a trust. The laws are not the King's laws nor the Parliament's laws, but the laws of England. More fundamental than the Constitution, than even the laws, is that supreme power which may change them. Such a power is arbitrary. It is as though a man had uncontested and irresistible power to do the thing he desires to do. He will certainly do it.

Thus he develops his conception of the Constitution as a living thing which must grow or die. Its end is, or ought to be, the *Salus Populi*, or, better, the good of the people; but circumstances may arise in which the *Salus Populi* must be sacrificed. Is there then any assured political 'fundamental' after all?

It is, however, the wit and observation of Halifax that are illustrated by the *Thoughts and Reflections*, rather than coherent political thought; and of these the following aphorisms may stand as an example:

Men who borrow their opinions can never repay their debts.

Some men's heads are as easily blown away as their hats.

Innocence [he is speaking of apologies] hath a very short style.

Popularity is a crime from the moment it is sought . . .; it is stepping very low to get very high.

The Government of the World is a great thing; but it is a very coarse one too, compared with the fineness of Speculative Knowledge.

Men are not hanged for stealing horses, but that horses may not be stolen.

Ignorance maketh most men go into a party, and shame keepeth them from getting out of it.

Laws are generally not understood by three sorts of Persons, viz., by those that make them, by those that execute them, and by those that suffer, if they break them.

In a limited monarchy prerogative and liberty are as jealous of one another as any two neighbouring states can be of their respective encroachments.

The first ground of prerogative was to enable the Prince to do *good*, not to do *everything*.

There is an accumulative Cruelty in a number of Men, though none in particular are ill-natured.

The angry Buzz of a Multitude is one of the bloodiest noises in the world.

So far we have been considering the works of the closing years of Halifax's life, works written in retirement in the reign of William III. We now turn to the works of his fighting days, the writings inspired by critical situations in the reigns of Charles and James. By his determined stand against

Shaftesbury in the debates in the Lords on the Exclusion Bill
Halifax had, as we have seen, kept the succession open for
James, who, had he shown himself capable of submission to
constitutional restraints, might have overcome Halifax's rooted
distrust of his Catholicism. James's obstinate folly culminated in the Declaration of Indulgence, an unscrupulous bribe
to Dissenters offered in the interests of the Catholics. So far
from being merely a politic act, this was nothing less than
a declaration of the absolute power of the Crown. Tempo-
rarily there was a wavering in the ranks of the Dissenters, and
Halifax met the danger by a pamphlet entitled *A Letter to a
Dissenter*, twenty thousand copies of which were distributed
throughout the country.

He suggests that Dissenters have cause to suspect their
new friends, and appeals to them to take thought for the public
safety. Can there be a true alliance between liberty and
infallibility? " The other day you were sons of Belial, now
you are angels of light." He hints at the next probable
revolution, and asks in what position they will then find themselves. " Let us be still, quiet, and undivided, firm at the
same time to our Religion, our Loyalty, and our Laws." The
King has failed to win the compliance of the Church of
England; is he to succeed in dividing Protestantism? Protestant disunion is not only a reproach, it is a danger.

Dissent had little cause to think of the Church of England
as a natural ally; but it responded to the examples of its own
best representatives, men like Baxter and Bunyan, and by its
resistance to the Declaration justified the appeal of Halifax.
A year later the King renewed his effort, offering now as an
equivalent to guarantee the establishment of the Church of
England. The refusal to read the Declaration in the churches
and the trial of the Seven Bishops were the result. Meanwhile
Halifax had returned to the attack in a second pamphlet
entitled *The Anatomy of an Equivalent*, opposing the bribe to
the Church. The acquittal of the Bishops was virtually the
condemnation of the King, and the fact that Halifax visited
them in their confinement is significant of his attitude to the
constitutional questions at issue. *The Anatomy of an Equivalent* is in some ways the most characteristic of his writings.
Apparently an examination of the elements of true bargaining,

actually it is a demonstration of the ulterior motives of the King. Halifax was less interested in the ecclesiastical than in the constitutional questions at issue. If he had allowed himself the liberty of expressing his own attitude toward the three ecclesiastical opponent parties he would probably have written something in effect not unlike Swift's *Tale of a Tub*; but the interests of Peter, Martin, and Jack were not as important to him as England and the King's encroachments on the liberties of her Constitution. An unlimited prerogative is the object of his attack, and he asks mischievously what equivalent or honest bargain one can hope for from a Catholic Church incapable of dealing equally without *betraying her prerogative*. To the Catholic in his dealing with heretics there can be no question of equality.

There remains to be considered the work by which Halifax is best known, *The Character of a Trimmer*. He was engaged when he wrote it in resisting the growing influence of James and the Tories in the closing years of Charles's reign. This Tory reaction may be dated from the meeting and dissolution of Charles's Third Parliament at Oxford in March 1681. A month later an entertaining daily paper was started by the famous Tory journalist, L'Estrange, with the title *The Observator: in Questions and Answers*. The interlocutors at first were indicated merely by a " Q." and " A." Later they became " Whig " and " Tory." Later again the " Observator " took the place of " Tory," and allowed himself to be referred to familiarly as " Nobs." In his absence his part was sustained by the " Courantier," and on November 13, 1682, " Whig " dropped out and the paper opened :

> *Trimmer*. Sir, at your Service, my Name is Trimmer.
> *Courantier*. What akin may you be to the Laodicean in the Revelation? Pray how came you at first to be call'd *Trimmer*?
> *Trimmer*. We write with an *Alias*: But I fancy the name originally had an allusion to the language of the River.[1] When a vessel does not row even, they'l cry Trimm the Boat. And so

---

[1] Compare the use made by Halifax of this metaphor in his *Character of a Trimmer* : " This innocent word *Trimmer* signifieth no more than this, that if men are together in a boat, and one part of the company would weigh it down on one side, another would make it lean as much to the contrary ; it happeneth there is a third opinion of those who conceive it would do as well if the boat went even, without endangering the passengers."

when one side is lower than t'other, 'tis our way to lean to the Upper Side, and still to make the best of things.

Two days later " Whig," " Tory," and " Courantier " have all disappeared, and for more than three years *The Observator* was to be a series of dialogues between the " Observator " and a " Trimmer." On December 3, 1684, " Trimmer " asks :

> And what is a Trimmer at last?

" Observator " replies :

> Why a Trimmer is a Hundred thousand things. A Trimmer, I tell ye, is a man of Latitude as well in Politiques as Divinity; An Advocate both for Liberty of Practice in the State and for Liberty of Conscience in the Church . . .

On the following day the sheet opens with :

> *Obs.* We gave off yesterday in the middle of a Discourse upon the *Character and Humour of a Trimmer.*
> *Trimmer.* Yes, Yes, I remember't very well; by the token that you were carping at Protestant Principles which looks very ill, let me tell ye, in a man that has taken the Sacrament upon't that he's a True Son of the Church of England.

It was at this point that Halifax, who, it must be noted, is nowhere attacked in *The Observator* by name, anonymously wrote his *Character of a Trimmer.* For two years the term had been held up to ridicule by a clever journalist to indicate a politician whose sympathies are always with the law-breakers and never with the law. Halifax turned the attack by assuming the title of reproach as one of which he was proud, and proceeding to justify himself in his character as " Trimmer."

Our " Trimmer," he says, greatly venerates the laws, but does not care to see them turned to the disgraceful office of destroying mankind. Unworthy judges—he is hinting at the political trials—are a discredit to the King who nominated them. Our " Trimmer " is not a commonwealth man nor a monarchist.

> Monarchy leaveth men no liberty and a Commonwealth no quiet. The Rules of a Commonwealth are too hard for the Bulk of Mankind to come up to; that form of government requireth such a spirit to carry it on, as doth not dwell in great Numbers.

Absolute monarchy is good only if the prince is good, wise, and powerful; but as heaven has willed that the good and bad are mixed in the world, there must be laws and rules to check the wantonness of princely power.

Our "Trimmer" thinketh that the King and kingdom ought to be one creature. The King therefore is not to be reduced to the single definition of a man; he must be surrounded with dignity. All force, however, is a "kind of foul-play." He who uses it "doth by implication allow it to those he playeth with."

Kings ought to beware of "employing small authors" to urge their unconstitutional claims. "It is the People that readeth these books; and the People that must judge of them." This is as near as Halifax comes to a reference to L'Estrange in the body of the pamphlet.

In his faith in the national spirit he rises to a height that has almost a religious fervour:

> When all is said there is a Natural Reason of State, an indefinable thing, grounded upon the Common Good of Mankind, which is immortal, and in all Changes and Revolutions still preserveth its original right of saving a Nation when the Letter of the Law perhaps would destroy it; and by whatsoever means it moveth, carrieth a power with it, that admitteth of no opposition, being supported by Nature, which inspireth an immediate consent at some Critical times into every individual Member, to that which visibly tendeth to preservation of the whole; and this being so, a Wise Prince, instead of controverting the right of the Reason of State, will by all means endeavour it may be of his side, and then he will be secure.

This passage, which is central in the teaching of Halifax, was, it must be remembered, intended to be read by Charles, and possibly to influence the question of the succession. The reference to the "Letter of the Law" thus becomes significant if Halifax had James and Monmouth in mind.

> Our Trimmer owneth a passion for liberty, yet so restrained that it doth not in the least impair or taint his Allegiance. . . .
>
> He admireth our blessed Constitution [in which] the Crown hath power sufficient to protect our liberties and the People have so much Liberty as is necessary to make them useful to the Crown. . . .
>
> Our Government is like our Climate, there are Winds which are

sometimes loud and unquiet, and yet with all the Trouble they give us we owe great part of our Health unto them, they clear the Air. . . .

Our Trimmer is a Friend to Parliaments [his last address was, as we have seen, directed to the electors of a Parliament that he did not live to see] notwithstanding all their faults, and excesses which of late have given such matter of objection to them.

He " cannot help thinking it had been better if the Triennial Act had been observed, because 'tis the Law "—and " all irregularity is catching." He would have had a Parliament, because it is an essential part of the Constitution. Nothing else can unite and heal us. All other means are mere shifts, " houses of cards."

Halifax must be thought of not as answering L'Estrange, whom he despised, but as addressing Charles, for whom he had a certain respect and definite liking.

So far we have been dealing with the " Trimmer's " opinion on the laws and Government. He next turns to the Protestant religion. To the Church of England our " Trimmer " is " very partial." How and by what methods can the Church best bear itself toward Dissenters of all sorts? First, there can be no true religion without charity, and though the late conspiracies are not easy to forgive and forget, moderate men will hesitate to involve a whole party in the guilt of a few. Our " Trimmer " therefore refuses to condemn all Dissenters because some have been conspirators; nor can he resist the feeling that their affectation toward separation from the Church is a kind of disease of the mind. In time the laws may change, and moderate men can afford to be patient. He urges Nonconformists to come into the Established Church of England, and he urges the Church to open the gate to the strayed sheep. There is much to forgive, but that must not cut off hopes of reconciliation. Our " Trimmer " supports the clergy in their lawful rights, but not in their political ambitions. " He thinketh that a nation will hardly be mended by principles of religion where *morality* is made a *heresy*." If devotion is misplaced when it gets into a conventicle, so too is loyalty in a drunken club. The liberty of the Commonwealth days had diffused light so universally among the people that " good resolute nonsense backed by authority " no longer prevails. Men are become good judges of what they hear;

" the world has grown saucy and expects reasons." Our " Trimmer " allows that hypocrisy arraigning vice among some of the Dissenting clergy is a most provoking sin, yet that very sin may help to save some of the company of listeners. That a Protestant Church should voluntarily elect a Popish king for their guardian, who must believe that it is a mortal sin not to endeavour to destroy that Church, is such a refined piece of breeding that he cannot help but smile at the preachers who prefer it to an understanding with Dissenters.

His attitude toward the Catholics is largely governed by considerations of policy. His whole genius lay in the direction of wise compromise in the national interest. With the Catholic clergy compromise was impossible : with the Catholic gentry, particularly the landowners, he urged the exercise of patience. It is only the laymen who are capable of being treated with. By a curious irony the lord of the Cistercian estate at Rufford suggests that a lay Papist will first consider that his abbey lands will sink in value the moment that Popery prevails. He would be prepared to mitigate such anti-Papal laws as have been made (" as it is said King Henry VIII got Queen Elizabeth ") in a heat against Rome.

> We must not always be smelling the match that was to blow up the king and both houses in the Gunpowder Treason.

Our " Trimmer's " opinion in relation to things abroad has particular interest as a serious study of our peculiar position as a balancing power. To support the weaker side was our historic policy until Cromwell chose to join the stronger, in order to suppress the power of Spain, which Halifax held he ought to have supported. His analysis of the foreign policy of France in relation to the Dutch and the English is a masterpiece of lucid exposition. It is in this chapter that the great passage occurs to which we have already referred as an important motive of his political conduct :

> Our Trimmer is far from Idolatry in other things, in one thing only he cometh near it, his Country is in some degree his Idol.

The one thing he dreaded—and it was the weightiest warning he could address to Charles—was a " general discontent."

LORD HALIFAX

Not long after he had read *The Character of a Trimmer*, Charles, for whom it was written, died, and Halifax wrote his frank but sympathetic *Character of King Charles II*. He shirks nothing; he admits that dissimulation was his fault. He talks of his amours and his mistresses. He writes of his habit of sauntering. He tells us that he had back stairs to convey informations to him, as well as for other uses. He has a delightful chapter on his wit and conversation, and he begins his analysis of his talents, temper, and habits by telling us that he had a " mechanical head," a natural inclination toward practical business, and a very good memory. " Let his royal ashes," he concludes, " then lie soft upon him, and cover him from harsh and unkind censures; which though they should not be unjust, can never clear themselves from being indecent. What private man will throw stones at him because he loved, or what prince because he dissembled? "

Halifax stands in a place apart among the politicians of his age. One alone challenges comparison with him. He and his friend Sir William Temple had much in common. Statesmen of remarkable prescience, men of acknowledged probity, independent and imperturbable, each in his own sphere of action laid down lines of conduct in foreign or home affairs that stand approved to-day as established precedents in statesmanship. If Temple's public conduct has the appearance of greater consistency it is because he held aloof from domestic politics. In his attitude toward foreign affairs Halifax was no less persistent than he in supporting the principles of the Triple Alliance or in his hostility to the ambitions and intrigues of France. In some respects Halifax was a forerunner of Burke, as a political thinker gifted with the power of enunciating political ideas in a form that has given them permanence. And in this connexion it may be noted that when the New England colonies were threatened by a Tory ministry with the loss of provincial government Halifax championed their cause against his colleagues in a manner that has won the admiration of historians. " He was a man of a great and ready wit; full of life, and very pleasant; much turned to satire. . . . He was punctual in all his payments and just in all his private dealings. But with relation to the public, he went backwards and forwards and changed sides so often that in conclusion no side trusted him." So wrote his friend Burnet, who, like most of his contemporaries, failed to understand Halifax's contempt of party loyalty and his virtues as a ' trimmer.'

A. W. REED

BIBLIOGRAPHY

Much is to be found of interest and value for the student of Halifax in Macaulay's *History of England* and his essay on *Sir William Temple*. The *Works* are accessible in a Clarendon Press edition by Sir Walter Raleigh, with a characteristically refreshing Introduction (1912). The best survey of his ideas is probably that by G. P. Gooch in his *Political Thought from Bacon to Halifax* ("Home University Library"). Last, but most important, there is the definitive edition in two volumes by Miss H. C. Foxcroft, entitled *The Life and Letters of Sir George Savile* (Longmans, 1898).

JOHN LOCKE

HE political theory of John Locke has been so frequently analysed in the past fifty years, and the arguments of his *Essay on Civil Government* have been so carefully scrutinised from the *Lectures on Political Obligation* to the brilliant essay by Professor Laski,[1] that it is an impossible task to add anything new to what has already been said on the subject. Nor shall I attempt to add one more to that growing number of epitomes of *Civil Government* which form the stock-in-trade of the class text-books on political ideas. I shall merely try to suggest one or two lines of thought concerning those general conceptions which formed the background of Locke's political reasoning, and which seem to be of significance when one is trying to place the man in his true setting in the history of the modern world. A recent penetrating article [2] has reminded us of the dangers of a merely abstract analysis of a thinker's work, apart from its concrete setting; and it would seem that a careful reading of Locke's journals and letters would suggest to any future historian of Western political theory some interesting ideas concerning the material in terms of which Locke attempted to answer the problems that confronted him.

In the century and a quarter preceding Locke's birth three great revolutions had shaken to fragments man's intellectual world and brought to chaos the neatly ordered hierarchy of purposes and beings of the mediæval system. The religious revolution had destroyed for ever the Catholic conception of the Church as an unquestionable and divine trustee of truth, and had let loose in the world the spirit of critical individualism. But the full significance of the Reformation only slowly dawned

---

[1] *Political Thought in England : from Locke to Bentham.*
[2] " The Philosophical Significance of Biography," by A. K. White, in *Journal of Philosophical Studies*, vol. i, No. 4.

upon the minds of men. Hampered by the despotism of princes on the one hand and the hesitant narrowness of the early Protestant doctors on the other, the critical genius of the Reformation did not come fully to self-consciousness until the seventeenth century. It was not until then that the spirit of rationalism, of individual judgment, and liberty of examination invaded all fields of thought and action, and that the religious soul began with mingled hope and terror to see open before it the bounds of new horizons.

A second revolution was shaking the fabric of man's world at the same time. The Copernican revolution had removed man from his proud position as the central figure and end of the universe, and had substituted for that picture the conception of man as an insignificant element on a tiny planet, among infinite worlds and in infinite space. The work of Copernicus was but a beginning; it was left to Tycho Brahe, Kepler, and Galileo, by accurate observation and mathematical induction, to establish experimental confirmation of the Copernican theory and to substitute for the Thomistic system of variety and gradation the notion of the uniformity of nature. It was in 1632 that Galileo's chief work, *The Dialogue on the Two Chief Systems of the World*, was published; and the following year —when Locke was but one year old—that the works of all these pioneers were put on the *Index*. The battle between the old view and the new was definitely joined.

But along with the Copernican revolution had gone yet a third and no less vast intellectual upheaval which is usually called the Cartesian revolution. The fragmentary conceptions of all the pioneers from Leonardo to Kepler were fused into a system by Descartes, and he, first of all moderns, sketched the clear outline of the new universe in which men now found themselves. He had made of nature a vast machine manifesting nothing but an inexorable mechanical order. His *Discourse on Method* was published when Locke was five years old; and his mathematical interpretation of the universe spread throughout Europe with the rapidity of a fierce enthusiasm.

Such were the revolutions, all three of which had reached something of a climax at the time of Locke's birth. It is in Locke's life that one sees the fierce and tragic efforts by an age to find a synthesis, and to find for man somewhere a place, something of a fixed home, in the vast and lonely stretches of an infinite universe. Without the realisation of this fact one cannot possibly grasp the significance of any of Locke's work. To take his politics in isolation is to misinterpret him woefully, and to deliver over to party his bequest to mankind.

John Locke was born at Wrington, ten miles from Bristol, on August 29, 1632. His grandfather was a merchant-draper who had prospered and acquired various small proper-ties in Somerset. His father seems to have led an interesting and varied existence ; he was a small landowner, solicitor, and clerk to the local justices ; typical of the lesser seventeenth-century gentry, and keenly interested in religious and political problems. Of this man we get a fascinating glimpse through a small notebook which chance has preserved to us, and which is now in the British Museum. It shows us something of the intellectual climate in which the future philosopher was born and bred. It was the habit of the elder Locke to carry with him a notebook of accounts ; but he recorded therein not merely the interesting trivialities of a country solicitor's reckonings, but also the thoughts on current topics which were agitating his mind at the time. One such entry is typical :

> Is the Episcopacy a divine institution? Is the voice of a people necessary to the election of a minister? Is the Roman Church a true Church?

The growing struggle between King and Commons was rapidly rising to a crisis ; but the problems were first presented in a religious guise ; and it was within the limited sphere of ecclesiastical organisation that the critical individualism of the Reformation first developed its capacity for social problem-solving. The notebook is eloquent of this, and we find the Puritan solicitor out of hostility to the policy of Laud debating within himself all manner of topics from predestination to the ceremonies of the Eucharist.

In such an atmosphere of critical reflection and doubt of official truths Locke became adolescent. His relations with his father were interesting and formative. While he was a child, he tells us, his father treated him with becoming Puritan severity ; but as the boy grew to manhood the father

71

relaxed by degrees, until eventually they lived together as close friends and comrades. Mr J. A. Hobson, in his recent great contribution to the process of social thinking, emphasises the enormous influence of paternal authority in determining the direction of social attitudes. John Locke's happy experience of a frank *camaraderie* was scarcely the soil in which one would expect Filmer's absurd notions of paternal despotism to flourish very successfully—a fact not to be forgotten when considering Locke's later outlook.

The Civil War broke out the week before John's tenth birthday. His father at once joined up with the Parliamentary forces, as captain under a family friend named Colonel Popham. After a year's suspense the decisive battle was fought at Roundaway Down, just before Locke was eleven, and the Royalists were completely victorious. The elder Locke barely escaped with his life in the general *sauve qui peut*. Henceforth he was practically a ruined man.

The tide turned, however, in time for Colonel Popham to be of service to the young John. In the October of 1645, when the boy was thirteen, Popham was elected to the Long Parliament for Bath. It happened that Westminster School had been put under a Parliamentary committee of control, and Popham seems to have used his influence to get John elected on the foundation in 1646.

Of his life at Westminster we know next to nothing. The fearsome Richard Busby of whom Evelyn speaks was headmaster, and gave the boys a ruthless and painful classical education of which Locke later spoke with much bitterness. But events without the school walls can assuredly not have failed to continue the political education begun down in Somerset. Westminster was the centre of that ferment which agitated the whole country; and the place of execution was within sight of the school windows.

All we know definitely is that Locke went up to Oxford with a scholarship, and was entered at Christ Church in the Michaelmas term of 1652, when he was twenty. At that time the Dean and Vice-Chancellor was John Owen, who had replaced the Royalist Dr Fell six years before. This don is one of the noblest figures of the Interregnum, and doubtless exerted no small influence on the maturing Locke. Originally a Presbyterian, but now turned Independent, he had been brought from some country retreat by Fairfax and appointed to Oxford. Called upon to preach before Cromwell the day after the King's execution, he advocated moderation and abstention from triumph. At Oxford he had given a remarkable example of the practical possibility of toleration, and his Vice-Chancellorship constitutes a unique moment in the seventeenth century. This experience of a momentarily tolerant Oxford was never to be erased from Locke's mind in after-life, even when Oxford herself refused to receive him.

In such surroundings Locke's contacts and his reading soon brought him to maturity. After taking his B.A. in 1655 and his M.A. in 1658 he was appointed to a series of lectureships in Greek, rhetoric, and philosophy. It was in those ten years from 1655 to 1665 that the final form was given to the cast of Locke's thinking. During that time the surging wonder of all three revolutions of thought mentioned at the beginning of the lecture agitated his soul before its direction was finally set. He read Descartes, and first gained a relish for the new philosophy, whereas the old scholasticism had nauseated him. He lost his original Puritanism, and became an Independent. And lastly he became fascinated by the ideal of experimental science and the codification of knowledge which the Copernican revolution had created, and of which Bacon had given such an eloquent formulation. His life henceforth is the attempt to fit the experimental method within the Cartesian framework, and to harmonise the whole synthesis with the simple form of Christianity espoused by the Independents.

Space does not permit the telling of the story of intellectual adventure in the fifties and sixties. One can but refer to two facts which certainly influenced Locke profoundly. The first is the resort to Oxford during the Civil War of that little group of scientists who had been wont to meet in London at Cheapside or Gresham College, and who ultimately became the founders of the Royal Society. Among them was Petty of Brasenose ; Wallis was lecturing in geometry, Seth Ward in astronomy, and Robert Boyle in medicine. Locke attended the lectures of all of them, and became an intimate friend of Boyle. Under the tuition of these men and others he caught the great enthusiasm of the age for experimental science, and never lost it. From 1660 to 1667 Locke was making observations and experiments on behalf of Boyle which that scientist incorporated in his work on *The History of the Air*; and on Boyle's death the lot of editing this scientific work devolved upon Locke himself. In 1668 he was elected a Fellow of the Royal Society. To the last his letters and journals are full of experiments watched or experiments made; and he managed to maintain a voluminous correspondence throughout with researchers in every field of natural science.

The second fact which influenced him was the rise of the Latitudinarians, who sought in the clash of creeds a philosophic Christianity, half-way between Puritan fanaticism and the semi-Catholicism of the Anglicans. The most famous of these were the Cambridge Platonists, with one of whom —Cudworth—Locke became very intimate. Rejecting the authority of councils and tradition, they sought in the application of reason to the Scriptures the sole source of ultimate truth. This school gave a permanent direction to Locke's mind, and many of his later theological pamphlets are but commentaries upon this thesis. His theory of toleration, indeed, is to a large extent but one corollary drawn from the fundamental Latitudinarian theorem. He embraced their teaching the more readily since, at the time when he met them, they had adopted with eagerness " the new philosophy," as they called the teaching of Bacon. Locke's friend and teacher Boyle was of their number, and along with them held an invincible faith in the future of science—an enthusiasm which Locke quickly shared. As early as 1651 Boyle had saluted " the dawn of a revolution which must exalt theology and make true philosophy flourish beyond human hopes."

Perhaps under the inspiration of this vision Locke had given up the idea of entering the Church, and in his early lecturing days had begun to study medicine. But up to 1665 there is nothing to show that he would have done otherwise than pursue a quiet, scientific, academic career. True he had made one journey abroad as secretary to Sir Walter Vane, ambassador to Brandenburg; but on his return he refused the offer of a similar post in Spain, and settled down at Oxford once more. Then occurred the accident which was to determine the whole of the rest of his career.

JOHN LOCKE

In July 1666 Lord Ashley came to see his medical adviser, Dr Thomas, of Oxford, but it happened that Thomas, who was a friend of Locke's, could not attend, and asked Locke to do so. Ashley was so charmed with Locke that he took him back to London as his doctor, and in June of the following year Locke performed an operation for tumour on Ashley which saved the latter's life. Henceforth Ashley became devoted to his doctor. Locke became *confidant* and secretary to his benefactor, and was entrusted with much intimate and important business.

It was at this time, in 1666, that Locke wrote his first political essay of importance. It was an *Essay concerning Toleration*, drawn up at Ashley's request in the summer of 1666. A brief analysis of it will illustrate the fact that Locke already had reached certain fundamental conceptions in his political thinking. The Clarendon Code had shattered in that year Locke's great dream of a National Church. Comprehension was dead, but what was to be done with the Dissenters? Locke argued for toleration along two main lines of thought. The first was an analysis of the nature of the magistrate's power, and the second was an analysis of the nature of opinions. The magistrate's function, says Locke, is to promote well-being and peace. He summarises his contention by this important statement:

> The whole trust, power and authority of the magistrate is vested in him for no other purpose but to be made use of for the good, preservation and peace of men in that society over which he is set; and therefore, that this alone is, and ought to be, the standard and measure according to which he ought to square and proportion his laws, model and frame his government.

The power of the magistrate is derived from men only, and cannot be considered as a delegation from a divine source. He says:

> There are some that tell us that monarchy is *jure divino*. I will not now disprove this opinion, but only mind the asserters of it that, if they mean by this, as certainly they must, that the sole, supreme, arbitrary power . . . is and ought to be by divine right in a single person, 'tis to be suspected they have forgot what country they were born in, under what laws they live, and certainly cannot but be obliged to declare Magna Charta to be downright heresy. If they

mean by monarchy *jure divino* not an absolute, but limited monarchy (which, I think, is an absurdity, if not a contradiction), they ought to show us this charter from Heaven, and let us see where God hath given the magistrate a power to do anything but barely in order to the preservation and welfare of his subjects in this life, or else leave us at liberty to believe it as we please.

This insistence on the *facts* of the Constitution such as Magna Charta must be borne in mind when considering his later and more mature work.

Locke now turns to consider the nature and kinds of opinions and beliefs. There are three kinds of opinion dealing respectively with God, the practical life, and the moral life. The magistrate cannot interfere between God and man, since he is dealing only with the material needs of the community. His function is specific and limited. Therefore speculative opinions and their manifestations are outside his sphere. Hence liberty of cult follows from liberty of conscience. As for anything touching the *practical* life, that is, indeed, an affair of the magistrate. When speculations impinge on this sphere the magistrate may prevent their spread and their manifestation, but he cannot, and must not, stop belief in them. Moral beliefs may or may not concern the magistrate. It is only a question of the degree to which the beliefs express themselves in conduct, and whether they are a hindrance to civil peace.

He then turns to consider the specific applications of this doctrine. Are Catholics to be tolerated? He answers no, because, in the first place, they have a foreign allegiance, and are therefore a state within the State; and, in the second place, they themselves are intolerant; and both these facts touch upon the practical problem of government which is security. Are Nonconformists to be tolerated? Locke answers yes, and the reasons he gives are purely utilitarian. The State must not be economically weakened by the expulsion of its skilled Nonconformist artisans, and, moreover, England ought to become the Protestant leader of Europe, ought to welcome refugees, and thus secure economic advantage. He concludes by one more plea for comprehension. Toleration ought to be the Government's policy so as to facilitate the return of the Dissenters to the single fold of a National Church.

JOHN LOCKE

The curious mixture in this essay of the contract theory and the doctrine of expediency is to be noted, for it is a mixture which we shall find also in Locke's later work. Before leaving the essay it may be observed that these theories were not prepared for Ashley's special consumption, since they are found again in all detail in Locke's own private journal, in 1673.

In the period from 1666 to 1675 Locke had his first taste of political life. He was made one of the eight Lords Proprietors of Carolina, and undertook the secretaryship of that body. In this capacity he assisted Ashley in drawing up the *Eternal Constitution*—which ceased to be eternal at its complete collapse twenty-three years later. We need not concern ourselves here with an examination of this curious fossil of political theory, beyond saying that the doctrine of toleration seems to reveal the influence of Locke; and noting that the oath of acceptance of the Constitution, which every Carolinian had to take at seventeen, seems to be an anticipation of the doctrine of acceptance which he himself was to put forward in his later famous essay.

We will not follow Locke in all his relations with Ashley during this period, or consider his various official positions. Throughout this time he was carrying on his medical work, and attending the meetings of the Royal Society, but the influence of the Shaftesbury connexion upon him was undoubtedly a profound one. Shaftesbury was an opportunist, and the two characteristics of opportunism are a scepticism of ultimate principles and attention to immediate circumstances with regard to a severely utilitarian end. Thus Locke saw applied to affairs of State something of the experimental method of science and the pragmatism of the Latitudinarian. This contact prevented his thinking from ever again becoming academic, and gave a permanent concreteness to all his ideas of State and Government.

In 1675 Locke's weak chest—his father and brother had both died of consumption a few years before—drove him to seek refuge in the South of France, and there he spent four years travelling widely, making detailed observations on social customs, political conditions, and the scientific work of Frenchmen. Reports on the silkworm industry in his journal and letters jostle financial statistics and figures of the peasant's rate of wages, but this period of travel was most important from our point of view, because it was a great period of mental activity. Locke was evidently feeling his way toward a synthesis of all the varied experiences, intellectual, scientific, and practical, of the previous ten years. His journal shows his constant preoccupation with this problem—whether he himself consciously realised it or not—and reveals the intensity of these four years of ferment.

It will be convenient therefore to notice the general nature of Locke's thinking at this point in his career, not merely because of the obvious fascination there is in watching a great thinker on the eve of an intellectual discovery, but also because out of that ferment was eventually to emerge the final synthesis of his political theory. It is said in a dozen text-books that Locke's theory was " in essence an apology for the Whig revolution." Now, " in essence " it was nothing of the sort. Years before the 1688 episode Locke had reached nearly every one of the positions maintained in his *Civil Government*. The most casual reading of his journals and letters in France will show that the driving force, the motive of Locke's thinking, was something far more compelling and far more significant than any party apologetic. If anybody had cared to make a careful correlation of the theories in Locke's journals and letters up to 1680—a task which, so far as I am aware, has never been yet performed—he would have discovered that Locke, the very embodiment of his age, was struggling toward a synthesis of the three great forces which were agitating the age. He was trying to harmonise into a working conception the Cartesian outlook of the philosopher, the experimental method of the scientists, and the utilitarian empiricism he had learnt from Shaftesbury and his contact with practical politics. And the resulting synthesis, even if lacking in detail, is clear and definable. It had been reached by a double process: by induction from his actual experiences, from observations, and from his reading of history; and by deduction from Christian, Platonic, and rationalistic conceptions. The two processes had gone on side by side, and were indistinguishable. But the result was that by 1680 a clear and stable attitude to existence had been reached, which remained fixed in all essentials for the rest of his life. He had found his own soul and discovered his own task. Henceforth his way was clear. It is of no small significance, therefore, to observe that nineteen-twentieths of Locke's voluminous work was produced after this date—indeed, after he was fifty years old. Let us turn therefore to consider the structure of his system.

He had accepted completely the new philosophy in its Copernican-Cartesian outlines. To him the universe is " the Great Machine." The puny human " finds himself lost in the vast extent of space " on the one hand, and rendered dazed by the " inconceivable divisibility of matter " on the other. His finite mind can " know nothing of those large bulks of matter we see floating in the abyss," nor can tell how "nature in this great machine of the world produces the several phenomena." [1]

This " Great Machine of the Universe " is the product of the " infinite power and wisdom " of the Creator, and it is "agreeable to His greatness" that the comprehension of it should "exceed our capacity and the highest flight of our imagination." Yet we know that the whole structure is determined by " a Supreme Ruler and a universal law." Behind all things, and immanent in all things, is inexorable law—the law of God, or, what is the same thing, the law of nature. This law is an " external immutable standard of Right."

Within this structure exists man endowed with the light of reason—" spark of the divine nature," as Locke calls it. It is only a flickering light:

> We are here in the state of mediocrity: finite creatures furnished with powers and faculties very well fitted to some purposes, but very disproportionate to the vast and unlimited extent of things. [2]

But finite though he is, he is capable of discovering something of those objective immutable laws under which he must live:

> Where anyone endeavoured to know his duty sincerely . . . scarcely anyone ever miscarried for want of knowledge. [3]

Or as he puts it later:

> The same spark of the divine nature and knowledge in man . . . showed him the law he was under as a man. He that made use of

---

[1] *Journal*, March 6, 1677.   [2] *Ibid.*, March 6, 1677.
[3] *Ibid.*, February 8, 1677.

79

this candle of the Lord so far as to find out what was his duty, could not miss reconciliation and forgiveness when he had failed in duty.[1]

One of the ways in which the law may be discovered is by deductive reasoning. " I cannot but think morality as well as mathematics capable of demonstration," [2] he says. And in the *Essay concerning Human Understanding* he sums up man's general relationship to the universe thus :

> The idea of a supreme being, infinite in power, goodness and wisdom, whose workmanship we are and on whom we depend, and the idea of ourselves as understanding rational beings . . . would, I suppose, if duly considered and pursued, afford such foundations of our duties and rules of action, as might place morality among the sciences capable of demonstration.[3]

Now all this is going to have a profound influence on Locke's social conceptions. By his acceptance of the infinity of the universe, and of the littleness of man, Locke comes to lose confidence in the possibility of determining rigidly the details of everyday conduct. It is only the general principles of existence which are discoverable; for the *minutiæ* of conduct, he says in one of his letters, there is no single rule. " We are not capable of living together exactly by one rule "; and " even the apostles themselves were not of one mind." God allows us " in the ordinary actions of our lives a great latitude " and many alternatives. What then is man to do when he leaves metaphysical speculation and comes down to the ordering of his everyday existence? In answering this question Locke leaves his Cartesianism and embraces a wholehearted utilitarianism, which is both empirical and experimental. The business of man is

> to be happy in this world by enjoyment of the things of nature subservient to life, health, ease and pleasure and the comfortable hopes of another life.[4]

Hence his programme is defined : discover the laws regulating the material world and turn them to the use of man. Man ought to bend his energies to becoming

---

[1] *Reasonableness of Christianity*, Works, vol. vii, p. 133.
[2] *Journal*, June 24, 1681.   [3] *Human Understanding*, vol. ii, p. 340.
[4] *Journal*, February 8, 1677.

well-skilled in knowledge of material causes and effects of things in his power; directing his thoughts to the improvement of such arts and inventions, engines and utensils as might best contribute to his continuance with conveniency and delight

' Between the lawful and the unlawful," says Locke, " there is a great latitude," and he " cannot imagine that God hath made anything with a design that it should be miserable."

Locke's utilitarianism is clear and unmistakable. Bentham himself could not be more explicit. He says :

> Happiness and misery are the two great springs of human actions, and though through different ways we find men so busy in the world, they all aim at happiness and desire to avoid misery, as it appears to them in different places and shapes.[1]

Locke has adopted this utilitarianism in order to bridge the vast gap between the insignificance of man and the vastness of the universe. Did it do so? And if it did, how did utilitarianism harmonise with those laws of nature which are the determining principles of the universal machine? Locke's answer is truly startling, for it anticipates Paley by a century. Morality is but pleasure; and pleasure is only conformity to universal law. " There is nothing morally good," he writes in his journal, " which does not produce pleasure." Utility is the sole thread in the maze by which man can find his way out of the conflict of circumstances into the freedom of universal law. His great difference from Bentham lay in the fact that he posited this law at the back of things and believed it the source of pleasure; whereas Bentham rested his philosophy on no such piece of cosmic speculation, but upon the simple pleasure-pain fact of experience.

The political consequence Locke draws from this is the grand rule of probability :

> The truths of mathematics and morality are certain. But whether this course in public or private affairs will succeed well . . . is only known by experience: and there is but probability grounded upon experience or analogical reasoning, but no certain knowledge or demonstration.[2]

---

[1] *Of Ethics in General*, Section I, p. 308 (King; 1858).
[2] *Journal*, June 24, 1681.

The theory of government expressed in these tentative early writings follows to a large extent from what has already been said. We have seen that in his earliest political tract he had defined the purpose of government as the preservation of peace among men in the society over which it rules. Could men but live peaceably with one another there would be no need, he tells us, of magistrates or politics. The magistrate, then, has a specific and limited function—" to preserve men in this world from the fraud and violence of one another." This leads him to make the great deduction that " what was the end of erecting government ought alone to be the measure of its proceeding." [1] We see him in that sentence trembling on the verge of a revolutionary conception ; and he wrote that, it must be remembered, in 1666. The end of government is limited and specific. But what if the specific became generalised and the limitation ignored? Locke never seems to ask that question in his letters. He was too concrete a social thinker to ask such questions before their necessity became urgent. He never allowed himself the seductive pleasure of toying with dangerous abstractions. But it is to be noted that the unmade deduction from that assertion that " the end of erecting government ought alone to be the measure of its proceeding " would have to be made as soon as a concrete situation demanded it. And by the time he wrote his famous letter on toleration he had drawn the obvious conclusion of the appeal to arms. And that was three years before the essay on *Civil Government*.

We find another element of the later theory too in his journal for 1678. He says :

> A civil law is nothing but the agreement of a society of men either by themselves or one or more authorised by them, determining the rights and applying rewards and punishments to certain actions of all within that society.

Such a theory, it must be noted, is completely divorced from a religious or ecclesiastical significance. We have seen how in his earliest work he had divorced Church and State. The same idea runs throughout all his letters. " Civil laws have only to do with civil actions." The Gospel " alters not in the least civil affairs." So when the New Testament says

---

[1] *Essay concerning Toleration*, printed in Fox Bourne's *Life*, p. 174.

" Obey your superior " it means nothing more nor less than existed before Christianity came into the world.

From first to last, it must be emphasised, in all Locke's journals, pamphlets, and essays the one idea runs like a thread of gold : " The public good is the rule and measure of all law-making." It was only a question of time before he would overcome his own native caution and ask himself the inconvenient question : Suppose the law does not secure the public good?

By 1680, then, the general outline of Locke's thought is clear. The universe is a machine run by immutable laws only partially discernible by our frail intellects. In the very structure of this universe there is an eternal standard of right and wrong—a law of nature, external to us, and not in any sense of our own construction. Our foremost task is to find that law and to live by it. It may be discovered in two ways : by a deductive process like mathematics, or by an experimental process. Man is so constructed that he pursues pleasure and avoids pain ; the universe is so constructed that the keeping of its laws produces pleasure and the breaking of them causes pain. Here, then, is both a policy and a method for man to pursue. Even though his natural reason—the candle of the Lord—may flicker and go dim, yet man may feel his way to something of order and something of attainment by empirical investigation alone. And as for government, that is but a tool like any other of the " machines and utensils " of man—whereby he seeks his own fulfilment and the gratifying of that deepest urge within him for the pursuit of happiness. It is a universe of wonder and mystery, says Locke, but by its very nature demands effort and adventure. Passive acquiescence in received opinions is utterly foreign to the whole conception. So as Locke wanders about France, fighting his consumption and defying his constant asthma, the function of the thinker in society becomes more apparent to him. The thinker must make inventions, for life is capable of much greater plenty and fullness than has yet been experienced by man. Moreover, since our task here is to live in peace with our fellow men, it will be the thinker's business to turn his attention to that problem, for happiness depends on " the ordering of ourselves in our actions in the time of our probation " on this earth.   Lastly, the thinker must speculate to a practical intent on the laws of existence—" what those actions are that man must do and must avoid."

Locke returned to England in 1679 at a time of great political crisis.   Shaftesbury's whole career was in the balance. Locke went back to Oxford and there was spied upon by Royalist dons who informed the Court regularly of his movements and actions.   The Shaftesbury friendship had rendered him suspect to all.   Eventually, finding life in England too dangerous to be risked longer, he fled to Holland in January 1683.   There he lived at first *incognito* as a hunted exile.   His name was on the list of the proscribed twenty-four refugees whom James II demanded of Holland, but by passing from town to town among his Arminian friends he managed to evade capture.   Later he lived more openly.

It was in these five years that his political thinking, hitherto scattered and fragmentary, became correlated and elaborated. The first essay on *Civil Government* had been written while he was still at Oxford.   Now, contact with refugee Huguenots and with the multiplicity of faiths to be found in tolerating Holland stimulated him to much thought and more expression.   A great intellectual friendship—such as he hitherto lacked—helped him to put some of his ideas into article form for publication.   His new friend was Le Clerc, a brilliant young Arminian professor of something the same cast of mind as Locke himself.   Through this friendship, essays by Locke began to appear in the new European learned journal—*Bibliothèque Choisie*.   And, having thus started to formulate his ideas definitively, Locke continued writing to the end of his days.   His fame—hitherto local and personal—began to spread both on the Continent and in England.   He now understood the *rôle* of the man of thought in society ; he had ceased to be the secretary of a minister, and himself had become a leader in the republic of letters.

The *Essay concerning Toleration* was written in Latin in the winter of 1685–86.   It contained nothing new, but was an elaboration of the general Latitudinarian position and an expansion of the ideas expressed in his 1666 work on the same subject.   In what was destined to be the last year of his exile he began and finished his famous essay on *Civil Government*.

The general occasion of its being written can easily be determined. Europe in 1685 was passing through a political and religious crisis such as she had not passed through since 1588. In February of that year James II had declared himself a Catholic. In June, on the death of its Elector, the Palatinate passed into the hands of the Catholic family of Neubourg. In October Louis XIV revoked the Edict of Nantes; and in December the Duke of Savoy withdrew his grant of toleration to the Vaudois. On every side the Reformation and liberty seemed threatened as never before. It was the last great attack of Catholicism and despotism in alliance. The doctrine of the Divine Right of Kings was utterly triumphant. In the gigantic struggle between two epochs—between the sixteenth century and the modern age—this was the March push of absolutism. Filmer was being widely read in England; and in France the Huguenots were prostrating themselves in terror before *Le Roi Soleil.* " There is not a single Protestant in the realm," wrote Jurieu just before the Revocation, " who does not venerate—I may say who does not adore—Your Majesty as the most brilliant image which God has made of Himself on the earth." And monarchs everywhere were acting up to the Huguenot-Filmer principles. In such a situation, fraught with momentous significance for the rest of history, Locke sat down to write his supreme appeals to the common sense of humanity and to plead for the spirit of the new world in the face of a triumphant old one. His *Toleration* and *Civil Government* are but two aspects of the same appeal.

The first essay on *Civil Government* need not detain us. Filmer had quoted texts to prove the hereditary transmission of royal power from Adam. Locke quotes texts to disprove the assertion. But one always feels that Locke was treating the whole question with something of a mock heroic spirit. A lambent irony plays over his caustic remarks; and he works the argument up to this great climax: Did Shem receive plenary power after Noah's death?

It is the second essay, however, which must occupy the rest of my space.

All political theory in the long run is a series of deductions from, and compromises between, a man's world-view on the one hand and his view of human nature on the other. That is to say, however logical a system may be, and however complete its structure, when traced back to its fundamentals those fundamentals will be found to rest on certain tacit assumptions —certain acts of faith—about the world as a whole and about man's nature and place within that world, which cannot in any strict sense be proved, but which must of necessity be granted. To borrow a mathematical analogy, they are the axioms which make the theorem capable of demonstration, but which render all deduction impossible when not conceded at the outset. Now the chief fact to observe in connexion with Locke's great polemic against Filmer is that the struggle between the two men is not merely one of opposing lines of argument and of debating points about the state of nature, but is a fundamental and irreconcilable conflict of general world-views. In short, it is the struggle between the modern type of mind and the essentially mediæval type. Plato would have understood Locke, even though he might have mistaken the Whig for a sophist; but he would have found Filmer utterly unintelligible.

Now we have seen that Locke by 1680 had reached a stable world-view. It was the scientific seventeenth-century conception, and it dominated his politics as completely as the theory of evolution and historical emergence dominates ours at the present day. Similarly he had reached a stable view of human nature—partly from experience and partly from the teaching of Latitudinarian Christianity. And this will determine his thinking no less than it determined that of Hobbes. From the combination of these two axioms we find in the whole of Locke's work, philosophical, religious, and political, a clear dualism which may reveal a fundamental disharmony, but is nevertheless pronounced and unmistakable. There is the line of experimentalism and of utility; and the line of deductive mathematics, of logic, of the Cartesian universe. We see this everywhere. In philosophy it produced his famous epistemological dualism which was the starting-point of modern philosophy. In religion it produced his compromise between a simple practical ethic and the doctrine of Revelation. And —most important of all, though least noticed—in politics it gives us the great compromise between (*a*) empirical organisation based on the sole criterion of utility, and (*b*) the idea of

86

a determinable and delimiting system of rights. Unless these facts are clearly realised a true assessment of the worth of Locke's *Civil Government* is quite impossible.

From the great emphasis on utility which we have seen in Locke's letters we shall be prepared to find in his politics an emphasis on the idea of the State as the tool for the attainment of human happiness. No idea of the monarchy as a divine institution will be possible from such an axiom. But a second corollary will follow. We shall not expect to find in his work a system such as a more purely philosophical or theological basis would give—such as we associate, for instance, with Hegel or Bosanquet, or with Filmer. Instead of a system we shall find a rather loose assertion of principles which will more or less cohere, but which leave a great latitude for subsequent deduction and interpretation; and some of which at any rate may be found to be mutually incompatible.

But above all we shall be sure to find in his teaching an emphasis on purpose; on the finite individual purpose, and not confident assumption of complete knowledge, concerning the divine purpose. Filmer had said that fear of the monarch (and Hobbes had said that fear of the sovereign) by the people alone would be an adequate safeguard against anarchy. Locke, emphasising individual purpose, will simply turn that thesis upside-down. The fear of the people by the monarch, he will say, is a far more potent safeguard, for the monarch will know beforehand what the purpose, what the will, of the community actually is. In that sense, by contrast with Filmer, will, not fear, is going to be the basis of the State. It is a more logical assumption—and certainly a more teleological one—than that of the great protagonist of Royalism.

Let us turn, then, from these premises with which he will approach his political theory to consider briefly his method. It is a simple one, and consists of that process which a contemporary philosopher calls the process of " mental subtraction." That is to say, in imagination he " thinks away the state "—conceiving of a " state of nature " and assessing its disadvantages. It is based on the plausible idea that " while we seldom realise the uses of habitual things (be they institution or bodily organs) while they are functioning properly, yet we quickly find out their uses when we are deprived of them. The purpose of an institution is that good which humanity would miss if that institution were absent or suspended."[1] Locke as a boy had actually seen that intellectual experiment as a concrete process between 1642 and 1649. And as a lecturer at Oxford he had seen a close approximation to it in that ghastly autumn and winter of 1659. So in spite of its dangers the method may be considered a legitimate one. To put it in the terminology that we have adopted throughout, we may say this: Locke had made certain observations which led him to think that man is naturally free. He saw independent princes free in regard to each other. He saw circumstances in which men were in analogous situations of freedom in the outposts of the colonies. He observed that the Governments of Rome and of Venice seemed to owe their constitution to the will of certain free men. From these different facts he induced a law which would explain them—the law, namely, of the social contract. In other words, he attempted to think away the variable, utilitarian superstructure in all societies that he might discover beneath the invariable and rational basis, which Kant was later to call the "regulative principle." The method was legitimised once Kant had given it a name. Nor need we suppose that Locke thought of it in historical terms at all. His historical justification of it is scanty as we should expect were he treating it as method rather than history. And it may be remarked that in this assumption we have the weighty support of Sir Frederick Pollock, who declares that the state of nature for Locke "was rather a perfectly conscious abstraction than an attempt to construct historical origins." Just as in Locke's scientific work he had learnt to posit scientific truth, or an invisible reality beneath the variable flux of concrete facts, which truth was to be discovered by observation and induction from the several particulars, so he carries over into politics the same method, and posits an underlying reality beneath the variable elements of particular organisations, and tries to discover that reality by the process just described.

It is possible to explain almost the whole of his essential theory of the State without any serious consideration of the contract hypothesis. The heart of his doctrine lies in his view

[1] W. E. Hocking, *Man and the State*, p. 152.

of human nature.   Men are not for Locke mutually repulsive atoms; they are not anti-social.   On the contrary—to continue the chemical metaphor—even though he thinks of them as atoms, they are atoms with very definite valency; with an inherent tendency, that is to say, to combine and associate. For Locke, man has four fundamental natural characteristics which are the very stuff of his being, as inherent as the various qualities of the chemical elements.   He is first and foremost social, and this social quality manifests itself in two clear ways. " God hath woven into the principles of human nature tenderness for offspring "—a fact which will lead to a constant increase of social affiliation.   And, also, man is by his very nature " bound to preserve the rest of mankind " from harm " when his own preservation comes not into competition." This amounts to saying, as Sir Frederick Pollock has recently pointed out, that the problem is not to account for the existence of society, but to ascertain its best and normal mode of existence.   This way of stating the case may not be as frank and clear as that of Aristotle, but as an appeal to a nominally Christian audience it was a master-touch of polemic.   On its face value, at any rate, this appeal to the innate social spirit of man was more in the direct line of Christian teaching than the views of either Hobbes or Filmer.

In the second place, man is born rational.   This did not mean for Locke what it was later to mean for Godwin.   Rationality for him was something which needed much cultivation. He saw that reason might be clouded over by many mists; might be " biased by interest and ignorant for want of study." One may observe in passing that throughout Locke's works and letters there are the elements of quite a comprehensive social psychology.   An essay on them has not yet been written, but if they were collated they would make fascinating reading, and reveal that Locke was far more critical an observer than is often supposed.   But the day of social psychology had not arrived.   Yet this view of man's nature was to lead him to devote much of his energies in after-life to the problem of education —that is to say, a social and rational education—for he saw, as Professor Dewey has so powerfully reminded us, that the roots of democratic theory must lie deep in educational method. The treatise on *Education* and the remarkable but almost unread manual of acute reflection called *Of the Conduct of the Understanding* remain as permanent monuments of his work in this connexion. As a study in the forces determining political beliefs this latter volume is truly penetrating, and anticipated much of Bentham's doctrine of fallacies by well over a century.

Man is social and rational, then. Two other characteristics follow. The first is freedom: " we are born free as we are born rational." The second is equality. Men are equal not in the sense of having equal capabilities, as Locke emphatically points out, but in the sense that nobody is born with a natural jurisdiction over another. The reference is obviously to Filmer; but so completely has this conception of jurisdictional equality become absorbed into the nature of our own thinking that we scarcely realise what a challenging assertion it was at the time. It is in striking contrast to the appalling contemporary Huguenot prostrations at the feet of the great Louis.

Since men are born social, rational, free, and equal, they have certain inalienable rights. These rights are but the individual correlatives of the vast law of nature. We have seen Locke in his letters trying to bridge the gap between man and the world; the same attempt can be clearly discerned in *Civil Government*. " The law of nature," he says, " stands as an eternal rule to all men." And again, " it is certain that there is such a law . . . intelligible and plain to a rational creature." " Reason is that law," we are told, and farther on we are informed that the law is " nowhere to be found but in the minds of men." Hence it cannot be miscited or mis-applied. Reason, right, and the eternal law are correlatives in the general structure of things. The universal right gives rise to individual rights.

There are two cardinal rights, according to Locke, which can be deduced from these principles. There is (*a*) the right of property, and (*b*) the right of punishment for those who transgress the law. Of the right of punishment, which he deals with fully, little need here be said, save that it follows directly from his conception of law, and also that it is a practical necessity consequent upon, and for the preservation of, the right of property.

This right of property is one of the most fascinating parts

of Locke's political speculation, and a full treatment of it has, so far as I am aware, never been made. Indeed, even Sir Frederick Pollock says of it that " this economic digression is of little interest." As a matter of fact, it is of profound interest, for however irrelevant it may be to the general scheme of his argument it was destined to cause repercussions in political theory for a century and a half, and finally to be absorbed by Karl Marx.

Locke said that property owed its origin to labour. At first all was common to mankind. Then, by effort, man ' mixed his labour ' with the soil and its produce, and that ' mixing of labour '—which was a sort of extension of his personality to the object concerned—gave him a right to own that object. " It is labour indeed that puts the difference of value on everything," he says. " This is the original law of nature," and the process still takes place. Little did Locke realise what an unexploded bomb he was dropping into the Arcadian pastures of eighteenth-century thought. After the Napoleonic wars this theory of his was destined to be rediscovered by the early English radicals, and to form the very core of all their theorising. Cobbett was going to teach it vociferously. Hodgskin was going to build a revolutionary doctrine out of it. Hall and Gray were going to inflame the imagination of the town artisans with it, and make it the yeast of a prodigious social ferment from 1815 to 1848. Lastly, Ravenstone was going to revive the doctrine, along with the emphasis on consent, and—Tory though he was—was going to make from it the first great utterance of the doctrine of the class war.

This is not the place to consider the story of the remarkable transmission and growth of that doctrine. It is a history which has yet to be written. But it serves to remind us that Locke's influence is not to be confined to certain rather academic deductions from a pseudo-historical contract, and that it contained within itself the elements of a great revolution of thought. Before leaving this labour theory of value, however, it may be as well to scotch one more of the misconceptions which text-books have heaped upon the memory of this man. It is always said that Locke's theory took care to placate the landed Whig gentry who had contributed to the National Debt. This is positively absurd, and nothing could be farther from the truth. I have tried to show Locke's thought as practically a rounded system before 1680. I have shown that its formulation was completed when he was an exile, and had no thought of placating anybody, but was simply building a defence against an all-victorious absolutism. But in addition there are Locke's own essentially dangerous words. In no gentle tones he proclaims that the law of nature concerning property has also set bounds to that property. " As much as anyone can make use of before it spoils," he says—that is the bound to property, and it is a devastatingly limiting one. If Locke had been the Whig pamphleteer that he is usually depicted, would he have been so foolish as to set such limits to property? The Whig landowners would have received little consolation from his emphatic and reiterated assertions.

From these fundamental assumptions, then, Locke constructs the rest of his theory. He has a theory of man as essentially social and free, but incapable of defending himself adequately without organisation. He has a theory of rights and of property ; but these too need some sort of organised protection. By thinking away the State he discovers that its functions are to preserve all these fundamental rights. The State therefore must exist as a purposive tacit agreement by the community to organise itself for its own protection. If you like, the State is a super-policeman ; but the emphasis is not on his function of force, as with Hobbes, but on his regulative function in the crowded thoroughfare of civilised life. That regulative function depends, and always will depend, on its being accepted by the fully socialised individual. But the necessity of the State does not imply the apotheosis of the policeman. Always to Locke the policeman-State is a servant, and never a master.

Government thus comes into being by agreement—by a contract. Nowhere in Locke do you find a theory of double contract, one to create society and the other to create government. Man by his nature, as we have seen, is already social. The only contract, or agreement, is that which creates government. Locke is not clear in distinguishing the State and its government, and he seems to regard them as synonymous. This government is endowed overtly or tacitly, for it matters not to the argument, with those powers of self-protection which each individual would have did it not exist. They give up, in other words, certain of their rights—not in order to lose them, but in order that they may be more fully preserved. The essential right they give up is the right of punishment, which, says Locke, has a dual aspect, viz., the right of restraint and the right to compensation. The State is the recipient of all the voluntarily conceded rights of punishment yielded up by every individual, which, without the State, each individual would exercise as best he could alone.

It follows from this statement of the case that the body receiving these rights is limited on all hands, and is not absolute. It is limited as to purpose; for its sole purpose is to prevent discord and preserve civil peace. The individual only concedes a part of his rights, and never the whole. Consequently the State can never invade the other rights of the individual. And it is limited also by the law of nature, for no transgression of the moral law by the Government can receive the support and obedience of the subject. The inevitable conclusion is drawn. Should either of these limitations be overridden the individuals constituting the community are perfectly justified in removing their Government. Government is a trust, and when that trust is broken rebellion must follow.

Of the rest of his theory little need be said : it is but a utilitarian superstructure built on these essentials ; and utility may cause its alteration where necessary. It is convenient to preserve the time-honoured distinction of executive, legislature, and judicature. It is convenient to give the executive certain powers of prerogative. It is convenient to work by majority vote. But all these details of actual organisation do not interest Locke very greatly. It is the life of society and not its machinery that preoccupies him. Nor is he concerned with the juristic problem of sovereignty. That word is not mentioned once in the essay. All he is concerned to emphasise with regard to these things is that " there still remains with the people," as he puts it, " the supreme power to alter or remove the legislature." That granted, the rest is but a question of utility.

It will thus be seen that Locke in every detail was in the completest possible opposition to Filmer. Locke saw that Filmer's dilemma of either despotism or anarchy was essentially a false one, and that it disappeared as soon as a less depraved view of human nature was assumed. He saw clearly also the inherent contradiction in Filmer's thought. The depravity of human nature was assumed by the Royalist in order to justify despotism; but straightway the passivity of human nature was assumed the moment that despotism had come into being, for its very existence could only depend on bovine passivity. Locke saw, too, that Filmer's scholastic structure would completely collapse if the question were asked: " Suppose man refuses to remain passive to tyranny? "

Locke's reasoning is more honest than Filmer's. The latter, once his despotic monarchy was constructed, sedulously ignored this question of possible disobedience within the absolute State. But yet, when he wanted to attack the contract theorists, he assumed that such disobedience would be normal in any State but his own. In the first case passive obedience was taken for granted : in the second its validity was questioned. His argument therefore was unsound, since it was not homogeneous. Locke, on the other hand, faced the question with open eyes. He realised something of the great difficulties of the problem ; but he also realised that man was not fundamentally anti-social. He realised that such scholastic sophistries as Filmer's would lead to political agnosticism—and political agnosticism from the days of the Stuarts to the days of Mussolini means either despotism or anarchy. That is not a solution of the problem. It is the abandonment of it. Consequently, with magnificent common sense, Locke sweeps aside the whole paralysing argument of Filmer by a simple assertion of the pragmatist's faith. No amount of logic, he declares in effect, will make a thinking human being submissive to the abuses of tyranny.

But the great contrast comes down ultimately to their respective views of the Deity. For Filmer God was known and absolute ; a Cosmic Stuart, whose commands were also known in all their details. But to Locke God was the impenetrable Mystery of a vast universe, who had endowed man with his little candle of reason, and left him to find his way as best he could. Confidence was consequently impossible. No divine command could be the basis of his theory, but only the voluntary choice of a rational will.

JOHN LOCKE

Thus thought Locke. His slim little anonymous volume containing the two essays on *Civil Government* is indicative of the age, for it looks before and after. In the first essay he looks to the past: his method is that of the past, and his argument deals with the thought of the past. But with that wearisome essay English political theory bade farewell for ever to the scholastic ideal and the method of quoting texts. In the second essay he looks to the future and the new construction of limited monarchy—written though it was when all his foes were in the ascendant and when he himself was exiled. It is the first great English common-sense statement that will and not fear nor divine intervention is the basis of our life in the community. Purpose is the cutting edge of social achievement. And with that assertion he changed once and for all Englishmen's idea of social necessity. Henceforth the quest of the immanent dialectic was to become more important than the quest of the historical contract. He stated an imperishable truth in the sober terms of common sense. And when modern England was presented with the alternative of either Filmer or Locke it chose without hesitation.

Locke himself, as much as anybody, realised that the work was only just begun. He had sketched the essentials of a political theory, but much remained to be done. The statement of the problems was his bequest to the future. As the old man lay dying in his Essex home he wrote to his young friend Peter King these words:

> Now, methinks—and these are often old men's dreams—I see openings to truth and direct paths leading to it, wherein a little industry and application would settle one's mind with satisfaction, and leave no darkness or doubt. But this is at the end of my day, when my sun is setting; and though the prospect it has given me be what I would not for anything be without—there is so much irresistible truth, beauty and consistency in it—yet it is for one of your age, I think I ought to say for yourself, to set about it.

And the work is not completed yet.

C. H. DRIVER

BIBLIOGRAPHY

A. PRIMARY SOURCE

The Works of John Locke. 10 vols. London, 1801.

B. SECONDARY SOURCES

BASTIDE, CHARLES : *John Locke : ses théories politiques et leur influence en Angleterre.* 1907.
FOX BOURNE, H. R. : *Life of John Locke.* 2 vols. 1876.
KING, LORD : *The Life and Letters of John Locke.* 1858.

V

JACOBITES AND NON-JURORS

THE subject of Jacobitism and the movement associated with the name of the Non-Jurors may appear to be of slight importance in comparison with the striking and outstanding developments which mark the progress of what is justly styled " the Augustan Age." Jacobitism, as viewed from the political standpoint, may be regarded as a perverse reaction; and the strongly worded denunciation of the Non-Jurors by Macaulay, who accused them of sacrificing " both law and order to a superstition as stupid and degrading as the Egyptian worship of cats and onions," will probably indicate the attitude of indifference which is commonly assumed to this subject, even by those who are interested in the various social, religious, and political problems which vexed the souls of our forefathers in the glorious years of the eighteenth century. It may be said, nevertheless, that the study of small and apparently trifling movements of human belief and practice, or even of eccentricity, has been known to yield valuable results, and I hope to be able to maintain the position that no account of the history of our country in the eighteenth century can be considered to be complete in which no place is found for the story of the devotion to the house of Stuart, and the far-reaching development in religious thought exhibited by the Non-Jurors. At the beginning of the era with which these lectures are concerned Jacobitism was a political problem of the highest importance, reached its most acute point of crisis at the death of Queen Anne, broke into new life in the rising of the '45, and did not cease to be a matter of concern to the British Government until the death of Prince Charles in 1788. The Non-Juror movement in the same way continued in a more or less organised form during the whole of the century, the last congregation, which met in a watchmaker's shop in Manchester, being dissolved in the year 1805.

G

The fact that the question of the relations between England and Scotland is involved in the Jacobite movement is in itself sufficient to raise the subject to a position of the greatest importance. If I may be allowed to speak for a moment from my own personal experience, I began my own slight researches into these matters by a study of a particular period in the history of the Non-Jurors strictly so called. As my sphere of vision grew wider and included the entire range of the beliefs and hopes of the Non-Jurors it became evident that no history of the movement could be written which did not take into account the close connexion which existed between the adherents to the house of Stuart in both the kingdoms, which, it should be remembered, were separate political entities at the time when Jacobitism took its rise. The union of England and Scotland in 1707, moreover, resulted in an accession of devotion to the Jacobite movement which has possibly not been sufficiently estimated. The appeal made by the Stuarts to the anti-English sentiment in Scotland was in itself of a powerful nature, with which is to be associated the friendship publicly displayed to the world by the shelter afforded to the exiled Stuarts by the head of the house of France. The days in which France and Scotland were drawn together as the natural enemies of England were not very distant as viewed from the end of the seventeenth century. These circumstances are sufficiently obvious, but there are at once presented to the view of the observer of these matters influences which greatly outweigh the strength of the appeal which was certainly made to traditional Scottish nationalism. The religion professed by the head of the house of Stuart was abomination in the eyes of the vast majority of the Scottish people, and inevitably extinguished any sentiments of national aspiration which might otherwise have been kindled in the hearts of those by whom Popery and prelacy were equally detested. Herein is an illustration of the many cross-currents of thought, sentiment, belief, and policy which mark the whole course of Jacobitism and make difficult in the extreme the task of the historian who seeks to present a clear and concise account of a movement which, as has been said, maintained its course throughout the whole of the eighteenth century. A further consideration of a different nature may be advanced in justification of the claim for " a place in the sun " which is being made on behalf of the obscure and self-contradictory body of men which forms the subject of this present lecture. The extraordinary devotion which was called forth in support of the claims of the Stuarts, and maintained to the bitter end, cannot and ought not to be passed over without notice. On the purely political side of the movement the words of the writer of the Epistle to the Hebrews may be applied to the sufferings of the many who counted their lives as of no value as compared with the success of the " good cause "—" They were stoned, they were sawn asunder [these words are literally applicable to the details of the barbarities practised upon the bodies of the unfortunate prisoners of 1746] . . . were slain with the sword : they wandered about in sheep-skins and goat-skins ; being destitute, afflicted, tormented." And in the more definitely religious or ecclesiastical development let the sufferings of the rabbled clergy in Scotland and the sacrifices made by the deprived clergy of England (to say nothing of the Non-Abjurors, among whom the names of Thomas Brett of Spring Grove, Timothy Mawman of Stockton, John Griffin of Sarsden, and William Law stand out pre-eminently) bear witness to a spirit of true devotion which, however mistaken, was certainly sincere, and as such deserves notice at the hands of those who set out to record the worthy deeds of the eighteenth century. We have in a word in the history of Jacobites and Non-Jurors the life-stories of multitudes of men who for the sake of what they believed to be true principles of government in Church and State risked their all—and lost it.

To come, then, to the exceedingly brief survey which is all that is possible within our present limits, let it be noticed that although both Jacobites and Non-Jurors refused to acknowledge the validity of the changes made at the Revolution in 1688, and remained loyal in their devotion and allegiance to the Stuarts, yet the two terms are not interchangeable. The following statement may be challenged on grounds of strict and theoretical accuracy, but I venture to put it this way. The Jacobite was a believer who dissembled, who frequently took oaths of allegiance to the Government in being, and not seldom occupied positions of importance under that Government. The Non-Juror, on the other hand, the term being

99

used in a strict and limited sense, was, to use a phrase of yesterday, a ' whole-hogger.' His conscience forbade him to take the oaths, and there was an end of it. *Ruat cœlum*, let the sky fall in, he could not be moved. Oxford, Bolingbroke, and Ormond were according to this definition, in varying degrees it may be, Jacobites, but no Non-Jurors. So in the ecclesiastical sphere Atterbury, than whom a more convinced Jacobite never lived, and who added to his belief in divine right a strong personal attachment to the unfortunate son of James II, cannot possibly be described as a Non-Juror. On the other hand, Hickes, Leslie, and Collier chose to carry out to the bitter and logical extreme what is described in the picturesque language of the time as " the Doctrine of the Cross." The names of these men are truly to be reckoned among the Non-Jurors, and in the case of Leslie and Collier among the outlaws to the end of their days. Thomas Brett, the most distinguished convert made by the Jacobite party in the years following the Revolution, in a very delightful autobiography written for the benefit of Richard Rawlinson, that insatiable collector of out-of-the-way information, gives a frank exposition of the successive changes of his personal belief and standpoint. Brought up as a Whig, he became a Tory, a Jacobite, and finally a Non-Juror, the last stage being reached after the making " of a penitential confession to Bishop Hickes." The important stages in this development were the acceptance of the Tory theory of divine right, the acknowledgment after considerable hesitation of the titular James III as the true and lawful child of James II and Mary of Modena (it may be noted in passing that on this point Brett expressed very great hesitation in believing in the legitimacy of the Old Pretender; it is evident that the stories circulated concerning the son of James and Mary obtained a considerable measure of acceptance), and finally the realisation of the impossibility of continuing " to pray for him as King whom he could not in conscience acknowledge so to be." [1]

It will have been observed that consideration of this part of the subject with which we are concerned has already taken on a decidedly ecclesiastical colour, and as a matter of fact it is only in this particular sphere that the distinction between

[1] Brett MSS., vol. 19, f. 33 *et seq.*

Jacobite and Non-Juror is clearly realised. It is to be remembered that subscription to the oaths of allegiance was demanded of ecclesiastical persons of every degree, which fact is sufficient in itself to account for the predominance of this particular atmosphere with which the consideration of our subject is surrounded. From a more general point of view, however, it is evident that the difficulties caused by the continued adherence of the Stuarts to the Church of Rome are largely responsible for the fact that to an historian of Jacobitism what is called 'the religious question' is never far away.

To return, then, to the distinction between our two terms, it is a matter of fact that many Jacobites remained in the communion of the English Church, while the stricter Non-Jurors set up and continued their own communion. The first separate congregation of Non-Jurors was set up immediately after the deprivation of Archbishop Sancroft in 1691, on the Whit Sunday of which year a farewell celebration of Holy Communion was held in the chapel at Lambeth Palace, and from that time for a hundred years onward there were in existence many separated meeting-places of those who with greater or less accuracy were called Non-Jurors. At the time of the death of Queen Anne this separate organisation was generally known by the title of the Communion of Dr Hickes. The differences between the Jacobites in the Church and the Non-Jurors in the wilderness were not in the early years of the eighteenth century felt to be of serious importance. There is an interesting account of the Annual Festival of the Sons of the Clergy in the year 1713 given by the Rev. Richard Foley in a letter written to Dr Thomas Brett, who was then well on the road to his complete conversion to the cause of the Non-Jurors.

> Dr Sacheverell preached before the Sons of the Clergy—afterwards a gathering took place where Dr Bisse, the Bishop of Hereford and the Bishop of Rochester honoured us by their presence—we drank a great many loyal healths, and the musicians were so foolish as to play a tune which they say is called *The King shall enjoy his own again*; however, it was received with universal approbations and was often repeated and when they offered at another tune they were as universally hissed.[1]

[1] Brett MSS., vol. 1, f. 594.

This will be accepted as an illustration of the fact that most of the London clergy were Jacobites, and the difference between the men who had taken the oaths of allegiance to the Government *de facto* and the more thoroughgoing believers whose consciences forbade them to take the oaths of abjuration against that Government which they believed to be *de jure* was not felt by either side to be of very high importance. The new developments which were coincident with the close of the reign of Anne tended, however, to define more clearly the position of the Non-Jurors strictly so called. The main position adopted in ecclesiastical matters by those who at that time enjoyed the title of " Extremists " is sufficiently well understood, viz., that the Non-Jurors and they alone were the Church of England as it stood before the Revolution, and that the prelates, clergy, and laity of the " Regnant " Church (to use another of the picturesque phrases current in the Non-Juror circles) were all in schism. This description was commonly adopted by all Non-Jurors until the accession of the house of Hanover. *E.g.*, Archibald Campbell, who was never a " Church of England màn " in the sense in which that title could be applied to Hickes, Collier, Brett, Spinckes, or Gandy, writing to Thomas Brett shortly before the latter's conversion to the Non-Jurors' communion, says :

> I am glad to hear that you are coming to a closer union with your old antediluvian friends. We maintain the old principles of the Church of England as it stood before the Revolution, and we suffer in so doing.[1]

It is necessary to stress the point that this claim to be the true Church of England involved a good many limitations. The pre-Revolution Church was certainly not free from State control, and the Act of Uniformity was generally regarded with a respect which is certainly not in evidence in these modern days of wide interpretation and mutual toleration. There were to be found among the stalwarts who claimed to be the Church of England some who were prepared to recognise these limits, beyond which, as they conceived, they had no right to pass. *E.g.*, Bishop Gandy in the year 1727 gave it as his deliberate opinion that no changes in the Book of

[1] Brett MSS., vol. 2, f. 191.

Common Prayer could be made except by the authority of a
"lawful Convocation called by a lawful Prince." [1] Some
thirty years later Bishop George Smith in a series of extraordinary letters to the Bishops of the Non-Jurant Church in
Scotland wrote: "The indiction of all National Synods of
your Church belongs to His Majesty by the prerogatives of
his Crown, and all Convocations of that kind without his
license are merely unlawful." [2]

There were not wanting throughout the whole course of the
movement examples of those who took what may be described
as the more Erastian standpoint, and in so doing brought upon
themselves reproaches from both clerical and lay members
of their own body. But as the weary years of separation
rolled on, and the prospects of a legitimist restoration in the
State or a Catholic reorganisation in the Church began to fade,
the Non-Jurors found their freedom even against their will.

The right of the Church to act on her own proper motion
received early illustration in the various consecrations to the
Episcopal office made by the Non-Jurors, which amounted to
twenty-nine in all. [3] In 1693 George Hickes and Thomas
Wagstaffe were consecrated secretly by the deprived Bishops
of Norwich, Ely, and Peterborough, to whom Sancroft, Archbishop of Canterbury, had resigned his authority. No further
steps in this direction were taken until twenty years later,
when George Hickes remained the sole survivor of the Non-
Juror bishops. It had long been a fixed plan of Hickes to
continue the succession, and in 1713 Jeremy Collier, Samuel
Hawes, and Nathaniel Spinckes were consecrated, being the
first bishops of a new series which was continued to the close
of the century. It is true that many of these consecrations
were fenced, so to speak, by the phrase *regio consensu*, which,
however accurately applicable to the case of the Suffragans of
Thetford and Ipswich, would need in the later cases to be
interpreted with considerable latitude, if by this phrase is to
be implied the actual consent of the head of the house of Stuart
for the time being. [4]

The actual effect of the performance of this long-continued

[1] Brett MSS., vol. 7, f. 67.   [2] Episcopal Chest Papers, No. 2092.
[3] See the complete list in *Later Non-Jurors*, p. 349.
[4] See *Later Non-Jurors*, p. 217 *et seq.*

103

series of consecrations was to lead the Non-Jurors to the belief in the inherent right of the Church to govern herself with or without the consent of the State. This tendency may be illustrated by the taunts which were levelled by the Usagers —*i.e.*, the advanced party of the Non-Jurors led by Collier and Brett—against their more conservative " old friends " Hawes, Spinckes, and Gandy. Thomas Brett in one of the interesting and illuminating letters to Johnson of Cranbrook which are preserved in the Brett MSS. states that " the other side could not throw off the Erastian notions which they had imbibed in the days of Charles II." [1] The same party had a further weapon of attack placed in their hands owing to the fact that " the other side," who in matters of liturgical reform contended that, under their present circumstances, no authority existed to alter one single comma of the Book of Common Prayer, were most careful to continue a succession of bishops of their own opinions, and in the year 1725 went to the length of sending one of their number, Henry Doughty, to Edinburgh to be consecrated by the Non-Jurant bishops of Scotland. Bishop Archibald Campbell, one of the stormy petrels of the movement, had some nasty things to say about this particular appointment. He extracted from Bishop Spinckes the interesting information that Mr Doughty was " pitched upon " because he was willing to go to Scotland, whereupon, says Campbell, " I told him I perceived that being a jockey was a principal qualification for a bishop on their side." [2] If the bishops had a right by virtue of their office to continue the succession and to ordain priests and deacons, how was it possible to contend that they had no right to enter upon the task of revising the Book of Common Prayer? Such was the argument of the Usagers, and the irregular prelates of a more conservative and Erastian turn of mind did not find it an easy task to make any convincing reply. It must, however, be confessed that the careful examination of the beliefs and practices of the Non-Jurors, which it has been my privilege to make, leads me to think that the statement made by Dr Johnson, that the Non-Jurors were incapable of reason, was not so much an exaggeration as the more perfervid admirers of the little body have led us to believe. Inconsistencies

[1] Brett MSS., vol. 15, f. 329 *et seq.*   *Ibid.*, vol. 6, f. 17.

both in belief and practice on the part of all Non-Jurors, and at all periods of their history, can easily be perceived by those who are prepared to search beneath the surface. It remains, however, true to say that the continuance of the ' succession ' which was felt to be a matter of great concern by all sections of the Non-Jurors tended to develop in their minds a clear conception of the " distinction between the allegiance which was due to the sovereign and the higher authority of Him, by whom kings reign." [1]

The question of the possibility of an alteration in the services of the Book of Common Prayer had no necessary connexion with Jacobitism or the tenets of the Non-Jurors, but became by force of circumstances a leading feature in the later history of many of those who in the political sphere remained faithful to the house of Stuart. There is to be noticed at the beginning of the eighteenth century a general revival of interest in the teaching and practice of the Primitive Church, which was by no means confined to the Non-Jurors, nor even to the more orthodox of their sympathisers in the Established Church. One of Rawlinson's many curious notes refers to a project of William Whiston.[2] It was a proposal to set up "a Primitive Library " in Cross Street, Hatton Garden. Whiston's idea was " that this library should consist of the best editions and of as many other editions as may be, of all the sacred primitive books of Christianity, and that in Greek, Latin, and English during the four first centuries and ending with St Austin." With this may be compared the statement made by Brett in his *Primitive Liturgies* regretting that

> Cranmer and his Colleagues sent into foreign parts for Bucer, etc., to interpret the Scriptures in our Universities according to their modern notions, and interpretations were placed upon them to alter the Liturgy and make it less agreeable to the consentient tradition of the Church and more agreeable to their modern doctrines and interpretation of Scripture [3]

This standpoint was adopted by many of the adherents to the Established Church, among whom Johnson of Cranbrook

[1] *Memoir of the Life of John Bowdler*, p. 72 *et seq.*
[2] Rawlinson MSS., D. 373, 13154, p. 103.
[3] Brett's *Dissertation on Primitive Liturgies*, Introduction (1720).

may receive special mention, and who, while refusing to follow the Non-Jurors into separation, nevertheless were in very complete agreement with them in their appeal to the authority of the Primitive Church, and particularly in regard to a reform of the Liturgy. There is here to be observed what may be described as a natural reaction against the more protestant and static conception of what was involved in the Reformation changes. It was a development which was perfectly loyal to the Book of Common Prayer as it stood, for the reason that in the book itself the appeal to the doctrine and practice of the Primitive Church is clearly enshrined as the justification of the position assumed by the English Church at the time of the Reformation. It did, however, represent a change from the position assumed by that typical individual who in our day is styled the ' plain man,' who was strongly opposed to any developments which, according to his opinion, meant going behind the Reformation—which standpoint is not entirely unknown at the present day. I may state as a matter of fact that I have heard in a Northern diocesan conference a lay representative contend that what the Primitive Church taught or practised did not matter at all—the appeal was not to the Primitive Church, but to the Reformation.

It is obvious that if this conception be adopted by men of minds static by nature and undeveloped by anything in the nature of liberal education, it inevitably leads to the belief in the troublous period of the Reformation without roots in the past, and without possibility of development in the future, and yet as the standard of teaching and practice for all ages to come. Such a conception was not in the sixteenth and seventeenth centuries held by any leading exponent of the Anglican Church, but it is of supreme importance for our purpose to note that in the eighteenth century the mantle of the earlier exponents of the claim of the English Church to appeal to primitive standards fell to a very large extent upon the little body of the Non-Jurors, and even upon a small section within that body. It is impossible within my present limits to go into the question of the disputes between the Usagers and Non-Usagers which led to the separation of the Non-Jurors into two or three groups, but let it be said in a word that the Usagers desired such a revision of the Book of Common

Prayer as would make it more conformable to primitive tradition. The newly awakened interest in primitive antiquity was developed with extraordinary learning by Hickes, Collier, Brett, Wagstaffe, and Deacon, all of whom, but for the unhappy and crippling influence of their separation into a tiny little sect, were fitted to illuminate the Church in any age. Here is an illustration of the keenness of the young men who surrounded Collier and Brett in 1718. Brett had written to Thomas Wagstaffe, the younger, announcing his plan for the production of a comprehensive book on the subject of liturgies, and asking that some of the young men in London should take their part by translating a number of them into English. Wagstaffe's reply was sufficiently encouraging.

> Mr Deacon and Mr Jebb will be glad to serve you, but I am not sure that Mr R. Rawlinson's business will admit of an avocation. However, if he should not be able to bear us company Mr Rutter has promised to supply his place.[1]

The learning and research which is here illustrated had result in the publication of the new Communion Office in 1718, and in Brett's *Dissertation on Primitive Liturgies* in 1720.

As the interest in these questions increased the political side of the movement tended to fall into the background, especially after the failure of the plans to bring about a Stuart restoration on the death of Queen Anne. It is not generally known that the trend of opinion in favour of reforming the Church on a basis of primitive beliefs led in the case of some of the Non-Juror leaders to a position which involved a complete breach with the English Church, even as it stood before the Revolution, and to the formation of a separate body of Non-Jurors who were known as Manchesterians and maintained a separate existence longer than any other section of the movement. As a Manchesterian myself, I am bound to feel some interest in this particular phase, and particularly as some fifteen or twenty years ago I devoted much time to the preparation of a biography of Thomas Deacon, one of the most extraordinary leaders of the whole movement, who was the first bishop to live in Manchester, preceding the present regular and lawful succession of Bishops of Manchester by more than a century.

[1] Brett MSS., vol. 3, f. 267.

The critical stage of this last development may be said to have been reached by the publication in 1734 of Deacon's *Compleat Devotions*, but the signs of this development are clearly to be perceived by those who will take the trouble to read the correspondence of the Non-Jurors from the time of the outbreak of the Usages Controversy in 1716. In 1747 Deacon formally authorised this book to be the standard of belief and worship for all those who in London and Manchester held communion with him. The main feature of this work is, as is well known, the so-called Clementine Liturgy, which was, however, at the time of the first publication in 1734 believed to be of very great authority by scholars both within and without the Church. But Deacon's divergence from the Church of England began at a very early period. In 1717 he wrote to Brett: " Bishop Hickes' principles were different from yours and mine, he did not believe there was any essential deficiency in our liturgy, though we do." [1] Four years later Deacon indicates a further advance of opinion, acknowledging that formerly he had tried to vindicate the Church of England, and adding: " I wish I could do so now. When I came to consult history the less defensible I found the Church of England." [2] The connexion of Deacon with the rising of the '45, involving as it did the loss of three sons, is well known. It is, however, surprising to find—that is, from the point of view of those who are not aware of the developments which have been explained—that immediately after these disasters Deacon issued an authoritative statement to the effect that those who desired to communicate with him were not expected to adopt any particular political basis whatever, as they went upon a totally different foundation.[3] Thirty or forty years later this standpoint was reaffirmed in plain language by William Cartwright, Deacon's son-in-law, and one of his successors, in a letter written to Dr Douglas, Bishop of Carlisle, at the time when the Scottish bishops were first seeking relief from State proscription. " Our difference with the establishment was not and had not been for a long time on any political ground, and we are loyal to the civil state and constitution upon Christian principles." [4]

[1] Brett MSS., vol. 3, f. 151.   [2] *Ibid.*, vol. 4, f. 285.
[3] See *Biography of Thomas Deacon*, p. 192.
[4] See *Later Non-Jurors*, p. 289.

This brief statement of a late and little-known development of the Non-Juror movement will help to explain the very last description given in a Manchester journal in 1804 in which a reference is made to " The Non-Jurors as they are generally termed, but as they denominate themselves The True British Catholic Church which once made a considerable noise in the world, but is now nearly extinct." [1]

Some words may fitly be said by way of conclusion with regard to the long continuance of the movement which has been under consideration. In the political sphere the problem is sufficiently simple. The great central and outstanding hindrance to a Stuart restoration was to be found in the adherence to the religion which had been embraced by Charles II and James II. On either side of this central and insurmountable difficulty there are to be noted two tendencies which worked in opposite directions. In the first place, the almost universal dislike of the Hanoverian succession gradually wore away, and by the time of the accession of the third George the new house had obtained a respectable tradition of its own. On the other hand, the later life of Prince Charles Edward could not be raised to a level sufficiently high to attract devotion even by the efforts of a few surviving Jacobite writers of songs, and on the succession to the claims of the house in 1788 by Prince Henry, Cardinal Duke of York, even the Scottish Episcopalians struck at transferring their devotion to one who in a curious and anonymous tract written in 1788 is described as a " Pope's man." [2] A curious piece of information has recently reached me which illustrates the hesitation felt by the Scottish Jacobites in continuing to pray for one who, whatever else he may have been, was certainly a Roman Cardinal. The prayers for Henry IX are reported to have been made on one knee only.

On the strictly religious side the duration of the movement in a more or less organised form may be assigned to causes which deserve more serious consideration. Broadly speaking, the Non-Jurors were, in the literal sense of the expression, High Church men. They were as a body essentially opposed to the theory which, as a matter of fact, was carried into effect

[1] Aston's *Manchester Directory* for 1804.
[2] Farquhar, *Three Bishops of Dunkeld*, W. pp. 69-71.

by successive Governments of the eighteenth century, viz., that the Church was a department of the Civil Service of the State. It is no doubt an exaggeration to say that the Non-Jurors were of one mind, even upon this subject. Richard Rawlinson and George Smith, at least in his later developments, were Erastians of a very pronounced type. It cannot, however, be doubted that the continuance of a separate organisation, long after any possibility of the realisation of the hopes with which the movement began, is to be attributed to the dread of the almost complete subjection of the Church to the State which is particularly associated with the name of Walpole. The controversy which was aroused by Brett's attack on Hoadly's *Plain Account* (1735) and Waterland's *Review of the Doctrine of the Eucharist* (1736) is an illustration of the conviction held by the small surviving body of Non-Jurors that submission to a Parliamentary Church was treachery to what Bishop Hickes described as " the faith of the purest and most primitive ages." The tone of Non-Juror literature is certainly very clerical, but the laity did speak sometimes, and the opinions of two laymen of distinguished Non-Juror families may be worth quoting in illustration of this particular point. In the year 1744 John Cotton wrote: " Bishop Smith's attitude to the Scottish bishops gives the Romish emissaries a handle to draw off persons by charging us with being a Parliamentary Church." [1] And apparently at the same period Thomas Bowdler declares : " I would not be thought to be a member of an Erastian Church, if I could help it, and I hope that the Church of England is not such as Mr Smith represented her." [2] It may be conjectured that apart from the Erastian tendencies of the earlier Hanoverian period the logic of Dodwell would have prevailed and the schism been brought to an end on the death of the last deprived bishop. The views expressed by Robert Nelson in a letter to Bishop Hickes in January 1709–10, " the only principle on which I think we can defend ourselves is the non-vacancy of the sees," [3] do not differ in essence from the opinion of Dr Brett given in a letter to Sir Richard Cox in January 1722–23, and written at the very height of the former's enthusiasm for the Usages.

[1] *Scotichronicon*, vol. 5, p. 199.   [2] Episcopal Church Paper 585.
[3] College Papers, f. 6, p. 2.

It is contrary to the law of God for the civil magistrate to make or ordain bishops, priests, and deacons, because Christ has committed that power to His apostles and their successors. Neither can he *dissolve the spiritual relation between them and their people*, because that also was committed to the apostles and their successors.[1]

So it came to pass that a movement which was originally a political issue developed into a protest against the intrusion of the State into matters concerning which it had no authority to deal.

Last of all, and more interesting, as bearing on a question of great interest in the present day, the Non-Jurors have left an enduring monument of liturgical reform. It is entirely beyond the scope of these lectures to indicate approval or disapproval of theological or liturgical questions. It is, however, a plain matter of duty to point out that objections to the reform of the Liturgy on the lines laid down by the Non-Jurors cannot be made on the ground that they are Popish. It is simply a matter of historical fact that the bishops of the English Church in 1927 in their revision proposals have laid aside the earlier Liturgy of Cranmer contained in the first Prayer Book of Edward VI, and have in all essential features copied what was first issued to the world by their irregular predecessors in the Non-Jurors' new Communion Office of 1718.

H. Broxap

BIBLIOGRAPHY

Books suggested for further reading :

Broxap, H. : *Biography of Thomas Deacon.* Manchester, 1911.
Broxap, H. : *The Later Non-Jurors.* Cambridge, 1924.
Dictionary of English Church History, edited by Canon Ollard. Article on the Non-Jurors. London, 1912.
Lang, Andrew : *Prince Charles Edward Stuart.* London, 1900.
Overton, Canon : *The Non-Jurors.* London, 1902.

For more detailed study :

The Brett MSS., being the Correspondence of Dr Thomas Brett. 20 vols. Bodleian Library.
The various MSS. in the Episcopal Chest in Edinburgh; also other MSS. in the care of the Scottish bishops entitled the *College Papers.*

[1] Brett MSS., vol. 16, f. 295.

VI

BENJAMIN HOADLY, BISHOP OF BANGOR

THE eventful fourscore years and five which saw the unfolding of the tragic fortunes of the Stuart monarchy in England witnessed also the progressive and irreparable crumbling of the Elizabethan creation of a National Church, wherein the entire people should be gathered in a spiritual unity " according to the pattern of God's own ancient elect people." From the outset indeed the Elizabethan Settlement had borne within its womb the seeds of two religious traditions, and before the end of the reign two parties had separated themselves within its communion. The struggle between ' reformers ' and ' innovators,' between the champions of Anglicanism and of the Presbyterian system, had resulted in the victory of the former chiefly because the power of the royal supremacy had been exercised heavily against the Puritan party. "By the goodness of Almighty God and His servant Elizabeth we are " was a thanksgiving as truly merited as enthusiastically offered by the grateful Anglicans. But the very closeness of the alliance between the monarchy and the episcopacy which had preserved hitherto the *via media* so straightly was to prove a source of disaster when the Stuarts succeeded to the throne. Within the Church the conflict of parties was accentuated by the growth of the new school of Laudian divines, who, in return for the protection of Charles I in religious policy, lent the support of their office to his claim to rule without consulting Parliament. The unhappy consequence of the coalition of Church and Crown became evident in the struggles preceding the Civil War, when the combatants ranged themselves largely according to their ecclesiastical allegiance, the Parliamentary party being resolved to destroy root and branch that order of episcopacy which had seemed to Hooker " the glue and soder

112

of the public weal, the ligament which tieth and connecteth the limbs of this body politic to each other." In the Civil War the two religious traditions born of the English Reformation joined in deadly issue; and during the Commonwealth the Puritans by their proscription of Anglicanism rejoiced to fulfil yet another Scripture: " By thy sword shalt thou live, and . . . when thou shalt break loose, thou shalt shake his yoke from off thy neck." With the Restoration came a reversal of fortunes, and the Church returned triumphant to be avenged of the enemy. Yet in the hour of its seeming rehabilitation complete victory was beyond its grasp. The Commonwealth had established organised Dissent as a permanent factor in the life of the nation. Before the Civil War there had lingered still the possibility of restored unity in the Church. Those whom persuasion could not win to peaceful conformity persecution might yet compel to come in. Of the spirit of persecution there was indeed a double portion resting upon the fervent Royalists of the Cavalier Parliament, who were the real authors of the miscalled Clarendon Code. But the collapse at the Savoy Conference of the attempted comprehension of orthodox Presbyterians— an attempt based upon the common belief of Anglican and Presbyterian in the necessity of a National Church and their cordial detestation of the excesses of the saints—presaged the failure of the persecuting laws against Nonconformists. Had Episcopalian and Presbyterian been bound into a solid phalanx it might have fared ill indeed with the sects. Instead, the issue by Charles II, within twelve years of his restoration, of the first Declaration of Indulgence for Dissenters signalised the establishment of a new element in the religious life of the nation. The Church had perforce to recognise grudgingly that the English nation, unlike the ancient people of God, was but " part of them the Commonwealth and part of them the Church of God," not " whole and entire " in allegiance to one National Church.

Less than a generation was granted to Churchmen to reverse the presuppositions of a century. After the bewilderment and chaos of civil war and proscription they had but twenty-five years in which to learn that the restoration of the Church, like that of the Crown, was conditional, and not

H

absolute. It is little surprising that the clergy failed to read the signs of the times; that they surrounded the throne with adulation and loyalty; that they refurbished and reiterated the doctrines of divine right and passive obedience; that they encouraged the revival of touching for King's Evil; and that they cherished still the hope that Dissenters might be suppressed. Nemesis came swiftly upon their blindness. Charles II betrayed them secretly, James attacked the Church openly; and though the true Israelites were content submissively to be martyrs, others of their countrymen shrank not from rebellion and from the invitation to William of Orange to save the liberties of the kingdom.

The Revolution of 1688 penetrated the confusion of English politics with the sharpness of a two-edged sword, piercing to the dividing asunder of precept and action. The practical exigency of events compelled the substitution of William III for James II, without regard to the difficulty of constructing a political theory which would conceal the vital fact that a dynasty ruling by divine hereditary right had been displaced by a monarchy created in a Convention Parliament of doubtful legality. The pious fiction of an abdication and consequent vacancy of the throne could not veil the essential breach of continuity; and the full force of its destructive logic fell upon the Church and the leaders of the Tory party. These allies had been drawn together by a natural sympathy of outlook, evinced in their support of Charles II during the struggle concerning the Exclusion Bill, and cemented by their common reverence for the principle of hereditary succession. Their alliance did not amount to complete identity, for the Church embraced a considerable number of Puritan incumbents who had survived the ejection of 1662, and who found an affinity with the ideals of the Whigs. But the majority of the clergy were in close sympathy with the Tories, and upon them the Revolution Settlement fell with devastating force. The conversion of a secular politician might conceivably be effected by the resolution of the Parliament which declared William and Mary King and Queen, distasteful though its consecration of the Whig theory of an " original contract " would be to Tory stomachs; but the sacred conscience of Churchmen could not render allegiance to a sovereign who had expelled the divinely appointed dynasty of the nation, and might also seek to introduce the Calvinistic Presbyterianism with which he was familiar abroad into the Church over which he must become supreme governor. Faced with the denial of both the principles which Caroline churchmanship had accounted essential to Church and State respectively, Archbishop Sancroft and four of his suffragans went into voluntary exile rather than perjure their conscience. But for the removal of three other bishops by death, their number would have been larger, and they were followed by about four hundred of the inferior clergy.

The schism thus effected had a far-reaching influence. The Non-Jurors received in full measure the respect accorded to those who had placed fidelity to principle above the advantage of compromise. To the Tories who had accepted office under William III there was a standing rebuke in the spectacle of their Fathers in God " being destitute, afflicted, evil intreated, of whom the world was not worthy." Politically the Non-Juror tradition exercised a fatal fascination upon their old party, drawing it back to the pursuit of causes lost. Nor was their influence confined to the force of silent example. Their schism aroused a fierce literary controversy, in which they themselves bore conspicuous part, concerning the foundations of civil government and the relations of Church and State—a controversy which sustained the vital issues of English politics until the rise under George III of a new Tory party divested at length of the Nessus shirt of allegiance to the Stuarts. In this warfare the Non-Jurors adopted an aggressive attitude. They stigmatised the new sovereigns as usurpers and the Church Establishment as schismatic. They declared the true episcopate to be continued among themselves, and the lawful monarchy among the exiles at Saint-Germain. The Whig writers, in rejoinder, took their stand upon the notion of an original contract between King and people, and defended the election of William III as necessary to preserve the liberties of the people. But the crux of the controversy centred in the position of the Church. Could the bishops intruded into the sees of the Non-Jurors be regarded as true apostolic bishops of the Church of God? Or had not the State, by its deprivation of the Non-Juring prelates, effected a breach of continuity in the episcopate as complete as that in the monarchy, and therefore created a new schismatic communion? Such questions were as much beyond the ability of the Whig writers to answer as the whole problem of ecclesiastical authority was beyond their temperament to comprehend. For the task of meeting the Non-Jurors upon their own ground there was need of a school of clerical Whigs; and by a singular irony of fortune the schism of the Non-Jurors itself provided the means for such a creation. No fewer than fifteen bishops were consecrated during the first two years of William's reign, and the King was not slow to take advantage of the opportunity to appoint divines of approved loyalty to his *régime*. Upon their shoulders devolved the necessary, and generally not uncongenial, duty of justifying their position against the aspersions of their opponents; and that duty embraced the auxiliary task of encouraging and promoting such of their clergy as were zealous in defence of the Revolution Settlement. The Whig cause could now count upon the support of a considerable part of the episcopal bench, and a Church-Whig party was in process of creation.

The heritage to which the Church of the Revolution succeeded was neither peaceful nor easy in character. Foremost among the practical problems which awaited solution was that of the position of the Protestant Dissenters. Having rejected the tempting indulgence offered by James II, they could naturally anticipate a measure of clemency not less complete from the new administration. Further, in the crisis of the late reign, a gesture of marked amity had been made by the National Church. Sancroft had issued Letters of Advice to his suffragans, to be communicated by them to their clergy, in which he had exhorted them to show " a very tender regard towards our brethren the Protestant Dissenters." He desired the parish clergy to visit the Dissenters in their homes, to assure them of the unyielding hostility of the bishops to Rome, and to invite them to join in earnest prayer for the union of all Reformed Churches, at home and abroad, against their common enemy. It was evident that something must be done for the Dissenters, and that the new bishops appointed by William would view their position with more sympathy than the High Church prelates whom they had succeeded. The

116

solution of this problem would affect also the relations of the episcopate with their inferior clergy, the majority of whom looked with suspicion upon the tendencies of William and his advisers in religious policy. Behind the difficulties of practical administration lay the controversy with the Non-Jurors, challenging the Church to vindicate its allegiance to the new *régime*, and to produce a convincing apologetic of its position as a condition of the nation's confidence. Moreover, the Church of the eighteenth century was already on the threshold of the conflict with Deism, which shifted the entire basis of theological debate and resulted in the rise of the powerful Latitudinarian school within the Church itself. It was against the background of the deistic conceptions of God that the questions of the relation of the King to the law and of the nature of ecclesiastical authority were argued. The prevalent ideas of the universal reign of natural law and of the improbability of miraculous intervention by the Creator helped still further to discredit the dispensing power of earthly sovereigns and to subordinate their prerogatives to the decrees of positive law.

The essential characteristic of the controversies thus evoked was their close correspondence with contemporary political events. The defenders of the Revolution Settlement were contending, not for an orthodox exegesis of happenings in an historic past, but for the maintenance of a position still fiercely contested, and by no means beyond the chance of reversal. The reigns of William III and Anne were pre-eminently the testing of Revolution principles. The generation after 1688 was called, not to garner the fruits of that victory in peace, but to wage unceasing battle for its preservation. The position of Dissenters, apparently secured in 1689, was successfully assailed by the Tories in the reign of Anne, and not finally established until the ministry of Walpole. The doctrines of divine hereditary right and of non-resistance reappeared under Anne with pristine vigour, and regained their old predominance in High Church pulpits. The prospects of the Protestant succession varied with the fluctuating fortunes of the war abroad and of the parties at home. During the Indian summer of High Church Toryism after 1710 there seemed a real possibility of a Stuart restoration, and not until the exile of Bishop Atterbury in 1723 was the Hanoverian dynasty secure upon the throne. The Whig controversialists who denounced the Stuarts and defended the Glorious Revolution were assuredly not *laudatores temporis acti*. They were protagonists in a conflict of which the issue was still uncertain.

II

The absorption of public interest in political debate must serve as justification or apology for the volume and vehemence of the writings of Benjamin Hoadly. In an age voracious of controversy his indefatigable pen must surely have sated the stoutest appetite. Gibbon justly characterises him as " the object of Whig idolatry and Tory abhorrence." Extravagant abuse and equally excessive praise were heaped upon him in his own generation. The pamphlets which issued from his hand with teeming fecundity were read with avidity and answered with acerbity. To present-day readers there is little to excite passion in the three folio volumes of his works. " His memorable sayings are proverbs of ashes, and his defences are defences of clay." But Hoadly is still worth reading for other qualities than that of splendid pugnacity.

It must be acknowledged that he was incurably combative, almost predestined to become a leader of controversy. Providence caused him to be born, in 1676, the second son of the Rev. Samuel Hoadly, who had himself been born in New England, whither the Bishop's grandfather had fled in 1639, returning in 1655 to become chaplain to the garrison of Edinburgh Castle. Such antecedents virtually predetermined the politics of young Benjamin, and the influences of his education confirmed the traditions of his fathers. After receiving early instruction from his father, who kept a school at Westerham in Kent, he proceeded to Catherine Hall, Cambridge, then under the rule of Dr John Leng, a staunch Whig who was made Bishop of Norwich in 1723 by Gibson because of his firmness to the Protestant succession and the house of Hanover. During his residence in Cambridge Hoadly incurred a lameness of leg, which caused him always to preach in a kneeling posture and to propel himself with the aid of a crutch or stick. At the same time he suffered from a tendency to consumption, from which he did not entirely recover until his later prosperity enabled him to "take the air daily in a chariot." In due course he became Tutor and Fellow of the college, and he was ordained deacon in 1698 and priest in 1700 by Bishop Compton of London, who had the distinction of being the only spiritual peer to sign the invitation to William of Orange in 1688. Hoadly resigned his Fellowship in 1701, on his marriage, and became lecturer of St Mildred in the Poultry. He remained in this office ten years, "till he had preached it down to £30 per year (as he pleasantly observed), and then he thought it high time to quit it." At the same time he officiated for Mr Hodges, Rector of St Swithin's, during the absence of the latter at sea as Chaplain-General of the Fleet in 1702. In 1704 Hoadly was appointed by the Dean and Chapter of St Paul's to the rectory of St Peter Poor, Broad Street, largely on the recommendation of Dr William Sherlock, the dean. The period of his ministry in the City coincided almost exactly with the reign of Anne, and in the heated atmosphere of party politics it was not to be expected that Hoadly would remain indifferent or impartial. On the contrary, he produced a considerable number of polemical works. As an inevitable corollary of his Whig pre-dilections he incurred the censure of the Lower House of Convocation in 1706, and received the favour of the Whig House of Commons. In a resolution of the Commons in December 1709 it was declared that Hoadly's writings in defence of the Revolution had "justly merited" their "favour and recommendation," and a request was made to the Queen that she "would be graciously pleased to bestow some dignity in the Church upon Mr Hoadly for his eminent services both to Church and State." Unfortunately for the favourite of the Commons the following year saw the rout of the Whigs in the General Election and the return of a strong Tory majority. From 1710 to the end of the reign the Whig partisans had to be content with exile, and the preferments of the Crown were bestowed upon good Tories. Hoadly had to rest satisfied with the smaller rewards which a private patron could offer. He became chaplain to the Whig Duke of Bedford, and so was able to accept presentation to the rectory of Streatham,

which became " his most beloved retirement." Thus he continued during the years of darkness and anxiety, in which the
problem of the Queen's successor was canvassed with much
searching of heart, until by a miracle of Providence the
accession of George I was secured.

The establishment of the house of Hanover on the English
throne opened the land of political promise to the Whig out-
casts, and not least to the clerical defenders of the unpromising
Georges and their train of German followers. Nobody had
merited their favour more than Hoadly, and nobody preached
with greater vigour against the Jacobite rebellion of 1715
than himself. His devotion was speedily rewarded. He was
made a Royal Chaplain on February 16, 1715, and the first
important promotion of the reign was his appointment to the
see of Bangor, to which he was nominated on December 20,
1715, and consecrated on March 18, 1716. He retained
both his livings *in commendam*, and omitted to visit or reside
in his diocese, two faults which have been accounted for a
peculiar reproach to the eighteenth century, though they
could with as much relevance be regarded as signs of convincing continuity with pre-Reformation times. At first
Hoadly was busy with other matters than those of episcopal
visitation. He signalised his promotion and the royal favour
by producing in 1716 his two most famous writings : first the
*Preservative against the Principles and Practices of the Non-
Jurors both in Church and State,* and secondly the sermon
preached before the King, on *The Nature of the Kingdom or
Church of Christ,* which occasioned the controversy associated
with the see which he occupied. From this time his name
was even more execrated than it had been before ; but with
one all-important difference. Henceforth his opponents
might rage together against him, but they could neither
hinder nor minimise his success. A zealous though not very
exalted *malleus hæreticorum,* who was beneficed in the City
of London, protesting upon occasion against the heretical
opinions of his ecclesiastical superiors, declared that Hoadly
" had, by his writings, done more harm to the Church of
Christ and to the Protestant cause than any man living " ; and
there can be little doubt that he commanded the assent of the
majority of his order. Nor can it be doubted that the Bishop's

success no less than his writings contributed to the speaker's verdict that " these things gall all honest clergymen and others who have a regard for religion." [1]   It is opportune therefore to examine in some detail the ground upon which such charges were founded.

Hoadly's first incursion into the field of controversy was in connexion with the position of the Protestant Dissenters. Their momentary union with the Established Church in opposition to the policy of James II had raised fresh hopes of the possibility of a restoration of the religious unity of the nation.   In 1689 this took the old form of a conference to consider the question of a comprehension.   A Royal Commission was appointed to prepare proposals, and a Bill was introduced into the House of Lords to the same effect.   But although the Commission showed a readiness to make concessions which should have satisfied moderate Presbyterian opinion, its report was ineffective, because the temper of the Lower House of the Canterbury Convocation was so hostile to the entire project that the matter was not allowed to reach discussion stage there.   The scheme was therefore still-born. Instead, the Dissenters had to be contented with the Toleration Act.   This Act, though removing the weapon of persecution, confined its benefits within narrow limits.   It allowed freedom of worship to all Protestant Dissenters who would subscribe the Thirty-nine Articles and register their meeting-houses in the archdeacons' courts.   No relief from the civil disabilities of Dissent was allowed, and the liberty granted was limited to orthodox Trinitarian ministers.   Despite these very material restrictions, the passage of the Act marked an epoch in the religious history of the nation.   The State, for the first time, had given formal recognition of the existence of religious communions outside the Established Church, and that Church had to accept, as the price of its continued establishment, the anomaly of legal toleration of the sects.   It was not unnatural that the compromise should be unwelcome to many Churchmen.   The High Church clergy, led by Atterbury, insisted that toleration could not take away the sinfulness of schism, and protested particularly against the

[1] Egmont MSS., vol. i, p. 444 (Hist. MSS. Comm.).

practice of occasional conformity, by which moderate Dissenters, while cleaving to their denomination, received the Sacrament according to the rite of the Church in order to qualify for civic office. Exasperated by William's favour to Latitudinarian divines, the Tory clergy nursed a growing resentment throughout his reign, and awaited the succession of Anne to embark upon retaliatory measures against the Dissenters. As early as the first November after her accession a Bill to prevent occasional conformity was introduced into Parliament, passed the Commons, but was held up in the Lords by a series of wrecking amendments. The temper shown in the Commons, however, was of ill omen for the Dissenters, and the fury of High Churchmen against them increased as the reign progressed. The wrecking of meeting-houses was a feature of the Sacheverell agitation, and in the Tory triumph after 1710 both the Occasional Conformity and Schism Acts were carried. Within twenty years of the Revolution its religious settlement had been reversed; and the responsibility lay with the Tory Churchmen, clerical and lay.

Hoadly had entered the lists of literary dispute on the side of the Dissenters in 1703, by the publication of his *Letter to a Clergyman concerning the Votes of the Bishops* in connexion with the Occasional Conformity Bill. His object was to defend the Whig prelates who had opposed the Bill in the Lords against the Tory attack which represented them as having betrayed the cause of the Church. He emphasised first the political aspect of the situation, urging the great unwisdom of introducing any measure which might divide the Protestant interest at home, at the moment when the nation was engaged in a conflict with Louis XIV, the champion of Catholicism, abroad. But apart from considerations of State, he denied that the interest of the Church could be helped by the Bill. He counted it indeed an honour that William's bishops had " been for alterations and concessions in favour of the Dissenters," in the hope of a comprehension; and so long as this ideal should be unattained the practice of occasional conformity was to be encouraged, as tending " to abate men's prejudices towards those small matters, the constant use of which is disliked, and to reconcile them still more to constant

Communion." [1]   Hoadly stoutly refused to acknowledge that the Church had lost ground since the Toleration Act, and argued that the practice now in dispute was actually beneficial to the Church, since it retained within negotiating distance those sympathetic Nonconformists who approved of episcopacy and a settled Liturgy.   For the rest he desired that the bishops should accept the " odious appellation of Moderate Churchmen," proving their right to the title by making " amendments and abatements in things truly indifferent " in order to win Dissenters over to constant conformity.

While urging thus the continuation of efforts toward comprehension, in other writings Hoadly exhorted the Dissenters with equal vigour to preserve the unity of the Protestant religion by a full communion with the Established Church. In a series of pamphlets addressed to Calamy, the eminent Nonconformist divine, he surveyed the whole field of controversy between the Church and Dissent.   The general tenor of his argument was to the effect that, while the Church might not be perfect either in doctrine or worship, its shortcomings were not so grave as to compel separation; that its admitted comprehensiveness was designed to include in its ministry men who could give a *general* assent to its teaching and liturgy, while retaining freedom to press for further reform; and that a limited subjection to authority in things indifferent was preferable to the scandal occasioned to religion by the setting up of separate Churches.   In expanding these principles Hoadly had of necessity to traverse ground which had been much controverted in the disputes of the preceding century.   In his *Reasonableness of Conformity to the Church of England represented to the Dissenting Ministers* he started from the agreed position that " episcopal ordination was the regular, orderly ordination settled in the Church of Christ," and argued from thence that presbyterian ordination could only be justified in case of proved necessity.   Such a case had existed during the Commonwealth; and therefore he granted freely that those Dissenters " who were ordained by presbyters without bishops, because episcopal ordination could not be had," must be acknowledged " to have had a real ordination, and their authority to have lasted as long as that necessity

---

[1] *A Letter to a Clergyman concerning the Votes of the Bishops* (Works, vol. i, p. 28).

lasted, and consequently all their acts valid, even as to the authority of them." [1] This was a wide and charitable interpretation, but Hoadly insisted that its force rested upon the readiness of the Dissenters to put an end to the irregularity by refusing to continue their separated ministry after the Restoration. He urged those ministers who had been ordained under the Commonwealth to regularise their situation by receiving an episcopal commission, and he insisted that none of the arguments adduced to support their position could possibly justify the continuance of non-episcopal ordination among their successors. This defence of episcopal ordination was elaborated in a later separate pamphlet, which was an able and orthodox statement of the Anglican position, especially from the pen of a " Moderate Churchman." [2] But besides the difficulty of ordination the Dissenters felt scruples concerning the subscription and assent to the Book of Common Prayer required of ministers. In regard to this point Hoadly adopted a distinctly minimising attitude. Disapproving of all attempts to present the Declaration of Assent and Consent in a " rigid and unreasonable " manner, he announced his own interpretation of its terms, insisting that the assent was confined to the use of the book, and that it did not imply consent to the truth of every proposition in it :

> The Declaration of Assent and Consent cannot possibly be extended to anything but the *use* of this Book; and the subscription concerns this Book, only as it is a Book directing the Minister what prayers and what ceremonies to use; and has no reference to anything in it that does not concern the Minister who is to use it. And from hence it follows that whoever thinks this Book fit to be used in the service of God, may very fairly make this declaration and subscription without putting a stretch either upon the words or upon his own conscience. [3]

It was evident that the validity of this contention depended upon the right of the individual to exercise a considerable latitude of practice in the conduct of public worship; and in this case what became of the oath of canonical obedience

---

[1] *The Reasonableness of Conformity to the Church of England represented to the Dissenting Ministers* (1703) (Works, vol. i, p. 193).
[2] *A Brief Defense of Episcopal Ordination* (Works, vol. i, p. 395 *et seq.*).
[3] *The Reasonableness of Conformity* (Works, vol. i, p. 199).

which priests had to take to their bishop? Was it not possible that the orders of the bishop might nullify the liberty claimed for the minister? To these objections Hoadly replied by a minimising explanation of the oath. By it a presbyter promised " true and canonical obedience " to his diocesan " in all lawful and honest things "; a promise which was now interpreted to mean " a true obedience . . . and such a sincere, ready, and submissive obedience, as by the Laws of the Church is required of a presbyter to his Bishop, in all things that, according to the best light I have, I apprehend to be lawful and honest." This exegesis placed a twofold restriction upon the obedience sworn: it made the individual " the judge of the lawfulness and honesty of every command," and it limited the application of the term ' laws ' to " those actually in force in the present and not to laws or canons which may have fallen into disuse or obsolescence."

Hoadly's argument was already distinguished by the insistence on the prerogative of private judgment, which is characteristic of all his writings, and which, exaggerated later, caused him to dissolve all the authority of corporate societies in his Bangorian sermon. Although arguing earnestly for the conformity of Dissenters to the National Church on grounds of the preservation of Protestant unity and of the manifest advantages of national solidarity in religion, he admitted fully that the decision must rest upon individual conscience.

> If there be persons who will be persuaded by no arguments that a compliance with these terms is . . . lawful, I confess it is my opinion that, whilst they are thus persuaded, it is as much their duty to separate from us, as it is our duty to separate from the Church of Rome. For they as much as we are obliged not to do what they judge to be unlawful; and they as much as we are obliged to assemble themselves together for the worship of God and the enjoyment of His ordinances.[1]

From the espousal of such principles there followed inevitably not only the abandonment of the attempt to achieve religious uniformity, and the need for full toleration, but also the enthronement of private judgment as the final arbiter in

[1] *The Reasonableness of Conformity* (Works, vol. i, p. 282).

matters of faith. It is therefore not a little interesting to observe that this same pamphlet contains an unequivocal defence of the right of spiritual governors to exercise authority over the members of their churches. Hoadly was arguing with the moderate Dissenters who admitted the need of a liturgy for the ordering of public worship, but who objected to details of the Book of Common Prayer. In reply to their objection he urged that the determination of things indifferent belonged to the rulers of the Church, and that their rulings should command obedience.

> This authority they have, as they received the care of the Church from their predecessors; as they are obliged to take the most effectual methods for the preservation of order and decency in the public worship of God; and as it results from the nature of all societies that the Governors of them should have a power of ordering what seems to them most for the beauty and advantage of them; that they should be judges of what conduces to this end; and should have a title to the obedience of the people under their care, in whatever does not contradict the laws of that society by which they are all to be governed.[1]

As a practical example of this power Hoadly advanced the regulation of public worship. He declared that Christ

> only designed to ordain that there should be publick assembly of Christians and that the Holy Communion should be celebrated in these assemblies. All the circumstances of them . . . He left to be determined by the governors of His Church and people, according to the notions of decency and customs of different nations.

But the framing of rules is an exclusive as well as an inclusive action. What is the position, then, of governors when opposed by dissenters from their orders? It is surprising to find a candid admission that Nonconformists must submit to exclusion from the society in this case. Hoadly stated plainly " that the Governors of the Church have authority to impose some unnecessary things; that it is not unlawful to prescribe things antecedently unnecessary under the highest penalty "; and that " if any truly honest man be excluded Communion by this means, the penalty is to be considered, not as the punishment of the scruples of an honest man (which he may

---

[1] *The Reasonableness of Conformity* (Works, vol. i, p. 205).

have unavoidably) but as a fence against disorder." [1]   These principles were invoked to justify the reception of the Communion kneeling and the use of the sign of the Cross in baptism, but their force extended beyond the instances of immediate application.   There are not a few passages from the writings of Mr Hoadly against the Dissenters which could be urged with cogency by the opponents of the Bishop of Bangor.

In other pamphlets addressed to Calamy the main points mentioned above were developed in more detail, but throughout his career Hoadly maintained a consistent attitude toward the Dissenters, and his actions corresponded with the principles he proclaimed.   He lived sufficiently long to see the disappearance from the scope of practical affairs of the idea of a comprehension which he desired, but he was a steady champion of toleration.   After his elevation to the episcopate he helped to secure the repeal of the Occasional Conformity and Schism Acts in 1718, and was one of the small minority of the Bench which desired also to include the Test and Corporation Acts in the measure.   The proposal could not succeed at the time, but sporadic efforts were made by the Dissenters themselves during the reigns of the first two Georges to induce the Whig Government to grant this concession.   In 1732 Hoadly at the request of Walpole undertook to represent to them the inopportuneness of the time for such an attempt, though his own opinions were in favour of their claims.   One of his last political writings was a pamphlet of 1736, in answer to a defence of the obnoxious Acts by Gibson, in which he protested against the whole principle of the infliction of civil penalties for religious opinion.[2]   In his attitude toward Dissenters, Hoadly deserved the credit of an unwavering and disinterested championship of toleration and liberty of religion, without consideration of its effect upon his own fortunes.   It is of interest to observe that his stout acceptance of Whig principles on this question did not induce the Walpole administration to adopt a bold policy.   Instead the restrictive Acts were continued in force, but the passing of an annual

---

[1] *The Reasonableness of Conformity* (Works, vol. i, p. 209).
[2] *The Objections against the Repeal of the Test and Corporation Acts considered* (Works, vol. ii, p. 971).

Indemnity Act from 1727 onward afforded a practical relief
from their provisions.

III

The struggle for the toleration of Dissenters was but an
aspect of the wider contest for the succession to the throne,
which constituted the central political interest of the reign
of Anne. Enthusiasm for the Revolution had waned by the
time of her accession, in consequence of the heavy taxation
caused by foreign war, of the aloofness of William from the
issues of domestic politics, and particularly of the alienation of
the Church party. Churchmen had accepted with a bad grace
the results of the secular theory of government which had
triumphed in 1689, and the possibility of a quiet termination
of the Non-Juror schism had been defeated by the last act of
William's reign, the passing of the Abjuration Act of 1702.
By this malicious shaft the clergy were required not only to
affirm the rightfulness of the title of the reigning sovereign,
but also to declare that the Pretender's claim was void of right.
From the cold, unsympathetic attitude of the Dutch Calvinist
monarch Tories and Churchmen turned with eagerness to the
pronounced favour of the new Queen for their cause. Anne
was beyond possibility of doubt both English and Anglican.
The Vicar of Bray did not need prophetic insight to see in her
" the Church of England's glory." But prophetic insight
was granted to the Tory party to perceive, beyond the prosaic
clauses of the Act of Settlement which had brought her to the
throne, the faint yet authentic tradition of divine hereditary
right. Once the whisper of the magic phrase had been heard,
the pulpits resounded with it as an article of faith. Faith was
forthwith strengthened by the practical test of the revival of
touching for ' the Evil,' and some odour of the balm of an
anointed Queen was borne into the common-sense Georgian
era by the touching of young Samuel Johnson. Simultaneously the cult of the Royal Martyr evoked a new enthusiasm
and devotion; and the political sermons preached upon
King Charles' Day and upon Restoration Day pointed out
the dangers of rebellion and the glories of the Restoration,
tarnished though the latter appeared to be by the principles
of 1689. Inevitably the doctrines of absolute monarchy and

of non-resistance returned to secure the authority of cardinal points of belief; and the High Church clergy raised the battle-cry of "The Church in danger." The danger in question was understood to proceed from the attitude of the Whig bishops who opposed the Bills against occasional conformity; and the defence thus called for was undertaken by the inferior clergy of the Lower House of Canterbury Convocation. Nor was the change of temper reflected only in wordy controversy. The offer of bishoprics by the Queen at the beginning of her reign to the two Non-Jurors, Ken and Frampton, was a sign of the reversion of the Church to its old political allegiance, as was the elevation in 1713 to the see of Rochester of Atterbury, the leader of the Tory clergy in their attack upon their ecclesiastical superiors. To the Whigs the whole tendency of events was a cause of increasing apprehension and alarm. The very fact that Anne's real title to the throne was based upon the Act of Settlement made more ominous the insistence upon her supposed hereditary right. At her accession she had already buried sixteen children, and the prospect of her having further issue was very slight. Whither could the preaching of an indefeasible hereditary right turn the thoughts of men save to the recognition of the Pretender? Yet the Pretender's cause was at the moment espoused by Louis XIV, against whom the Grand Alliance was at war. Further, the party controversy within the Church had led the defenders of the lower clergy to espouse the tenets of the Non-Jurors, and to strike at the principles of the Revolution Settlement by proclaiming the ideal of the Church as a *societas perfecta*.

In truth there was a gathering of forces for a massed attack upon the principles to which the Whigs were irrevocably wedded. For several years the battle was left to the literary controversialists, and proceeded with a steady *crescendo* of vigour. But in 1710 the Whig Ministry unwisely resolved to force an issue by an open challenge to its adversaries. The impeachment of Sacheverell was designed simply as a public platform from which the defence of the Revolution could be solemnly promulged, and in argument the Whig advocates undoubtedly had the better of their rivals. But the incident aroused an incredible popular ferment, which resulted in the Tory victory at the elections of 1710 and the disappearance

I

of their opponents for the remainder of the reign. During the ensuing period of Tory reaction all questions of foreign and domestic politics were subordinate to the single interest of the succession to the throne. On the one side were the legal provisions of the Act of Settlement; on the other the principles of indefeasible right. For four years it seemed an open question to which course the Ministry would incline; and in the meanwhile the hearts of many Whigs were failing them for fear.

The part played by Hoadly in the debate is represented by his most ambitious essay in political theory,[1] and by a series of spirited pulpit pieces, which were remembered long after the occasion of their delivery as " the old cocks that fought the battles of liberty in good Queen Anne's days." [2] The champions of divine right and of non-resistance appealed constantly to the writings of St Paul in support of their thesis. In particular the thirteenth chapter of his Epistle to the Romans seemed the *fons et origo* of their beliefs. Such precepts as " Let every soul be in subjection to the higher powers: for there is no power but of God; and the powers that be are ordained of God. Therefore he that resisteth the power, withstandeth the ordinance of God. Wherefore ye must needs be in subjection, not only because of the wrath, but also for conscience sake "—these and similar passages seemed convincing proof both of the Apostle's attitude and of the Christian's duty. Nothing daunted by the High Church exegesis, Hoadly, preaching on Michaelmas Day 1705 before the Lord Mayor and Aldermen of the City of London, proceeded to attack the doctrine of non-resistance at its source, and to dispute the appropriation of St Paul by the Tories for their own advantage. Accepting the text " Let every soul be in subjection to the higher powers," he developed an interpretation of the apostolic counsel which actually justified the Revolution. After a preliminary observation that the words would apply to all public officers, high and low, and that St Paul did not affirm the divine prescription of any particular form of government to the exclusion of others, Hoadly pointed out that the function of rulers was stated to be " not a terror to the good work, but

---

[1] *The Original and Institution of Civil Government discussed* (1709).
[2] E. Pyle, *Memoirs of a Royal Chaplain*, ed. Hartshorne, p. 217 (London, 1905).

to the evil," and to be " an avenger of wrath to him that doeth evil." From this it followed that a governor who should violate his commission by protecting the evildoer and oppressing the righteous forfeited his claim to obedience on the part of his subjects. For although absolute obedience was due to rulers who exercised their authority aright, to render submission to those who betrayed their commission would be to assist them to thwart the purpose of God in their institution. The Apostle must be understood therefore to imply that submission was " due to governors, not for their own sake, but merely for the sake of public happiness "; and that the duty of obedience binding upon individuals was " only in relation to the public interest." " If their submission help to destroy or ruin that, it cannot be a virtue." It was an easy step from this to the triumphant conclusion that resistance to a prince who strives to ruin his people is " without shadow of a crime, nay with honour and glory." [1] Inevitably the enunciation of such opinions brought many replies from the High Church partisans. The Lower House of Convocation requested " that some synodical notice might be taken of the dishonour done to the Church " by the sermon; a warm reply appeared from the pen of Atterbury, and Hoadly retorted by a *Defence of the Doctrine of the Sermon*, in which he elaborated and illustrated the principles laid down.[2]

To carry the offensive a stage farther, he took advantage of the delivery of an assize sermon at Hertford to flagellate his opponents with another whip, by appealing to the practice of St Paul as recorded in the Acts as the best interpreter of his precepts in the Epistles. At Jerusalem the Apostle had protested that, being a Roman citizen, he ought not to be scourged; on a later occasion in the same city he had called the High Priest a " whited wall " because he had commanded the Apostle to be smitten " contrary to the law "; and at Philippi, having been wrongfully scourged and imprisoned, he had refused to accept the release offered by the magistrates, and had insisted upon their coming in person to hear his protest against the ill-usage to which he had been subjected.

---

[1] *The Measures of Submission to the Civil Magistrate considered* (1705) (Works, vol. ii, pp. 18–25).
[2] *Ibid.*, p. 26 et seq.

This conduct had plainly established the three great principles of liberty : the superiority of the law to the executive power ; the right of the individual to be the judge of the invasion of his own privileges ; and the duty of resistance to oppression and to magistrates who indulge in arbitrary acts. Insisting again that the same rules of judgment must apply to the behaviour of all governors, whether deputed or supreme, Hoadly proceeded to relate the instances to the circumstances of English politics. "How contrary" was the Apostle's conduct " to such as make written laws only an encroachment upon the absolute power instituted by God, and study to make their power as contemptible as they can, that the necessity of absolute monarchy may the better appear"! Were not St Paul's principles identical with those of the Revolution, since the latter were directed " chiefly to rescue our laws from a dispensing power, and to divert the executive from all pretences to superiority over the Legislature"? Did not the Apostle's "zeal for the laws shew that he thought both the Will of God and the good of Society to require another scheme than that of an unlimited executive power"? [1] By such arguments Hoadly not only defended, but glorified the Revolution Settlement ; and the two sermons are among the most entertaining as well as the most convincing of his writings. His style both of argument and of composition was better suited to the shorter scope of the sermon than to the longer compass of a sustained treatise. In his sermons he generally stated his position with lucidity and power ; but in the detailed defences and elaborations which were evoked by controversy his manner was laboured and unconvincing.

One of the most difficult tasks of the Whig divines was that of preaching on the "State Holy-days," especially those appointed by authority to commemorate the Restoration, or still more the Decollation (by some called Martyrdom) of King Charles I. Such occasions were welcome opportunities to Tory preachers to denounce the evil of rebellion and proclaim the duty of submission. A Whig must pick his way with care betwixt the Scylla of approving the regicides and the Charybdis of slighting the Revolution. In 1703 Hoadly,

[1] *St Paul's Behaviour towards the Civil Magistrate* (1708) (Works, vol. ii, pp. 118-125).

preaching upon King Charles' Day, delivered a moral discourse upon the virtue of moderation. Deeming the occasion
" to be observed most according to the design of it, when such
material points are insisted on as, if they had been heartily
embraced, would have prevented the effects of that violent
spirit, the character of which it now bears," he made no
reference to the events of 1649 until his concluding paragraph.
Even there he found it sufficient to mention generally their
tragic character, "not enumerating them, but rather praying
that the records of them in our Histories may make us
on all sides more in love with true Christian Moderation." [1]
Similarly in 1709 he turned the commemoration of the
Restoration into an occasion for discoursing upon the divine
overruling of the actions of men, as exemplified by the
restoration in 1660 " of that envied constitution in which the
commands of the prince and the obedience of the subject are
equally regulated by laws." Further, when foolish men
"took occasion to use their best endeavours to transform it
into an absolute and arbitrary tyranny," Providence again restored " the ancient form of government " in 1689.[2] After
the accession of the Hanoverian line, however, Whigs could
speak with greater boldness upon the political anniversaries.
On Restoration Day 1716 Hoadly dealt faithfully with the
passion of Royalist enthusiasm which had characterised the
Caroline age. "An universal madness of loyalty (falsely
so called) . . . took place; and the people came pressing in
throngs, beseeching to be accounted slaves rather than subjects." As for the blessings of the event, which the preacher
was appointed to commemorate that day, " where should we
now search for the blessing . . . if we did not see it in the
blessing of the Protestant Succession," which, as his hearers
well knew, had only been secured by a second expulsion of
the Stuart line.[3] In 1721 Hoadly preached before the House
of Lords on King Charles' Day, and expounded an interpretation of the events of 1649 which justified the happy measures
of 1689. In reprobating the execution of the King he
observed that such a crime had not been possible " till the
freedom of Parliament was totally destroyed, . . . the balances

[1] *Sermons*, XVII (Works, vol. iii, p. 659 *et seq.*).
[2] *Sermons*, XX (*ibid.*, p. 680 *et seq.*).   [3] *Sermons*, XI (*ibid.*, p. 632 *et seq.*).

which keep our government in an even situation torn asunder; and an armed force made the support of what remained of civil government." How great was the contrast with the Parliamentary Revolution of 1689! "The one ended in the ancient form of legal government, and a stronger establishment of the rights of subjects and Parliament; the other in a direct avowal of arbitrary power." The oration concluded with a triumphant affirmation of "the perfect consistency between a well-founded disapprobation of that scene of things" which ended in regicide, and "a settled and hearty approbation of that great transaction" of more recent times, "upon which the present happy establishment of the Constitution was founded." [1] A perusal of "the old cocks that fought the battles of liberty" thus handsomely must induce the reflection that modern politics and the modern pulpit are alike the poorer by the disappearance of the "State Holy-days," on which such entertaining fare of ancient example and modern application was wont to be furnished.

In the meantime Hoadly had penetrated into the more recondite sources of the controversy concerning the origins of civil government. Not content with invoking the authority of St Paul, the combatants carried back the argument to the original power conferred upon Adam. From his unlimited authority as father of the race the defenders of absolute monarchy deduced the powers of kings as fathers of their people. Nor did the quest for precedents rest with Adam. Some apologists argued from the monarchy of God to that of earthly kings; and hinted that Whig principles took their rise from that First Crusade in which "Michael and his angels fought against the dragon and his angels." Indeed, some of the versions were "as particularly related"—to quote the amusing phrase of Hoadly—"as if the historian had been a traveller in those blessed countries, and present himself at that remarkable transaction." On the other side the Whig writers traced the origin of civil government to a voluntary contract, and they had the advantage since 1689 that the Convention Parliament had sanctioned their thesis. Hoadly was drawn into this branch of the debate by a sermon of Bishop Blackhall of Exeter, defending the High Church

[1] *Sermons*, XVI (Works, vol. iii, p. 653 *et seq.*).

position, to which he felt compelled to reply. In his *Considerations humbly offered to the Bishop of Exeter* he laid down the two basic principles of his political position : that paternal authority differed in kind from that of civil governors ; and that the latter had its origin in a voluntary contract. He had little difficulty in arguing that paternal authority could exist in its plenitude in a state of society without any civil government, and therefore was distinct in origin and scope from political power. The institution of civil government he traced to the need of organised self-defence on the part of societies of men.

> A community or neighbourhood of people living together have a right to defend themselves against robbers, murderers, and enemies. . . . But finding this a state of no regular established security, they resolve to transfer this right of self-defence to some particular persons, reserving only to themselves the exercise of self-defence in those cases in which the magistrate cannot act for their safety.

This reservation of right could be legitimately applied to " the case of public impending ruin from the magistrate himself," especially since " the right of defending the community in this case was never given away by it, or taken from it by God." [1] Hoadly was here taking up the orthodox Whig attitude, which was based upon the dictates of common sense more than upon the historical reality of the fictitious contract. But since the argument for absolute monarchy sought justification from the Old Testament he was not unwilling to investigate that point also, which he did in another spirited assize sermon preached at Hertford in the same year. Seizing upon the account in the first Book of Samuel [2] of the request of the Hebrews for a kingship instead of the theocracy, he observed that this was the sole authentic occasion " given to Almighty God by mankind to declare His mind plainly concerning the institution of absolute monarchy." Therefore in the picture drawn by Samuel of the sort of monarchy they would receive men could " know the thoughts of God " concerning that matter. The details of the account were truly

---

[1] *Some Considerations humbly offered to the Lord Bishop of Exeter* (1708) (Works, vol. ii, p. 126 *et seq.*).
[2] 1 Samuel, viii, 9-18.

" sad and lamentable," and could be " all summed up in one comprehensive word, and that is, slavery." Such was the warning of God when His people desired to copy the surrounding nations and to have " an absolute monarch, governing by his single will, without the restraint of any co-ordinate legislative power." Nor was this the sum of discomfiture to Tory theorists from the appeal to the highest possible authority. Hoadly continued to point out that, even when the monarchy was instituted, the succession was not regulated by primogeniture; for David was the youngest of many brethren. " So that in this kingdom established by God Himself, it was so ordered that there never was one king lineally descended from that branch which alone could lay claim to pre-eminence and government by right of primogeniture." After thus slaying the notion of a patriarchal scheme Hoadly enunciated his own principles of government. "The great end of government is the happiness of the governed society "; and " the happiness of a governed society consists in the enjoyment of liberty, property, and the free exercise of religion." There was little difficulty in showing from these axioms that whatever liberties England had she owed " entirely to the late Revolution and those principles upon which it was founded." [1] Once again Hoadly had scored a distinct hit by his pulpit pieces.

His design, however, moved by an attack upon him by Atterbury, was to explore fully and in detail the origins of civil government, which he did in *The Original and Institution of Civil Government discussed*.[2] In this ambitious treatise he set out to refute in detail the patriarchal scheme, and to justify the opinion of Hooker in the *Ecclesiastical Polity*, that government was founded upon the contract. The work is very tedious and laboured. Furthermore it covered ground already trodden by Locke, and added nothing new to his argument. Hoadly unfortunately did not belong to the heroic age of this particular controversy. There were giants on the earth in the days of Locke, and the writers of Hoadly's time were but pigmies in comparison. Of Hoadly's major political treatises Sir Leslie Stephen says: " In them he once more slays the slain. . . .

---

[1] *The Happiness of the Present Establishment and the Unhappiness of Absolute Monarchy* (1708) (Works, vol. ii, p. 109 *et seq.*).
[2] Works, vol. ii, pp. 182–284.

The details of such a discussion may well be swept to the dust-heaps! The general tendency needs alone to be indicated." [1] None the less it was the publication of *The Original and Institution of Civil Government* which earned the resolution of thanks from the Whig House of Commons. In the following year, 1710, came the Sacheverell trial and the Whig downfall. Hoadly, however, was true to his allegiance, and published during that year a series of simple political pieces defending the Revolution Settlement. Some of these were satirical, such as *The True, Genuine Tory Address*, others were straightforward propaganda for the Whig cause, such as the *Serious Advice to the Good People of England, shewing them their True Interest and their True Friends*.[2] For a space there was darkness over the land; and the light did not dawn again on the party of Hoadly until the Elector of Hanover had arrived in England and been crowned by Tenison.

It should not be supposed, however, that the accession of George I was the end of the trouble from Jacobite sources. The first decade of Whig domination was a time of peculiar misfortune which brought little satisfaction to its supporters. Foreign affairs were troubled by difficulties with Sweden and Spain; domestic politics by a Jacobite rebellion, by the schism and feud within the Ministry itself, and by the scandal of the South Sea Bubble. A revival of Tory hopes and Jacobite plotting was caused by the birth of the Young Pretender in 1720, and even the trial of Atterbury, though resulting in his banishment, was eloquent of the extent of disaffection in the Church. The fact that Hoadly's attack upon the Non-Jurors did not appear until 1716, being provoked then by the posthumous publication of the papers of Dean Hickes, the most celebrated Non-Juror of his day, was not an indication that fear or prudence had compelled him to keep silence hitherto. In his *Preservative against the Principles and Practices of the Non-Jurors both in Church and State* Hoadly undoubtedly made his most serious contribution to the vindication of the Revolution Settlement. His attack was thorough. He

---

[1] Sir L. Stephen, *English Thought in the Eighteenth Century*, vol. ii, p. 153 (3rd edition, London, 1902).
[2] *A Collection of Several Papers*, printed in 1710 and reprinted in 1718 (Works, vol. i, p. 601 *et seq.*).

assaulted the threefold claims of his opponents, and asserted that the Revolution was justified as a civil transaction, breaking through the direct line of succession to the throne; that the State had full and lawful power to deprive any ecclesiastics whose tenets aspersed the legality of the Settlement; and that the Non-Juror doctrines of the Church as a *societas perfecta* were subversive of the true nature of the religion of Christ.

Dealing first with the political change, he insisted that the nation, faced with imminent ruin in 1688, had acted rightly in expelling James II. All parties to the controversy admitted that natural incapacity, such as insanity, justified the deposition of a particular ruler. From this Hoadly urged that " all incapacity is the same, in the effects and consequences of it to the concerns of a nation. It is of no importance whether it be natural or moral." To a Protestant country there could be no greater incapacity in its ruler than the profession of Popery, which bound him to attempt the extirpation of heresy. Therefore James' deposition was amply justified; "and the incapacity in him having arisen solely from his religion, the same incapacity must arise from the same religion in others, because there can be no difference in the obligations which it laid upon him and those it must lay upon any of his successors." [1] If this be granted, the rest would follow. " The Popish branches of the royal family were set aside, upon no other consideration than the safety of the whole nation; and the very first Protestant branches in the same royal family were declared heirs, and the succession from them declared and confirmed." [2] Since many of the Tories had proposed a regency, they had acknowledged the principle of incapacity upon the ground of religion. Hoadly therefore affirmed that, granting the necessity for the removal of James, the only alternative to the election of William was the institution of a succession of regents so long as the Stuarts should remain Papists. This being absurd, " necessity, reason, prudence,

---

[1] *A Preservative against the Principles and Practices of the Non-Jurors both in Church and State* (Works, vol. i, pp. 566–567). The sole exception to Hoadly's support of religious toleration was in regard to Papists, whom he wished to exclude from its benefits on the ground that they owed allegiance to a foreign political power which endeavoured to overthrow the Revolution Settlement. *Cf.* Works, vol. iii, pp. 52–72.

[2] *Ibid.*, p. 560.

the nature of human society, the ends of government and the voice of God ever approving these great arguments, all conspired to promote and justify what was done." [1]   Thus far the argument could be little contested.   Much more delicate was the justification of the deprivation of the Non-Juror bishops by the secular power, and the nomination of others to their sees during their lifetime.   Yet on this point also Hoadly would tolerate no half-measures.   He abhorred the attitude of those who " kept to the Establishment . . . as a thing barely lawful," and who " acknowledged deprivation by the Lay Power to be invalid, and only pleaded against carrying the matter to a separation upon that account."   His own argument was free from equivocation.   He appealed to " the right which the Supreme Power hath to all things necessary to its own defence and preservation," which embraced the " right inherent in it and inseparable from it, to guard the society from being undone by ecclesiastical officers as well as by laymen." [2]   This general power of the State to preserve itself from dissolution was especially valid against schemes of treason ; and Hoadly boldly stigmatised the Non-Juror principles as " treason made ten times hotter by religion."   Even so the doctrine thus laid down was only the general law of *salus populi suprema lex*.   Might it not be argued that the State could only take away what it had conferred ?   Had not the episcopal office a spiritual character conferred only by the act of Consecration and therefore beyond the power of any State to take away ?   Further, were not the principles of the Non-Jurors matters of religion, and was not the action of the Government a persecution of religious opinion ?

These considerations were swept aside severally by Hoadly as unworthy sophistries.   In the first place he pointed out that whatever the character imparted by consecration " the right of exercising this authority in their particular dioceses ariseth originally from the nomination of the King."   All that deprivation meant, therefore, was the inhibition of particular bishops " from the right to execute the episcopal office " within any diocese of the Church of England. [3]   The State had

---

[1] *A Preservative against the Principles and Practices of the Non-Jurors* (Works, vol. i, p. 569).
[2] *Ibid.*, p. 574.   [3] *Ibid.*, pp. 570, 572.

only taken away what it had conferred. This reservation, however, did not imply that the power was lacking to the Government to take away what it had not given. Such action was taken every time a criminal was executed or an individual's property confiscated. Nor could the clergy claim any superiority over the secular power by reason of a supposed supernatural commission. " As God approves of everything necessary to civil government, it is necessarily implied in that, that He approves of no powers or privileges in any persons upon earth, which are in such sense independent upon it as to be inconsistent with it." [1] The Non-Juror bishops were deprived by the same power of the Crown which Solomon had exercised in deposing Abiathar from the high-priesthood and in appointing Zadok in his place (1 Kings, ii, 27, 35). As for the contention that the deprived prelates had suffered for religious scruple, Hoadly answered that, though the origin of their objections might have been of a spiritual character, the State had cognisance not of motives, but of the effect of opinions. "Whatever affects the Civil Power becomes a matter of a civil nature," so that " public praying and preaching against a civil government is to that government entirely of a civil nature." Therefore he concluded that " deprivation by the Civil Power is a point of a civil nature, and ariseth not from any mixing of two incoherent powers, but from the one undoubted and undeniable principle of self-defence ; and from this plain maxim, that the Civil Power could not be the Civil Power without having a right (properly so called) to do everything necessary for its own preservation from ruin and for the support of its civil authority." [2] Thus a defender of the Revolution need not hesitate to communicate with the Established Church for fear of the sin of schism, since demonstration had been made that, the Non-Juror bishops " having been rightfully deposed, their successors were the regular bishops and the Church of their successors the true Church."

Unhappily for the credit of Hoadly with his brethren the debate could not stop upon the particular matter of the deprivation of the Non-Jurors. Behind the instance discussed

[1] *A Preservative against the Principles and Practices of the Non-Jurors* (Works vol. i, p. 579).
[2] *Ibid.*, p. 582.

lay the general question of the relations between Church and State, and the definition of the nature of ecclesiastical authority. The vigour of Hoadly's reasoning against the Non-Jurors suggested the doubt as to whether he ascribed any authority to the spiritual society. He had affirmed that " if the ecclesiastical power is not under the Civil Power in cases of the aforesaid nature [*i.e.*, the extrusion of the Non-Jurors], the Civil Power must be under the ecclesiastical," a position which he declared to be sheer Popery.[1] In the last section of his polemic he turned to the problem of Church authority, a subject also dealt with in the famous Bangorian sermon, and treated satirically in *The Dedication to Pope Clement XI.*

The Non-Juror clergy, disowned by the Established Church and deprived by the State, appealed from the decrees of the secular power to the principles of Catholic Order. Fortified by the possession of the apostolic commission handed down in regular succession to their bishops, they claimed to pronounce an authoritative absolution and to offer a true eucharistic sacrifice. They vindicated their position against the charge of schism by asserting that they alone had retained the Catholic Anglican heritage, in which the State could have neither part nor lot to confer or deprive. Such a scheme of doctrine was anathema in its first principles to Hoadly. He denied that God could possibly require all men as a condition of salvation to belong to " one external communion," and declared it blasphemy to conceive that He would commit the power of absolution to any fallible mortal. " To make the absolutions of weak, fallible men so necessary or so valid that God will not pardon without them, and that all are pardoned who have them pronounced over them, is to contradict the natural notions of God as well as the plain tenor of the Gospel."[2] To possess such authority to absolve implied the gift of an infallible knowledge to direct the use of this power aright. The logical result of the claim was witnessed in the Roman Church, to which consistency of argument would lead the Non-Jurors. " But they who are first infallible may certainly claim the power of what is called authoritative absolution.

[1] *A Preservative against the Principles and Practices of the Non-Jurors* (Works, vol. i, p. 582).
[2] *Ibid.*, p. 594.

And therefore it is very consistent in the Church of Rome, if they are resolved to have the latter, to suppose and claim the former, which may undoubtedly be claimed, wherever the other is allowed to be." [1] In contradiction to this authoritarian scheme Hoadly upheld the principle of unfettered private judgment. " Every one may find it in his own conduct to be true, that his title to God's favour cannot depend upon his actual being or continuing in any particular method ; but upon his real sincerity in the conduct of his conscience and of his own actions under it." " The favour of God therefore follows sincerity considered as such ; and consequently equally follows every equal degree of sincerity." [2]

This bold affirmation of the cardinal principle of Protestantism engendered a natural suspicion that Hoadly's position rested upon the basis of unrestricted individualism. What was implicit in the *Preservative against the Non-Jurors* became explicit in the famous Bangorian sermon, delivered on March 31, 1717, from the text " My kingdom is not of this world." The preacher began by observing that the lapse of time produced such alteration in the meaning of words that the simplest of terms became fenced around with a labyrinth of incongruous associations. As examples of this tendency he contrasted the meaning of ' religion ' in the New Testament with the conventional ceremonies of ' external religion ' ; and that of ' prayer ' in the Gospels with certain contemporary conceptions. This was unfortunate for his purpose, since a good deal of controversial energy was diverted to attacks upon these points, and Hoadly in return embarked upon justifications of his words. The main purpose of the sermon was to rescue the idea of the Church from such confusion and accretion ; and this was to be achieved by identifying the Church with the Kingdom of Christ, and deducing the characteristics of the former from the meaning to be attached to the word ' kingdom.' Two conditions were plain at the outset. In the Kingdom of Christ " He is Himself sole lawgiver to His subjects, and Himself the sole judge of their behaviour in the affairs of conscience and eternal salvation." Further, the

[1] *A Preservative against the Principles and Practices of the Non-Jurors* (Works, vol. i, p. 595).
[2] *Ibid.*, p. 593.

Kingdom of Christ being not of this world, the difference consisted in the fact that " He had in those points left behind Him no visible, human authority ; no vicegerents who can be said properly to supply His place ; no interpreters upon whom His subjects are absolutely to depend ; no judges over the consciences or religion of His people." [1]   The position taken up by Hoadly, the hater of unlimited monarchy in civil societies, was that of defender of the most Absolute Monarchy in the Church, qualified only by the paradoxical difference that Christ was an absentee Ruler, who neither intervened personally to interpret His laws, nor commissioned any other person to act in His stead.

> For if this were so, that any such absolute vicegerent authority, either for the making new laws or interpreting old ones, or judging His subjects in religious matters, were lodged in any men upon earth; the consequence would be, that what still retains the name of the Church of Christ would not be the kingdom of Christ, but the kingdom of these men, vested with such authority.   For whoever hath such an authority of making laws is so far a king; and whoever can add new laws to those of Christ, equally obligatory, is as truly a king as Christ Himself; nay, whoever hath an absolute power to interpret any written or spoken laws; it is he who is truly the lawgiver to all intents and purposes, and not the Person who first wrote or spoke them. [2]

The general tenor of the argument seems plain from this passage ; and Hoadly's words were generally understood, as William Law stated, " to dissolve the Church as a society," and to exalt the principle of pure private judgment.   But it is noteworthy that the qualifying epithet, ' absolute,' occurs twice in the passage, and this furnished a way of retreat for Hoadly in the controversy which followed.   The quibblings even went so far as to dispute whether the adjective had been originally used in the sermon, or had been added later on the advice of White Kennett.   It is unnecessary to pursue this line of argument.   Though it may be true that Hoadly used the word ' absolute ' with deliberate purpose, yet other passages in the sermon confirm the general impression that his object was to dissolve ecclesiastical authority, and to rest

[1] *The Nature of the Kingdom or Church of Christ* (Works, vol. ii, p. 404).
[2] *Ibid.*, p. 404.

the whole edifice of Church organisation upon the basis of voluntary individual consent. He stated that the Monarchy of Christ involved the equality of all His subjects, so that none could claim lordship over another. "All His subjects, in what station soever they be, are equally subjects to Him; and no one of them any more than another hath authority, either to make new laws for Christ's subjects or to impose a sense upon the old ones; or to judge, censure or punish the servants of Another Master in matters relating purely to conscience or salvation." [1] The Church therefore became an invisible society, consisting of "the number of men, whether small or great, whether dispersed or united, who truly and sincerely are subjects to Jesus Christ alone, as their Lawgiver and Judge in matters relating to the favour of God and their eternal salvation." [2] From these premises Hoadly drew certain conclusions, as startling in their provenance from a bishop of an Established Church as the entire argument was to the majority of Christian believers. He affirmed that the profession of Christianity should be associated with no temporal rewards; that it had "no tendency either to the exaltation of some in worldly pomp or dignity, or to their absolute dominion over the faith and religious conduct of others of Christ's subjects." [3] Here again the insertion of the epithet 'absolute' may save the appearance of the Establishment, despite the contrary tendency of the argument. But the evil of coercion was unequivocally condemned in the statement that Christ taught "no calling upon the secular arm, whenever the magistrate should become Christian, to enforce His doctrines or back His spiritual authority." [4] Consistently with this, Hoadly desired individual Christians to derive their rules of religious life from their reading of the New Testament, without recourse to any interpreters, while he stigmatised a reliance upon the definitions of any Church as the setting up "the idol of unintelligible authority both in belief and worship and practice; in words under Jesus Christ, but in deed and truth over Him." The summary of the matter was contained in his distinction between those Christians who "seek all these particulars in those plain and short declarations of their King and Lawgiver," and those

---

[1] *The Nature of the Kingdom or Church of Christ* (Works, vol. ii, p. 405).
[2] *Ibid.*, p. 406.   [3] *Ibid.*, p. 406.   [4] *Ibid.*, p. 407.

who " hunt after them through the infinite contradictions, the numberless perplexities, the endless disputes of weak men in several ages " [1]—that is, between reliance upon the unaided individual judgment, and acceptance of the *consensus fidelium*, in whatever form expressed.

Confirmation of the general tenor of the Bangorian sermon may be found in *The Dedication to Pope Clement XI*, prefixed to Sir Richard Steele's account of the state of the Roman Catholic religion throughout the world. In this preface Hoadly wrote satirically of the Protestant Churches, which he considered to have inherited, though in lesser degree, the persecuting and intolerant characteristics of Rome. Starting with the Church of England, he observed that the High Church party claimed to have an unbroken episcopal succession, "and upon this bottom, which makes us a true Church, we have the right to separate from you, but no living persons have any right to differ or separate from us." [2] In this regard the Established Church was almost as exclusive as Rome. Nor were the Protestant Dissenters any more enlightened. Having by the Toleration Act escaped from persecution for Nonconformity, they proceeded with zeal to turn the engine of coercion against heretics. " Being themselves but very lately come from experiencing the convincing and enlightening faculty of a dungeon or a fine," they were eager to prosecute the unorthodox Dissenting ministers who could not sign the Article concerning the Trinity. In practice, therefore, if not in theory, each of the sects adopted the position of inerrancy, so that the difference between Rome and the Reformed Churches was slight. "You cannot err in anything you determine and we never do; that is, in other words, you are infallible and we are always in the right. We cannot but esteem the advantage to be exceedingly on our side in this case, because we have all the benefits of infallibility without the absurdity of pretending to it." [3] Therefore Hoadly assured the supreme Pontiff that despite the apparent rejection of Popish principles, the Protestant Churches paid Rome the compliment of slavish imitation. " I believe in time no man

---

[1] *The Nature of the Kingdom or Church of Christ* (Works, vol. ii, p. 409).
[2] *The Dedication to Pope Clement XI* (Works, vol. i, p. 536).
[3] *Ibid.*, p. 535.

K

of sense will be able to see any difference between your Popery and that of many amongst us, but that ours is Protestant popery and yours is Popish popery." [1]

The same satire contains a contemptuous reference to authority, which again illustrates the Bangorian sermon. Hoadly scorned the attitude which sought truth in the opinions of past ages. " What is Truth is determined for us and settled before we were born, by our forefathers and superiors in the ages of illuminated understandings and unprejudiced judgments." " The voice of Authority is this : Hitherto shalt thou come and no further." [2] Similarly, in his *Answer to the Representation of the Committee of the Lower House of Convocation*, Hoadly wrote with bitter satire of the baneful effects of the exercise of ecclesiastical authority:

> It is indeed the greatest and most irreconcilable enemy to truth and argument that this world ever furnished out since it was in being. . . . It is authority alone which keeps up the grossest errors in the countries around us.   And where truth happens to be received for the sake of authority, there is just so much diminished from the love of truth and the glory of reason and the acceptableness of man to God, as there is attributed to authority. [3]

From these confirmatory passages there can be little doubt that the Bangorian sermon represented the true sentiments of its author concerning Church authority; and despite the cloud of verbiage which obscured the real points at issue between the Bishop and his opponents, the main outline of his position is clear.   The argument of the sermon would not only dissolve the claims of the Non-Jurors that the Church was a *societas perfecta*, but would lead to the disestablishment of the Church of England.   Further, apart from the question of Establishment, there could be no rational ground for its retention of any of its peculiar characteristics, episcopate, clergy, or sacraments.   If private judgment alone constituted the tribunal of religious doctrine, there could be no occasion for Hoadly to examine such candidates as came to him for ordination, nor indeed to confer Orders upon them, since an inner conviction

---

[1] *The Dedication to Pope Clement XI* (Works, vol. i, p. 544).

[2] *Ibid.*, p. 545.

[3] *An Answer to the Representation of the Committee of the Lower House of Convocation* (Works, vol. ii, p. 571).

of sincerity would be an adequate seal of their commission. This conclusion was perceived and stated succinctly by William Law, the most important opponent of the Bishop.[1] " Your lordship is ours, as you fill a bishopric ; but we are at a loss to discover from this discourse what other interest we have in your lordship." Nor was it easy to see how, upon Hoadly's premises, any organised churches could be formed. If they were not under any obligation to fashion themselves upon the historic pattern of episcopal government, or to accept any credal statement of belief, it would be impossible to urge grounds for the creation even of a voluntary society of believers. The only credential required was that of sincerity, which alone, as Law observed, " will help us to the communion of saints hereafter, though we are in communion with anybody or nobody here." Again, Law showed that the discussion concerning the epithet ' absolute ' was but a subterfuge to conceal the real problem in debate. No Church claimed absolute authority in the sense of binding God by its decisions ; but this did not imply that conditional authority was either unreal or absurd. Hoadly's argument, to have effect, must therefore be directed against the conditional authority exercised by visible Churches ; and so considered, his enunciation of the principle of unlimited private judgment would dissolve all corporate authority whether of civil or ecclesiastical societies. Law indeed observed with irony that the Apostles were " furious High Church prelates, who aspired to presumptuous claims and talked of conferring the graces of God by their own hands." Certainly St Paul conceived himself to be founding societies with disciplinary powers in regard to the conduct of their members. If no authority were to be exercised until God Himself interposed, then all human society would disintegrate. Finally Law ridiculed the idea that sincerity could be the sole test of religious belief. " If the favour of God equally follows every equal degree of sincerity, then it is impossible there should be any difference . . . between a sincere martyr and a sincere persecutor ; and he that burns the Christian, if he be but in earnest, has the same title to a reward for it, as he that is burned for believing in Christ." Plainly, sincerity could not be a test of intellectual truth, but only of

[1] William Law, *Three Letters to the Bishop of Bangor* (8th edition, London, 1721).

moral integrity. From this position Law built up his apologetic for historic Christianity and the authority of the Church. Hoadly's scheme of religion, resting upon the conscience of the individual aided only by the words of the New Testament, bore more resemblance to the new fashionable Deism than to the historic tradition of any Christian Church.

The ominous combination in the *Preservative against the Non-Jurors* and the Bangorian sermon, of emphasis on the supreme power of the State and of ridicule for the authority of the Church, occasioned much disquietude as to the position of the Establishment under the Whig *régime*. At first there seemed to be good ground for apprehension. In view of the controversy aroused, a company of bishops met together at the request of the Archbishop to consider what measures should be taken in regard to Hoadly. Among other recommendations they urged " that no business . . . should be entered upon in Convocation until the present jumble was over." This was not done, and the Lower House of Canterbury Convocation proceeded to attack the famous sermon, only to be frustrated by the intervention of the Crown to prorogue the synod. It is certain that Hoadly did not desire this action, and it must be acknowledged that the record of Convocation since the accession of Anne had made some such step inevitable as a temporary silencing of strife ; none the less the actual circumstances of the prorogation suggested an unpleasant foretaste of the application of the principles advocated in Hoadly's recent writings, by the State against the Church.

IV

The deliberate depression of the position and powers of the clergy, which characterised the discourse on the *Nature of the Kingdom of Christ*, proceeded less from the political necessities of the situation than from the influence of Deistic principles, which were coming in full tide to dominate religious thought of the eighteenth century. This most important intellectual movement of Deism was in part a reaction against the theological squabbles of the preceding century, and in part a natural outcome of the renewed interest in natural science, which had been awakened by the activities of the Royal

Society. In particular the nation was wearied of the conflicts of the sects, and passed with relief from their disputes as to the interpretation of passages of Scripture to contemplate the new scene of order and majesty revealed by the starry heavens. "The universe which had been potentially infinite was becoming actually infinite." Its Creator was evidently the author not of confusion, but of law; and men sought for a correspondence between the harmony of nature and the precepts of religion. The result of this search was the discovery that true religion consisted in the notions of the obligation of morality and of the worship of God, which were supposedly common to all men and to all religions. A wave of religious optimism took possession of men, comforted by the belief in the Father-hood of God and the beneficence of His creation. Before these two cardinal truths all differences of ecclesiastical order or creed sank into insignificance. Hence the Latitudinarian school within the Church of England, infected with the pre-valent mode of thought, tended to obliterate the distinction between the Establishment and the Dissenters, and in particular to ignore divergencies of polity. To the patristic studies of the Caroline era there succeeded a contempt for historical theology, and an attempt to reduce and resolve Christianity into a few simple principles of practical morality.

Hoadly added to his other titles to the hatred of the clergy a championship of Latitude principles in theology. He was not the best representative of the school, for his friend Dr Samuel Clarke clearly outdistanced him in learning; but in the succinct and provocative statement of the Lati-tudinarian position he had few superiors. His views of sacerdotal claims and power were greatly coloured by the general tendency to break down barriers of polity, and by his conviction that matters of domestic organisation within a Church, such as episcopal ordination, were unimportant in the wider scheme of Christianity. In his political writings there are not a few interesting illustrations of the effect of this theological outlook upon his opinions regarding Church order. In meeting the arguments of the Non-Jurors from certain texts of the New Testament, which seemed to lend support to their claim to possess the power to absolve, Hoadly rarely con-sented to descend to a particular exegesis of the disputed

passages. He was content to appeal to another court.
" Whatsoever contradicts the natural notions of God and the
design and tenor of the Gospel cannot be the true meaning of
any passage in that Gospel." [1] Any text therefore was to be
interpreted not according to the context in which it occurred,
but according to contemporary ideas of the nature of God. In
an incidental phrase in the Bangorian sermon he revealed the
essentially Deistic basis of his thought by defining religion as
" virtue and charity under the belief of a Supreme Governor
and Judge." His theological position was fully set forth in
a series of sermons preached in his turn as Royal Chaplain,
which form a lucid and reasoned statement of the Latitudinarian position, and which earned much approval from Queen
Caroline and the *entourage* of the Court. In 1735 Hoadly
applied his critical methods to the central office of the
clergy, the celebration of the Eucharist, since the sacerdotal
powers claimed by them rested upon their exclusive right to
perform the sacred mystery of the consecration of the eucharistic elements. His *Plain Account of the Nature and End of
the Sacrament of the Lord's Supper* struck at the basis of these
claims by denying that the rite was anything more than a
memorial feast, observed in remembrance of an absent Master.
At the outset of the inquiry he ruled out the opinions of all
writers beyond the New Testament. " It is of small importance to Christians to know what the many writers upon this
subject since the times of the Evangelists and Apostles have
affirmed," since " it cannot be doubted that Christ Himself
sufficiently declared to His first and immediate followers the
whole of what He designed should be understood by it or implied in it." [2] Therefore " the writers of the New Testament
must be the best, or rather the only writers for us to depend
upon." From this limited field of authorities Hoadly reached
the following conclusions : that " the end for which our Lord
instituted this duty was the remembrance of Himself; that
the bread to be taken and eaten, was appointed to be the

---

[1] *Cf.* his refusal to consider the claim of apostolic succession, because he " had
not such notions of God as to think it consistent with His Nature to wrap up the
most important of all points in clouds of obscurity and uncertainty " (Works, vol. i,
pp. 592, 594).

[2] *A Plain Account of the Nature and End of the Sacrament of the Lord's Supper* (Works,
vol. iii, p. 846).

memorial of His body broken, and the wine to be drunk was
ordained to be the memorial of His blood shed."[1] Hence
the followers of Christ were faithful to His command only
while " considering it as a rite to be seriously performed in
remembrance of an Absent Saviour, and taking the bread and
wine as memorials of His body broken and His blood shed,
and not as the Things themselves in remembrance of which
they were ordained to be received."[2] Those Christians on
the other hand who " attempted to introduce into this Rite the
natural Body and Blood of Christ, and a real sacrifice of a
present Body, had not only endeavoured to introduce endless
absurdities into a plain duty, but had presumed to destroy, as
far as they could, the whole nature and end of our Lord's
institution."[3] This denial of the mysterious character of the
Eucharist completed the destruction of sacerdotal claims to
which Hoadly had set his hand, for, if the function of the
minister was merely to declare the remembrance of the death
of Christ, he needed no peculiar consecration to his office.
Inevitably the subject of the tract provoked controversy, and in
addition to the disapprobation of orthodox prelates, even the
Queen uttered censure of the author because, " being got to
the top of his preferment, he ought to have kept his notions
to himself, and not to have drawn all the clergy on his back."[4]
The pamphlet had this positive advantage, however, that it
evoked one of the most powerful defences of the traditional
doctrine from the pen of Waterland.

It must be insisted throughout that the controversies in
which Hoadly was engaged were not matters of academic
speculation, but had an immediate practical relation to the
politics of the time. Just as the Non-Jurors were drawn into
association with the Jacobite cause, where they mingled with
colleagues who had little sympathy with their religious scruples,
so Hoadly's polemic against their tenets was allied with the
fortunes of the Whig party in the State. This closeness of
alliance gave an added importance to his words, which, it was

---

[1] A Plain Account of the Nature and End of the Sacrament of the Lord's Supper (Works,
vol. iii, p. 852).
[2] Ibid., p. 854.　　　　　　　　[3] Ibid., p. 854.
[4] Egmont MSS., vol. ii, p. 188 (Hist. MSS. Comm.).

suspected, might influence the religious policy of the Whig Ministry, by whom he had been promoted to the see of Bangor. His stout avowal of the right of the civil power to adopt any measures judged necessary to its defence against Popery, without respect of persons, might bode ill for the Church at their hands. It was clear that the logic of his principles would involve the removal of all civil disabilities resting upon the Dissenters, and might even lead to some alteration of the position of the Church, whether by a process of disestablishment, or, as was more unwelcome, by the carrying through Parliament by *force majeure* of a comprehension scheme to sacrifice its distinctive characteristics, upon which Hoadly laid little store, to secure a united Protestant front against Jacobitism. Nor did the first measures of the Ministry do anything to allay such fears. Hoadly himself was the Court favourite, promoted " to sit in state at His Grace's right hand," and the attack upon him in the Convocation was forestalled by its prorogation. In 1718 the repeal of the Occasional Conformity and Schism Acts was carried, which opened the way for further concessions to the Dissenters. But the adoption of Hoadly's programme was not practical politics for the Whig administration. The Bishop's pen might divest the clergy of their sacerdotal status, but it could not destroy their political influence at elections, and it was this latter power which the Ministry wished to control in its own party interest. Especially after the trial and banishment of Atterbury, which showed the extent of clerical disaffection, the Whigs decided that they could not maintain themselves without the support of the Church interest. Walpole and Townshend therefore cast aside Hoadly, and gave their confidence to Gibson, Bishop of London, whose policy of judicious rewards for loyal Whig clergy, and of careful maintenance of the Revolution Settlement in regard to the relative position of Church and Dissenters, replaced the era of polemic by that of promise.

Notwithstanding the failure of Hoadly's principles in practical affairs of State, his personal position was secured, and in the region of thought he lived to witness the permeation of the Church by Latitudinarian tenets. Bangor being a see not much coveted by divines, in 1721 he was translated to Hereford, resigning his City living. Two years later he was translated to Salisbury, and resigned the rectory of Streatham. After the accession of George II Hoadly enjoyed the favour of the Queen and the especial patronage of her *confidante*, Lady Sundon. At the meetings in the Queen's closet to debate divinity his genius found a more congenial *milieu* than in the councils of State. His attitude to Lady Sundon was characterised by a servile flattery more distasteful to modern than to contemporary ears. The alliance of the royal and episcopal admirers of Latitudinarian theology had also an important political relation, for their object was to secure a strong Latitudinarian element on the Bench, in order to undertake the necessary task of revising the Liturgy and Articles in accordance with modern thought. The attempt to promote the ablest divine of the school, Dr Samuel Clarke, to the episcopate was successfully resisted by Gibson, supported by Walpole; and the unceasing opposition of Gibson was responsible for the failure of the project to dominate the Church by adherents of Hoadly and Clarke. Even Hoadly himself was restricted by his rival. In 1730 the see of Durham was vacant, upon which Hoadly had set his heart, but it was awarded on the advice of Gibson to his friend, Chandler. Four years later Hoadly was translated to Winchester as a compromise; and though exhorted by his friends " to behave as if there never was nor had been such a thing as a bishopric of Durham, but only to reflect that he was made Bishop of Winchester," yet Lord Hervey, the author of the advice, confessed his private opinion that " Winchester, now reluctantly conferred, atoned not for Durham, formerly unjustly conferred upon another."[1] At Winchester however Hoadly had to remain until his death in 1761 at the advanced age of eighty-five.

An enthusiastic panegyrist proclaimed that his writings had served to disengage the nation

> from the dread bonds of many an age,
> And to new habits mould the public mind.

In more modest prose his biographer stated that

> he was so happy as to live long enough . . . to see his Christian and moderate opinions prevail over the kingdom in Church and

---

[1] Lord Hervey, *Memoirs of the Reign of George II*, vol. i, p.446; Mrs K. Thomson, *Memoirs of Viscountess Sundon*, vol. ii, p. 268.

State; . . . to see the general temper of the clergy entirely changed, the bishops preferring few or none of intolerant opinions, and the clergy claiming no inherent authority, but what is the natural result of their own good behaviour as individuals, in the discharge of their duty; to see the absurd tenet of indefeasible hereditary right and of its natural offspring an unlimited non-resistance (demonstrated by him to be founded neither in Scripture nor Reason) absolutely exploded; and the Protestant Succession in the present royal family as firmly fixed in the hearts and persuasions of the people as in the Laws of God and the land.[1]

Substantially this summary is correct, though it is doubtful how far the results enumerated are to be ascribed to Hoadly's influence. The Jacobites were defeated by the obstinate Popery of the Old and Young Pretenders, and the Tory clergy who remained in the Church were converted more by the policy of Gibson than by the preaching of Hoadly to a quiet acceptance of the Hanoverian dynasty. The progress of Latitudinarian principles was undoubted, and in this regard Hoadly may claim real significance, though rather as an influential representative of a dominant tendency than as an original thinker. His position in its main outline secured a noteworthy vogue. The negotiations of Archbishop Wake with the Protestant Church of Prussia, and the indifference of John Wesley to matters of Church organisation, despite his High Church doctrine of the Sacraments, are illustrations from dissimilar sources of the widespread disregard for divergencies of ecclesiastical polity. Throughout the century there was a notable tendency to mark the differences between Protestants along the lines of Calvinist *versus* Arminian, not of Episcopalian *versus* Presbyterian. To this extent Hoadleian principles gained a considerable triumph. But his theological scheme, which Secker wittily termed Christianity *secundum usum Winton*, was a strange amalgam, unlike the tradition of any historic Church; and it found few apostles in its logical fullness. It was impossible as a practical programme even for the Whigs, who had to conciliate the Church interest and refused to alter the Revolution Settlement in religion. So the Church of England retained its position of privilege, its principles of Church order, and its historic creeds. The victory

[1] *Life of Hoadly* (Works, vol. i, p. xii).

of Latitudinarian opinions affected the intellectual temper rather than the constitution of the Church.

Of Hoadly himself it is more difficult to judge. It cannot be doubted that he was the friend and defender of liberty of conscience in all relations.[1] Nor was it always to his discredit that this attitude brought upon him a stream of clerical abuse and denunciatory epithets. Pope satirised his sermons, with their " periods of a mile," in his humorous inquiry :

> Which most conduce to soothe the soul in slumbers,
> My Hoadly's periods or my Blackmore's numbers ?

On the other hand, many of Hoadly's pulpit pieces constitute examples of telling and pointed polemic. His talent excelled in the production of short, incisive pamphlets, while in his more sustained works he was ineffective and unconvincing. As a bishop he suffered from the handicap of lameness, and, in the exercise of his diocesan duties, could not challenge comparison with his admired predecessor at Sarum, Burnet. His influence as bishop was further diminished by his alienation from the standpoint of the majority of his clergy ; and this lack of sympathy was reflected in the mediocre character of his visitation charges. It was as a controversialist that he chiefly distinguished himself. In an age of exuberant party controversy he was an indefatigable partisan of the Whigs. His services to their cause were neither small nor unworthy, nor were the rewards bestowed upon him incommensurate. But the literature of controversy is notoriously ephemeral, and the fame of its leaders generally short-lived. Notwithstanding, the readiness of Hoadly to engage in controversy and his zeal to pursue the adversary to the death suggest that perhaps the best summary of his character is to be found in his name. Few men have been called more appropriately after the youngest son of the patriarch Jacob, of whom his father testified : "Benjamin is a wolf that ravineth: in the morning he shall devour the prey, and at even he shall divide the spoil." Which things are for an allegory and an epitaph of Benjamin Hoadly, Bishop of Bangor.

NORMAN SYKES

---

[1] With the exception of Papists, as noted before, whose position he regarded as not religious, but political.

BIBLIOGRAPHY

A. Primary Sources

Hoadly, Benjamin : *Works.* 3 vols. London, 1773.
Law, William : *Three Letters to the Bishop of Bangor.* 8th edition. London, 1721.

B. Secondary Sources

Abbey, Charles J. : *The English Church and its Bishops, 1700–1800.* 2 vols. London, 1887.
Hunt, J. : *Religious Thought in England.* 3 vols. London, 1860.
Laski, H. J. : *Political Thought in England from Locke to Bentham.* London, 1919.
Overton, J. H. : *William Law.* London, 1881.
Stephen, Sir L. : *History of English Thought in the Eighteenth Century.* 2 vols. London, 1902.
Sykes, N. : *Edmund Gibson, Bishop of London.* Oxford, 1926.

VII

DANIEL DEFOE

DANIEL DEFOE wrote *Robinson Crusoe*; and the
names of the other works of Daniel Defoe fill fourteen
pages of the *Cambridge History of English Literature.*
At least fifty works may be described as political, while almost
every item might be classified as social. In order to write one
article, therefore, some limitations must be made. I cannot
profess to treat Defoe as a whole, nor to discuss the many
phases of his strange career. What may be attempted,
perhaps, is an estimate of the political thought of the great
novelist (in contradistinction to his political practice), and a
further estimate of his ideas on the subject of social reform.
Here is ample matter for investigation. In point of date some
limits also may be laid down. Most of Defoe's avowedly
political writings fall before 1714; the most theoretical of
them before 1702. That is to say, in estimating his thought
it is possible to stop short of the period in which his political
and journalistic practice was the most tortuous. His social
ideas and testimony are not so readily limited; broadly speaking, the romances and works of fiction have been excluded
and the moral and didactic treatises included. By this means,
we exclude the more dramatic part of Defoe's writing, and
have the greater chance of arriving at his serious opinion.
Moreover, social reforms in the early eighteenth century were
not within the programme of either party, and Defoe's expression of opinion in the world of ' projects ' would seem to
have been unbiased.

So much for necessary limitations. The essential background of Defoe's life is the birth and growth of the English
party system. What happens between the years 1660 and
1730 must always be tried against the touchstone of the two
great parties which arose to replace the long feud of Puritan

and Cavalier. The issue is continually confused by religious divisions; the nation is partly Anglican, partly Nonconformist, partly Roman Catholic, and the three religious groups do not fit harmoniously into the political system of two parties —Whigs and Tories. Compromise was essential. If the Protestant succession was to be maintained something, both of principle and of prejudice, must be sacrificed. Compromise, it has been said, means accepting a great deal of what one knows to be wrong in order to obtain a little of what one hopes will be right. The ages of compromise are unheroic ages, and Defoe is an unheroic figure, who nevertheless had his moments of courage, and finally sought the expression which was denied him in life in the creation of a whole gallery of adventurers, rogues, and vagabonds.

The life of Defoe is very imperfectly known; even those facts which are autobiography have been gravely suspected, and the interpretation of many undoubted events presents serious difficulties. It must suffice here to set down a few bare dates.

He was born probably in 1659, in the parish of St Giles, Cripplegate; his grandfather had been a yeoman of Northamptonshire, and that combination of two naturally allied occupations, cattle-grazing and butchering, which the Tudor Governments so bitterly hated, had brought his father to the City as a butcher. Little more is known of the family, though Defoe frankly acknowledges his father's generosity in educating him for five years at the " Dissenting Academy " of Mr Morton at Newington. Defoe wrote *Robinson Crusoe* when he was nearly sixty. At fourteen years of age he was being trained for the Nonconformist ministry. We have here no artificial paradox, but rather one of the clues which lead toward an understanding of the most enigmatical of English political writers. Defoe, however, decided against the ministry, and was enabled to set up in business in the City, probably not as a hosier, but as a wholesale trader. He was emphatically Protestant, was 'out with Monmouth' in 1684, and joined William III's army in 1688. In 1692 he was bankrupt. In 1695 his fortunes were improving; he had a minor post under the Government, owing to his having gained the favour of William III, and he was concerned with a successful tile-factory at Tilbury. His literary activity grew year by year. The *Essay upon Projects*[1] is his first serious work. *The True-born Englishman*,[2] the pamphlets arising out of the Kentish Petition,[3] and *The Shortest Way with the Dissenters*[4] fill in the years before 1703. In 1703 he was tried, fined, pilloried, and sent to Newgate for libelling the Church and disturbing the public peace. His offence consisted in the fact that he had written a satire, which, clumsy though it is, was too well disguised for the Tories. In his *Shortest Way with the Dissenters* he had advocated their complete extirpation. The Dissenters themselves hardly relished such ambiguous championing, while the Tories read his advice in all seriousness, and betrayed themselves so ignominiously that " libelling the Church " was a natural enough retort and accusation.

From this time forward there may be noted a certain change of moral attitude ; Defoe's experiences made him by no means anxious to " go on his travels again," and his connexion with ministers in power—Harley, Godolphin, Harley again, and Bolingbroke—marks the end of his sturdy independence of thought and action. The years 1706 to 1708 and part of 1709 were spent mainly in Scotland, acting as a kind of Secret Service agent to promote the Union. To these years belong his most famous journal, the *Review*. In 1713 he was in prison again for writing on the Hanoverian succession, though his satire was certainly not intended to be hostile. From 1714 to 1719 Defoe's journalistic work is particularly questionable, and it seems impossible to defend his good faith ; he apparently agreed to take over and write for a Tory organ with the privately avowed intent of watering it down in the Whig interest. From 1719 to 1728, toward the end of his life, comes that amazing burst of fiction, romance, adventures, intermixed with social and didactic works : *Robinson Crusoe* (1719), *Captain Singleton* (1720), *Moll Flanders* (1722), *Colonel Jack* (1722), *Roxana* (1724), *Jonathan Wild* (1725), together with the *Journal of the Plague Year* (1722), the

---

[1] *An Essay upon Projects* (1697).

[2] *The True-born Englishman : a Satyr* (1701).

[3] *Legion's Address* (1701) ; *The History of the Kentish Petition* (1701) ; *Legion's New Paper* (1702) ; *The Original Power of the Collective Body of the People of England, Examined and Asserted* (1701).

[4] *The Shortest Way with the Dissenters* (1701).

Memoirs of a Cavalier (1720), *The New Family Instructor* (1727), *The Compleat English Tradesman* (1726–27), the *Tour through Great Britain* (1724–26), and *Augusta Triumphans* (1728)—a sketch of the City of London. The mere volume of work, of which these are only a selection of the more familiar items, is almost incredible.

In 1724 Defoe was prosperous, with a handsome house at Stoke Newington, four acres of land, and three lovely daughters; by 1730 some catastrophe had occurred and Defoe had gone into hiding, and was evidently feeling betrayed and deserted; in 1731 he died, apparently alone, in Ropemakers' Alley, Moorfields—in obscurity, though probably not in poverty.

These appear to be agreed facts. In detail almost every point has needed to be scrutinised and revised by his biographers. Defoe either could not or would not tell the truth about himself. Perhaps he was mainly careless, for the critical works of Professor Trent or of Mr G. A. Aitken have for the most part lessened his fame for " splendid creative mendacity " and increased his reputation for vivid reporting of current stories. The deceased Mrs Veal's Ghost was not the product of Defoe's imagination, and the historical value of *The Journal of the Plague Year* has been vindicated in great measure by Professor Watson Nicholson.

II

The more serious charges against his honesty are largely irrelevant to our purpose. Defoe's ' political thought,' such as it is, belongs to his earlier life. His ' social thought ' or social observation has throughout a certain courageous originality, mingled with sincere conventionality, untouched by fear or greed. The question of his essential honesty must, however, be discussed later. It is by no means clear that Defoe *is* a political thinker in any strict sense. What is apparent at first sight is that he is a social reformer, one of the earliest social reformers of modern times, immensely and vividly interested in social conditions, in economic development, in the growth and decadence of social classes, in all that the modern thinker terms sociology. However, it is perhaps wise to examine first what evidence we have of Defoe's political ideas. To read about Defoe produces a conviction that he was one of the worst charlatans in our history, but to read Defoe himself produces a yet stronger belief in his sincerity and in the consistency of his basic ideas. He might change his opinion only too readily as to the expediency of a war, or the wisdom of a monarch, but his belief in sovereignty, in a mixed constitution, in the origins of authority, or in the need for toleration stands firm through all vicissitudes.

Nevertheless, Defoe's political thought was frankly eclectic, rather than original. He had obviously read Hobbes, and accepted his abstract theory of sovereignty. He had learned much from Locke, and he quotes Harrington, Filmer, James I, Raleigh, Coke, Grotius, Milton, and Algernon Sidney. Probably he owes most to Locke and to Sidney. It is unfortunate, however, that he was moved to write his one serious tract on the theory of politics in an unpleasant form of doggerel verse, which has not even the merit of being concise. The *Jure Divino* of 1706,[1] if carefully perused, does give something like a consecutive statement of political ideas, but to read it is an heroic measure. The prose footnotes form a more tolerable and more complete outline of Defoe's views on the nature and origin of the State. As to the verse, let me quote a few lines and pass on !

> But how did Families and Nations rise,
> Join for Defence and form Societies ?
>
> .　　　.　　　.　　　.　　　.
>
> If Families united by Consent,
> There we come back to Laws of Government;
> Compact and mutual Treaties of Accord,
> Between a willing People and their Lord.
>
> .　　　.　　　.　　　.　　　.
>
> It quite destroys the Nature of the Thing
> That Heaven should so uphold a Monster King.

From the prose notes, however, and from a pamphlet on the *Original Power of the Collective Body of the People of England* (1701) we can deduce Defoe's opinion without such acute torture : " The Original of all Humane Power is in the People governed, because in all Societies they are prior to the Government." The whole work is dedicated to " the most

---

[1] *Jure Divino : a Satyr*; in Twelve Books (1706).

serene, most Invincible, and most Illustrious Lady, Reason,"
because Reason's right of government alone is *jure divino*.
Men had joined together in society for safety and the general
welfare, and the patriarchal element in government was tem-
pered by the facts of conquest. So far he might have been
following James I. Authority or power is divine in its origin ;
Defoe debates only of " its being committed to any Body but
the People, for whose use . . . it is appointed." There must
be some power *prior* to the power of King, Lords, and
Commons, and Defoe perhaps goes back to the first " Agreement of the People " [1] in the sharp distinction which he draws
between the represented and their representatives ; the represented are clearly superior, and to them reverts the supreme
power, which they have delegated by mutual consent, whenever the use made of this power is such as to deny its whole
raison d'être. All power must centre somewhere, either
inherently and originally or by deputation, but the hands in
which it will centre will be determined by circumstances and
by expedience. The genius of this nation has always appeared
to tend to a monarchy, " a legal limited Monarchy, and . . .
there was not discovered the least inclination in any party
towards a Commonwealth." Nevertheless, the consecration
of a king " must have its original in Faith, for I can see nothing
of it in Common Sense." Defoe's idea of monarchy is not
unlike that of the *Patriot King*; he has abandoned the idea of
divine right, but in the unfinished treatise *Of Royall Educacion* [2]
he assigns to the monarch functions of considerable importance.
He is probably satirical in the remark that the souls of princes
are " oftentimes furnished thus in an extraordinary manner
from a superior hand," but he emphasises more sincerely the
need of education to enhance the original endowments. " A
fool knows not the beauty and excellence of a just, mild, and
mercifull Government, and is almost made a tyrant by the
nature of the thing and because he is a fool."

In place of divine right Defoe relies upon a contract theory
closely parallel to that of the Middle Ages ; his contract is
implicit rather than historical, and it is eventually limited by

[1] See S. R. Gardiner, *Constitutional Documents of the Puritan Revolution*, p. 333 (2nd
edition, 1899).
[2] *Of Royall Educacion : a Fragmentary Treatise*, ed. K. D. Bülbring (1895).

its end, and by reason. The end is more worthy than the means, and if the end be threatened the contract is revocable, and *ipso facto* void. " Reason is the test of the Law ; for Laws which are contradictory to Reason are void in their own Nature."

He does not, however, enter upon the complexities of natural law and the law of nature. In *The Original Power of the Collective Body of the People of England* Defoe goes on to apply his theory to the actual constitution of the kingdom. Sovereignty rests ultimately with the people, but the limits of *legal* authority have been left somewhat vague. Conditions perhaps ought to have been laid down, declaring that " King, Lords, and Commons, if they invert the great end of their Institution, the Public Good, cease to be in the same public capacity." Defoe, like Sidney, had no fear of permitting the people to be judge in their own cause. Have they not " the same right against any of the three Heads of the Constitution as they had against the King"? "The Parliament of England, consisting of the king, Lords and Commons, are to me the Supreme Channel of Power, the Great Collective Body in Miniature." " Their right is derived from their Propriety in the Freehold." " The Power of every Branch of the English Constitution is so shared out that every part is assistant to one another, and yet every Part is a Check to one another " ; " a due Ballance." But although Defoe thus pays homage to the orthodox doctrine of a balanced constitution, he sees quite clearly the need for some definition of the relations between the three parts thus balanced ; the limit of consent, as he calls it, between the three parts, and again between the Government and the governed. Perhaps he hardly appreciates the logical difficulty of binding a legal sovereign by legislation—a difficulty which has led to the growth of the Conventions of the Constitution. The method he would advocate is clearly a much greater precision in the Bill of Rights, and the practice of treating it as a written constitution, until such time as the people should express themselves otherwise. Defoe has no delusions as to the strength of a rigid constitution. A ' fundamental ' to him is a principle, not a law. The legal sovereign may always err ; " no collective body of men whatsoever . . . are or can have been infallible " ;

" 'tis possible for even a House of Commons to be wrong."
" You may die, but the People remain."   " Each Branch may
wrong and oppress the other, or altogether may do wrong
to the People they are made to govern."   The difficulty of
regulating relations between the three parts of Parliament is
clearly seen by Defoe, but his remedy is merely that they
should be directed by the law, and, where that is silent, by
reason.   If for reason we may read convention, it may be
suggested that Defoe knew all that could be known on this still
vexed point.

To understand the particular turn which Defoe gave to his
political thought, and his vivid interest in the attempted
tyranny of the House of Commons, we must look for a moment
at the circumstances in which his theoretical pamphlets had
their birth.   It was the sharp controversy over the dramatic
presentation of the Kentish Petition in 1701 which supplied
Defoe with his text.

In an age of rotten boroughs and all-pervading political
corruption, the county representation had maintained a higher
degree of purity and vigour than the borough systems.   The
county gatherings at the hustings or for Quarter Sessions
probably represented, in many districts, the freest expression of
public opinion that could be obtained.   It is natural to find
the county of Kent taking an independent attitude and main-
taining it with the characteristic Southern courage and tenacity.
In 1701, at the Quarter Sessions at Maidstone, the justices,
country gentlemen, and large numbers of freeholders, drew
up, through the Grand Jury, a petition requesting the House
of Commons to support King William by " turning their loyal
addresses into Bills of Supply "—in other words, to enable
him to get on with the war by voting him adequate supplies.
They based their right to petition not only upon the vague
words of the Bill of Rights, but upon statute.[1]   They were
petitioning the appropriate branch of the legislature, and they
felt, like Queen Elizabeth of famous legend, " We have made
you what you are."   Moreover, they backed their petition
with the practical consideration that the coasts of Kent were
the earliest exposed to French hostility, and ought to be pro-
tected by a vigorous offensive.   One of the members for Kent,

[1] 13 Charles II.

on pretext of consulting the member for Sussex, showed the petition to several other members, and then refused to present it. Eventually the other member for Kent presented it to an already enraged House, which proceeded to vote it scandalous, insolent, and seditious, and ordered its bearers to be taken into custody by the Sergeant. So soon had the seven Bishops and the Bill of Rights been forgotten. A few days later an outspoken paper, *Legion's Memorial*, was presented to the House, apparently by Defoe himself, who had written it. " Our name is Legion, for we are many," so the memorial declared, and indeed they were too many to be arrested, and the storm gradually petered out, until the prisoners were released on the prorogation of Parliament. The citizens of London entertained them to a great banquet in the Mercers' Hall, where Daniel Defoe joined them as a guest of honour. They thereupon started upon a triumphal progress to their homes in Kent, and so ended " the first occasion that ever the English nation petitioned to be taxed." Defoe had apparently played a perfectly straightforward and courageous part in these amazing scenes, which form the text on which much of his political thought is based. From it he drew the moral :

> Nature has left this tincture in the blood,
> That all men would be tyrants if they could.

The *Memorial* itself is an outspoken statement by " them that made you members " ; it follows the lines of the Bill of Rights by giving first a long series of grievances, and ending with a corresponding tale of *desiderata*, ranging from a request " that all the public just debts of the nation be forthwith paid and discharged " down to a final demand that the Kentish petitioners should receive the thanks of the House. What is impressive in the midst of such specific controversy is Defoe's clear-sighted analysis of the causes of the trouble. He sees unhesitatingly that Parliament, and the Commons in particular, ought to be the " Servant of the People " ; he denounces unsparingly the manner in which

> The Court, the King, the Church, the Parliament,
> Alternately pursue the same intent,
> Under the specious name of Liberty,
> The passive injured People to betray.

The alternate oligarchy of Whigs and Tories, the encroach-ments of the House of Commons on the rights of electors, the need for sounder choice of representatives—all these Defoe saw as clearly as if he were looking back upon the eighteenth century, rather than looking forward. This prophetic insight is admirably illustrated in a paper addressed by Defoe to Harley, during the year 1704, and first printed from the manuscript in the British Museum in 1907.[1] The greater part of the memorandum is taken up with questions of Secret Service and foreign intelligence, but it has also some remarkably bold and far-seeing judgments on political develop-ment. Defoe decides roundly in favour of a Prime Minister, and declares that the English people will easily be reconciled to it. The Secretary of State must be Prime Minister (and Prime Minister with applause, as Defoe puts it), and the two Secretaries with perhaps the Lord Treasurer or " a well qualifyed Chancellor " must form an inner Cabinet to the Queen. " Cabinets of ten or fourteen are monsters and use-less." This limited number, however, would make possible " a Prime Ministry without a grievance." When one recalls the sharp dissensions over both the title and the office which marked the fall of Walpole, it is clear that Defoe's opinion was far in advance of his times, and it is strange that it has been so little noticed by historians.

In spite of all party attachments, Defoe was neither a Whig nor a Tory ; he was one of the earliest members of the Radical party—an ancestor, perhaps, of John Wilkes—though he believed somewhat too devoutly in the sanctity of freehold to be a perfectly sound Radical. His attitude toward parties has perhaps been unduly obscured by our custom of reading backward. After all, parties were little older than Defoe himself. The party system was still in the throes of birth, and no man could as yet say whether or not it represented a merely temporary schism in the nation which could be healed. The Protestant succession was the one indispensable principle

---

[1] *English Historical Review*, January 1907. Although this reprint is far more accessible to historians than most of Defoe's writings, it has not, I believe, been used by any of the historians of the Inner Cabinet ; it is not mentioned by either Mr Temperley or Sir William Anson in their articles on the Cabinet in the *English Historical Review*, 1912–14. Defoe is not mentioned by either Professor Trevelyan or Principal Grant Robertson in their respective volumes of Oman's *History of England* (Methuen).

of politics to Defoe. William III was his hero ; Queen Anne, in spite of Dr Sacheverell, was better than the Pretender, and, moreover, his benefactor ; the Hanoverian succession was the only available security for Protestantism. Nevertheless, he was too critical and too open-minded for his fellow Dissenters. He was honestly shocked by their practice of occasional conformity, and he lost much of their support by his open disgust at their unscrupulous profanity, as he termed it. (If Defoe was not honest in this, then words are not only without meaning, but also without power to betray the secret of the heart.) Moreover, he could see some uses even for the Church of England, and his hatred of Roman Catholicism was not bitter enough for either party. He stood always a little aloof—an attitude no doubt encouraged by the pillory !

All the best men of his day were inveighing against the party system—Defoe argued that he belonged to no party ; Bolingbroke talked loftily of a reunited nation ; a century later the Duke of Wellington was still acting upon the belief that the Queen's Government must be carried on. " Though I don't like the crew, I won't sink the ship," as Defoe had put it. The difficulty in defending Defoe is that the two ignoble elements of fear and subserviency do undoubtedly enter into his politics and his writing, mingled with perfectly natural gratitude. Fear and subserviency, I believe, explain far more than the hypothesis of deliberate dishonesty. Defoe wanted to write, and his indulgence in clumsy satire led him more than once to prison and the pillory. Since the desire to write was his strongest impulse, some modification of his early honesty and independence was pressed upon him. He was still at the stage of declaring " *Il faut vivre*," and had not yet reached the heights of being able to say with conviction " *Je n'en vois pas la nécessité.*" This weakness he shared with perhaps the majority of mankind. His other weakness, subserviency, is harder to forgive, and its root did not entirely lie in fear. Honesty had caused him to abandon the ministry as a profession, but he had never reconciled himself to the position of a tradesman or a ' paid servant.' He was just Tory enough to long for Norman blood—not Tory enough to rest content with, or be proud of, his own station in life. Hence the exaggerated and rather boring criticisms which he launches

167

at the "Compleat Gentleman." He was an unsuccessful prototype of "the Great Mel" in *Evan Harrington*. His early attitude toward Harley was compact of both gratitude and subserviency, not unmixed with fear. But Harley, it must be remembered, was keeping him out of prison, and at the same time consistently forgetting to send him the necessary supplies for his Secret Service. The long series of letters printed in the *Portland Papers* [1] abundantly testifies to this attitude. As time went on, and Defoe became genuinely interested in Scottish politics and in reconciling public opinion to the Union, the abject tone drops from his letters, and finally he writes as man to man. " I could make you merry " with stories of North Country bigotry, or again " I have acted a true spy to you." Unless Secret Service ought never to be justified—a harsh position to take up—Defoe played an honourable part during the years which led to the Union with Scotland. His two great interests, toleration and trade, are constantly in question, and his zeal for constitutional definition has full play. " The very word, Parliament of Britain, is grown terrible here." It is interesting to notice how far Defoe respects the Scottish religious scruples about the Union, though his disgust with a ' clerical ' party was not disguised. The " implacable parsons " are going mad, and the people are out of their wits, and the country is united in universal discord. But Defoe does not scorn their scruples, he merely derides their suspicions—the suspicions of a " proud, passionate, ignorant and jealous people."

Defoe's transference of his services to Godolphin, when Harley fell, would seem to have been justified by Harley's suggestion, and by the fact that he was driven, of necessity, to seek the protection of a minister, and the emoluments of a secret agent. He could not take up a purely independent line, and during most of Queen Anne's reign, when the division between Whigs and Tories seemed to lose its original meaning, he was at least working for causes in which he himself believed. If he modified his opinions about the war with some rapidity, that is an experience to which the present generation is not entirely a stranger.

After 1714 the journalist in Defoe is uppermost, and

[1] *Hist. MSS. Comm. 15th Report*, vols. iv and v.

genuine thought on politics is hardly to be detected in his work ; from this date, therefore, I propose to treat mainly his social ideas. But I cannot leave the subject of his attitude toward parties without a word on the sympathy which is so marked a feature of his writing. Defoe had in him something of the quality of a dramatist, yet without the slightest power of expression. His fairly frequent excursions into dialogue, in his didactic work, are intolerably dull and overladen with repetition. Yet he had the dramatic imagination, the sympathy that could put itself in another's place. Ardent democrat though he was, and staunch Dissenter, he could see the dignity of Charles I, much as Marvell saw it, and could admit that he died for his Church. He could admire the cynical good sense of Charles II, whom he frequently quotes with approval : " Not the best governor of the country, but the man who understood it better than any other ruler in History." He saw that the fate of James II was infinitely more tragic than that of Charles, king and martyr ; " Death is an immediate Gate of Deliverance to such Pressures as are beyond the Power of Flesh and Blood to support." His fervent admiration for William III, " the best of monarchs and of men to me," did not blind him to the true qualities of the Stuarts.

Again, though his fictitious atheist husband in *Religious Courtship* [1] is compounded of vices, his Roman Catholic is a man of such charm and sincerity as to place his young wife in imminent danger of conversion if he had not opportunely died young ! The picture displays a remarkable and unusual sympathy—worthy of the boy who while still at the " Dissenting Academy " could not find it in his heart to pray that the Turks should defeat the Papists. The same boy, grown old, reports in one breath that " popish vestments " are still used in the cathedral at Durham, while he rejoices that Roman Catholics go openly to Mass in peace and unmolested under the beneficent rule of the Anglican bishop—a degree of tolerance not very usual in the early eighteenth century.

It would be easy to multiply such instances of genuine sympathy coming to the surface in unpremeditated words and phrases ; they must be taken into account in any attempt to

---

[1] *Religious Courtship : being Historical Discourses, on the Necessity of marrying Religious Husbands and Wives only* . . . (1722).

estimate Defoe's loyalty. He did not hold, and could not hold, the political creed or programme of either party. He was essentially an eclectic. If he could have inherited £5000 a year and a great name, while retaining his early experience, he would have ranked in history at least alongside of the Victorian Lord Shaftesbury. In saying this it must not be forgotten that Defoe is sometimes unable to rise above the conventional standard of his day ; certain cruelties leave him unmoved. Like Gladstone in his unregenerate days, Defoe saw no objections to negro slavery, and indeed suggests that the trade ought to be extended. Nevertheless, it is far more often that the prince of journalists stands out as a great social reformer, unlimited by party.

To sum up Defoe's contribution to political thought, perhaps I may quote the words of the late Master of Balliol, Mr A. L. Smith : [1]

> Short of originality in theory, Defoe contributed to political progress in almost every other direction. Much cant he laughed out of court; many prejudices he shamed into silence; on fallacies and misrepresentations his common sense came down like a sledge-hammer. The work he did in his numberless writings—some of them, such as the *True-born Englishman* and the *Shortest Way with the Dissenters,* permanent in their historical importance—the work of writing single-handed the whole of the *Review,* even to the fictitious correspondence, was work of the first value; it was educating a nation into political sense and morality. It was Defoe who applied and popularised Locke, and drove home the philosopher's principles.

Chalmers indeed declared that *The Original Power of the Collective Body of the People of England* was equal to Locke in reasoning and superior in style.[2]

III

Defoe's views on economic questions are somewhat difficult to determine, and his fame as an economist would certainly

---

[1] *Cambridge Modern History,* vol. vi, p. 817.

[2] That his style was at least different from Locke's is readily illustrated. His political thought is enlivened with such vivid phrases as " playing Bo-peep with the Almighty " and " making a mock of human misery "; " snakes in the grass are daily snarling "; the tyrant is he who can " pray with his lips and murder with his hands "; while there is a cheery reminiscence of Luther in his exhortation, " Sin like a lord ; little sneaking sins won't serve turn."

have been greater if he had set himself to produce a comprehensive treatise on the subject. He had, indeed, sufficiently clear and comprehensive ideas to have been a not unworthy forerunner of Adam Smith, but they must be sought here, there, and everywhere among his writings. Trade is his starting-point; he is immensely interested in every detail of overseas trade; he refuses to adopt the pessimistic view that it was declining, and he devotes much of his *Plan of the English Commerce* [1] to a precise description of the varieties of trade and their routes. The trading paper, *Mercator*,[2] though Defoe denied its authorship, without doubt expresses his views and owes to him its existence. He refused to take up either a whole-hearted Free Trade or a thoroughgoing Mercantilist point of view. Export and import duties were in themselves neither good nor bad, save as circumstances should prescribe. A ' prohibition ' might be the soundest policy under William III, and the " maddest thing a nation could do " under Queen Anne. Export of raw materials, of which we might have a monopoly, was little short of distraction, in face of the unemployment with which he was continually concerned, and for which he believed ' relief work ' to be no remedy. He did not deny the theory of the balance of trade ; he simply asserted, and provided statistics to prove, that the balance was always in favour of England. He will have nothing to do with any doctrinaire view ; it is the statesman's business to adjust and control the course of trade, in such manner as to promote the general welfare of his country. Theoretically he had made little or no change in the doctrines of Burleigh ; in practice he tends often, almost insensibly, toward the side of freedom. In matters of finance he represents, clearly enough, the more enlightened opinions of his day ; the *Essay upon Publick Credit*,[3] ascribed to Harley, but undoubtedly Defoe's work, gives a lucid analysis of the causes of the rise and decline of credit. " Credit is a consequence, not a cause ; . . . It is produced and grows insensibly, from fair and upright Dealing, from honourable performance of contracts and covenants." Money itself cannot " purchase

---

[1] *A Plan of the English Commerce* (1728).
[2] *Mercator, or Commerce Retrieved . . .* (1713–14).
[3] *An Essay upon Publick Credit* (1710).

the thing called Credit." " Publick Credit is the consequence of honourable, just, and punctual Management in the matter of Funds and Taxes or Loans." Defoe sees clearly that credit may flourish as well under one Ministry as another, one party as another, if its essential conditions are present. He does not in this pamphlet pursue the subject far enough to analyse the function of credit, but his opinions were outlined very early in life in the *Essay upon Projects*, where he deals with the system of banking and its advantages. Defoe's essay on banks was published within three years after the foundation of the Bank of England ; he therefore had not much experience on which to test his good opinion of it. Nevertheless his arguments appear to be lucid and sound. He speaks of " that part of a Stock we call credit, which always is or indeed must be, the most essential part of a Bank " ; essentially he thinks that banks are nothing but so many goldsmiths' shops, but he criticises the banks for being " so awkward in lending, so strict, so tedious, so inquisitive and so public " as to defeat their own ends. Their advantages, however, to a trading people ought to be manifest, in that they lower interest ; a " Royal Bank " could be exceedingly useful in time of war, by advances made to the Exchequer on Parliamentary security. The Royal Bank, however, was not as yet large enough in its operations to control the rate of interest, as did the banks of Amsterdam and Genoa, nor was it yet sufficiently provided with ' stock ' to be able to do all the business required. Defoe was willing to admit that a multiplicity of banks might supply these defects, but only if a perfect understanding could be secured between them, so that all their bills might be interchangeable. He looked forward, however, to one great Bank Royal, which, with its county branches, should preside over the whole cash of the kingdom.

Defoe's *Tour through Great Britain*[1] cannot here be examined in detail because, although it is first-class evidence for economic history, it combines the maximum of facts with the minimum of thought. Defoe is a shrewd and sensible observer, though sometimes fantastic, as when he describes the fifteen or twenty successive wives required by the marsh-dwellers of Essex.

[1] *A Tour thro' the Whole Island of Great Britain* (vol. i, 1724 ; vol. ii, 1725 ; vol. iii, 1726).

(The ladies came from the hill-country, and could not survive the ague!)

Defoe knows much of the conditions of industry in England and he reports with simplicity; the well-known descriptions of the West Riding of Yorkshire or of Stourbridge Fair will occur to every reader. He knows the actual market-day scenes at Leeds, and makes the small clothier live again before our eyes. He knows precisely where to turn north from Hastings to find the famous iron workings of Sussex, and he notes acutely enough that the Elizabethan outcry against decay of timber would seem to have been exaggerated and unjustifiable, in the eyes of a traveller who had to cross the Weald.

But it must be noted that Defoe was not above perpetrating one of the hoary fallacies of economic history. To him England's woollen industry begins in the sixteenth century, at the wise behest of Henry VII, and by the example of the Flemings. Against that error historians struggle almost in vain. It has had too long a start of us. Defoe writes:

> He [Henry VII] justly inferred that Heaven having been so bountiful to England as to give them the Wooll, as it were, in a peculiar Grant, exclusiv of the whole world, it was a meer rebellion against His Providence, and particularly ungratefull to His bounty that the English nation should reject the offer, giv away the blessing, and by an unaccountable neglect send their wooll abroad to be manufactured, and even buy their own clothing of the Flemings with ready money.[1]

Defoe thus attributes to Henry VII the first encouragement of the woollen industry, and very greatly exaggerates the influence of the Flemings. The whole passage is almost a travesty of the facts, and it is a warning that Defoe's evidence, precise though it sounds, always needs scrutiny. His assertion that wool is sent from East Anglia to Westmoreland to be spun, and thence returned to the East Anglian clothiers for weaving, seems to bear on its face all the marks of improbability. The economic historian, although naturally disposed to defend Defoe, must keep an eye upon that " splendid creative mendacity " which may crop up anywhere in his writing.

In his economic writings Defoe makes certain notable

---

[1] *Of Royall Educacion.* See above.

omissions—natural enough perhaps at the time. He has no discussion of rent, no question as to its origin or payment. Five shillings an acre seems to him a suitable rent for a reclaimed New Forest, after twenty years rent free during the process of reclaiming, but he makes no analysis of the reasons for the payment of rents. In like manner he does not touch upon the nature of profits; usually he seems more concerned to avoid bankruptcy than to anticipate profits, but he knows and names all the wealthier citizens and merchants of London, and appears to treat profits as almost invariably the result of foreign trade. Consumption he believes is good for trade, and he does not condemn luxurious expenditure except when it is beyond a man's resources, or contrary to good morals. Higher wages, he admits, increase consumption, and so would go far to abolish unemployment. All available labour, he believes, could be employed, if consumption could be more widely extended. Defoe's evidence on the subject of wages is often interesting, and deserves to be collected and analysed. But he has no theory of wages. His idea that poverty is mainly a family matter, closely associated with questions of population, would seem to suggest a family wage as the solution, but he never hits upon this expedient. Indeed, Defoe has no original ideas on the subject of wages. He does not follow up his suggestion as to increased consumption, and his picture of the " malice of servants " generally follows purely conventional lines. It is on account of such omissions that the reader finds himself asking for yet one more treatise from Defoe— a systematic work on economics which should have led him to follow up his own stray thoughts to their conclusions.

IV

Turning to Defoe as a thinker on questions of social reform or social well-being, we are confronted with an initial difficulty. Defoe's didactic works are packed thick with evidence of social conditions. So too are his novels. Yet in this he can hardly be ranked as a thinker; he is rather a peculiarly vivid photographer, to whom nothing is too humble or too sordid for his camera. If we are to speak of Defoe as a thinker, we must confine our attention to his deliberate and conscious reflection on social questions; it may be impossible to avoid noting some of his pictures, but it must be clear that they are pictures, not projects.

Defoe himself was anxious to be accounted a reformer—in religion, in manners, in economic methods. Sometimes he appears to modern taste to confuse the relative importance of his reforms. His genuine love of toleration has been shown in connexion with politics; it was certainly his strongest principle, and it led him again and again into an impatient anti-clericalism, directed impartially against Anglican " Highfliers," Scottish Presbyters, or his own Dissenting brethren. But over and beyond this love of toleration his writings have a certain religious fervour which is somewhat alien from the usual conventional picture of eighteenth-century religion. Robinson Crusoe's Puritanical musings will occur to every reader: the wearisome dialogues of the *Family Instructor* follow almost identically the same lines as Early Victorian works of pious fiction, such as *The Fairchild Family*. Defoe does not scruple to use the word ' ecstasy' in speaking of dawning convictions of sin in a child of six; nevertheless, when an unbelieving son returns home maimed from the wars his Christian father refuses to receive him, and assigns to him a solitary lodging and an allowance, until such time as he shall be converted.

It is of course almost impossible to say when Defoe is speaking in his own person, but evidently such works supplied a felt want, and not only among the Nonconformists, for Defoe's typically pious families go indifferently to church or meeting, united in heart by their condemnation of all recreation.

Defoe's desire for the reform of manners marks all his writing early and late, and it has every appearance of being sincere, and not to have been exploited for journalistic purposes. He castigates all the vices in turn, and inveighs against the disorders of the London streets. This, however, was common form in all serious writing of his day. He is more original in his vigorous defence of women, and in his plea for improvement in their position. His best-known work on this topic is the section in the *Essay upon Projects* where he pleads for an academy for women in the shape of a much secluded college, where they might learn to cultivate their capacities, which indeed are not negligible. It looks, says Defoe, " as if we denied women the advantages of education for fear they should vie with the men in their improvements." Defoe was not strictly original in this desire to see whether women's natural gifts, like those of Man Friday, could not be trained to greater heights. Mary Astell, an obscure lady, who had observed that " Piety is often offensive when it is accompanied with indiscretion," had already worked out a scheme for a women's college, and rumour went forth that the Princess Anne was on the point of endowing it with £10,000. The plan is said to have been quashed because Bishop Burnet thought it savoured of Popery. Nevertheless, everything points to Defoe's sincerity, if not to his originality. Throughout his writings there is a certain respect for a woman's share in the social group, a certain sense of justice which is rare. If a man takes a couple of thousand pounds of his wife's portion and puts it into his business he ought not to keep her in ignorance of the fact that he is approaching bankruptcy ; he ought never indeed to keep her in such ignorance that she cannot adapt her expenditure to her husband's circumstances. Defoe was ready to anticipate the Married Women's Property Acts by some hundred and fifty years, and he does not mince his language in describing the various ways in which women have suffered at the hands of their husbands.[1] Defoe carries this attitude into most of his casual remarks on women ; almost the only criticism to which he is moved is the remark that " Women are inordinately desirous of going to Heaven " (in contrast with Dissenters, who are " somewhat desirous of going to Heaven "). It is because this excessive desire appears to him a little morbid that he eliminates Mary Astell's idea of making her college a partial revival of the " religious life " for women. When he suggests that women have an unfortunate influence upon the education of their sons, as being far too much inclined to pamper them and retain them at home in ignorance, he is merely echoing a complaint already centuries old. So, too, he makes purely conventional objections to silly women led away by priests, and in their turn leading away yet sillier men ! It is Defoe's indignant defence of women that is original, though one can only hope that his zeal for reform sometimes exaggerates—as in his estimate of the

[1] *Good Advice to the Ladies* (1702).

numerous husbands who put their wives into lunatic asylums in order to have a freer hand for those ' diversions ' which marriage might hinder but could not replace. Like most moralists of all ages he warns the young women of his day that they should be " a little more modestly dressed . . . a little less curious, less extravagant, less exotic, and abated a little of their excesses " (of tea, drams, and late hours). But this is not one of Defoe's more original lines of thought. He deprecates resentment at his attacks on manners neatly enough. " If I have fallen upon our vices, I hope none but the vicious will be angry."

Defoe was always intensely interested in " the changes and chances of this mortal life," and for this reason, quickened no doubt by his own vicissitudes of fortune, he showed a keen appreciation of the value of insurance and assurance schemes of many kinds. He was not original in this, but he was perhaps the first popular writer who saw the possibilities of insurance against accidents, and all the commoner types of provision for a ' rainy day.' As a practical reformer he had little desire to turn the world upside-down, but he propounded a surprising number of expedients for preventing the reverses of mankind. " Man is the worst of all God's creatures to shift for himself. No other animal is ever starved to death."

Life insurance he did not approve in England, though he thought it might be desirable in a land of sudden death such as Italy. His scheme of insurance for widows has, however, many of the merits of life insurance. Friendly societies and a Pensions Office will meet most of the hard cases. Improvement of the law relating to bankrupts and debtors was another practical scheme in which Defoe had a close personal interest. His analysis of the problem of poverty and unemployment seems to lead him to two main conclusions. Poverty is the result either of unforeseen emergencies, or of temperament. The emergencies can no longer be met by charity, and they ought to be remedied by a vast extension of the principle of insurance, based on sound actuarial calculations. So far as poverty is caused by temperament, Defoe is not very hopeful. " Good husbandry is no English virtue . . . it neither loves nor is beloved by an Englishman." " We are the most lazy, diligent nation in the world." " English labouring people will eat and drink, but especially the latter, three times as much as any sort of foreigners of the same dimensions in the world." Idleness and drink, Defoe suggests, lie at the root of all poverty except that caused by accidents. Consequently he points out very vigorously that giving alms is no real charity, and that " Relief works " only succeed in diverting capital from one channel to another. It is significant that Defoe's tract *Giving Alms no Charity* [1] was reprinted by the Charity Organisation Society in 1893 ; it is more truly significant that Defoe in his stress on insurance and on education has seized upon the two remedies which appear to-day to have the greatest future ; his other cure for ' temperament,' the reformation of manners, suffers from being unduly Puritanical in its exclusion of reasonable recreation. The insubordination of servants is another vice which gives its name to a substantial didactic treatise ; [2] it is chiefly valuable as illustrating the numerous forms of ' combination,' at an embryo stage, which existed among servants and craftsmen in the early eighteenth century. Throughout Defoe's writings we get evidence of the surprising variety of wages paid in different districts and in different occupations ; the need for greater mobility of labour is clearly indicated, though Defoe draws only the moral that greater contentment is required.

It is Defoe's all-pervading interest in problems of poverty and unemployment that is remarkable in the early eighteenth century, and there is a striking consistency in all his works on social topics. In the *Essay upon Projects*,[3] written in 1693 or 1694, he advocates an Academy of Culture comparable to the French Academy, a military academy, and an academy for women. In *Augusta Triumphans*,[4] written very near the end of his life, he is busy with projects for an Academy of Music, a Foundling Hospital, and a University of London. The curious work entitled *The Protestant Monastery* [5] elaborates very minutely a scheme for founding a kind of refuge or club for old age, differing from almshouses mainly in being a joint-stock venture, intended for self-supporting old age, and

[1] *Giving Alms no Charity* (1704).
[2] *The Great Law of Subordination consider'd* (1724).
[3] Published in 1697.   [4] *Augusta Triumphans* (1728).
[5] *The Protestant Monastery* (1726).

controlled by its members on a democratic basis. The scheme provides generously for physical comfort and convenience and abundant domestic service, but hardly seems to meet the psychological needs of old age. It is designed, however, as a means of avoiding the cruelty and harshness which, Defoe asserts, were habitually meted out to the old. Puritanism, it would seem, had not been able to bring into play the kindliness and humanitarian feeling which followed the great religious revivals of the eighteenth century.

Defoe's *Compleat Tradesman*,[1] though not remarkable for original ideas, yet constitutes a very notable piece of historical evidence as to the conditions of retail traders in the early eighteenth century. It illustrates well the transitional and uncertain conditions of trade and capitalism at this time. London and the greater towns had large numbers of tradesmen who had ceased to be mediæval, and had hardly become modern, though they certainly possessed many of the characteristics we are apt to term Early Victorian or provincial. Defoe takes it for granted that the making of wealth is the final object of a tradesman, but it is evident that he is more concerned to avoid failure than to heap up riches. Retail trade was in a somewhat dangerous state of flux; foreign trade only half understood, and credit a ticklish matter, much at the mercy of politicians, as Defoe well understood. Versatility in trading is therefore a supreme virtue, while idleness is as the sin against the Holy Ghost. In his fear of financial failure the good tradesman would seem to have been in some danger of failing to be a man. Customers appear to have been extraordinarily trying; the arrogance which Defoe describes in fashionable purchasers is an almost incredible offence against good manners. Perhaps only the naturally obscure were guilty of it! Subserviency becomes exalted into a virtue; a good tradesman must dissemble his rage, even if he is obliged to run upstairs and kick his unoffending family to relieve his feelings. But indeed all vices, virtues, and customs are to be judged by their capacity to create and to maintain financial stability. The " compleat tradesman " at that time lives over his shop and keeps a small group of assistants and apprentices for whom he provides a kind of family life, conceived on

---

[1] *The Compleat English Tradesman* (vol. i, 1725 ; vol. ii, 1727).

tolerably generous lines of reasonable supervision. He reads prayers to them every evening, unless he is so much given up to ostentation as to be unwilling to serve even his Maker. In that case he offers a small salary to the parish reader ! He has a country house for his wife and children, but he sends them away alone and continues to attend to his business. He ought not, if he is to be successful, to ride or hunt, or learn " to talk dog-language." A good man of business must take his recreations in his wife's parlour behind the shop. Indeed, a striking feature of Defoe's description is the utter lack of any reasonable recreations or limitation of hours. The master should be accessible from 7 A.M. till 12, and again from 2 P.M. till 9 P.M. The country gentleman's horses, dogs, and gardens are inappropriate ; the society man's coffee-house, gaming-table, balls, or facilities for drinking were pernicious and a waste of time. Politics were impossible. If he wished to put his country first, let him give up business and enlist. His hours were inconsistent with the playhouse. His wife's main diversion would seem to have been display of wealth—only too often non-existent wealth. It is true that in London the churches seem to have called him every morning at 6 A.M. ; he could evidently hear a sermon before breakfast if he would, as we learn from the story of the over-zealous tradesman who, when dispatched by his wife to fetch an urgently needed mid-wife, found his way in at the open doors of a church, and com-pletely forgot his errand in the earnestness of his attention to the sermon then proceeding ! But Defoe insists that a craving for sermons should be kept in due subjection to the needs of customers. The fear of bankruptcy leads him to lay perhaps unnecessary stress upon common sense.

The Compleat Tradesman has been condemned as an im-moral book. It is an unfair criticism. The tradesman exists, Defoe would say, for the purpose of being successful. If he fails he is of no use in his chosen *métier*. Therefore if he is to act in a manner inconsistent with success, let him choose another profession ; let him fight for his country instead of selling for it. Within these limitations Defoe examines the whole question of commercial ethics. Is the standard of honesty in a tradesman the same as that of an ordinary honest man? " Is the good man necessarily the good citizen? " was much the same question in another form. Defoe invites criticism by admitting that there *is* a distinction in the standards of honesty, " and though the distinction is very nice, yet I must say it is to be supported." Yet, when all is said and done, Defoe asks extremely little latitude, and that mainly formal. " The rectitude of the soul must be the same." The actual liberties he desires are few. There is the liberty of asking more than he is prepared to take. Defoe notes the Quaker protest against this custom, but declares that the Quakers have been obliged to acquiesce in it. Defoe has here no theory of value, either mediæval or modern, to help him. Secondly, there is the liberty of making promises to pay, which shall tacitly be considered as conditional promises, with a contingent dependence upon circumstances. The trouble here perhaps is the need for a more extended system of credit, though Defoe hardly realises it. Customary frauds he denounces unquestioningly as " knavish and dishonest." He has a special dislike of what he calls " Shop rhetorick," but he succeeds in showing that it has become a kind of convention, and that to translate it into bare and truthful English might hopelessly shock his customers, though he has the wit to see that in some cases a " grave middle way of discoursing " would actually be more attractive. In more serious matters, compassion to the miserable is a debt of charity, while the strictest honesty is to be required in a bankrupt.

These appear to be the only points of ethics concerned, and it is a little difficult to see why Defoe should have been abused by Charles Lamb as commending " the meanest, vilest, wretchedest degradations of the human character." Lamb continues :

> The pompous detail, the studied analysis of every little mean art, every sneaking address, every trick and subterfuge (short of larceny), that is necessary to the tradesman's occupation, with the hundreds of anecdotes, dialogues (in Defoe's liveliest manner) interspersed, all tending to the same amiable purpose, namely, the sacrificing of every honest emotion of the soul to what he calls the main chance—if you read it in an ironical sense, and as a piece of covered satire, make it one of the most amusing books Defoe ever writ. It is difficult to say what his intention was in writing it. It is almost impossible to suppose him in earnest, yet such is the bent of the book to narrow and

to degrade the heart, that if such maxims were as catching and infectious as those of a licentious cast, which happily is not the case, had I been living at the time, I certainly should have recommended to the Grand Jury of Middlesex, who presented *The Fable of the Bees*, to have presented this book of Defoe's in preference, as of a far more vile and debasing tendency.[1]

It is perhaps the whole tone of the book that roused Lamb's ire, its jog-trot platitudes, its solid common sense, its eternal insistence upon the " happy medium." What is at the root of the trouble is Defoe's tacit assumption that it is the first duty of the tradesman to remain solvent. It is equivalent to Machiavelli's assumption that it is the first obligation of the statesman to remain in power. Neither assumption (if absolute) allows for any higher loyalty or obligation. It is only fair, however, to Defoe to notice that he does not believe success involves the ignoring of religious or ethical standards. Charity, justice, honesty remain. Defoe differs from both the mediæval and the modern world in his view of the implications of the great fundamentals of morality, but he never denies their obligations. He is merely arguing within the limits of the conditions he has already laid down. No one knew better than Defoe how *not* to remain solvent. Many of his exhortations as to ignoring politics, coffee-houses, " dog-talk," and so forth are merely preaching from his own experience ; while his intimate knowledge of customers to whom courtesy was a purely one-sided virtue, and truth a totally inacceptable asset, shows itself in every line.

Before condemning Defoe in Lamb's wholesale manner, we ought to pause for a moment over an opponent's description of his behaviour as a bankrupt. John Tutchin writes :

I must do one piece of justice to the man, though I love him no better than you do : it is this—that meeting a gentleman in a coffee-house, when I and everybody else were railing at him, the gentleman took us up with this short speech, " Gentlemen," said he, " I know this Defoe as well as any of you, for I was one of his creditors, compounded with him, and discharged him fully. Several years afterwards he sent for me, and though he was clearly discharged, he paid me all the remainder of his debt, voluntarily and of his own accord;

[1] " The Good Clerk " in *The Reflector*, No. 4 (1812).

and he told me that, as far as God should enable him, he intended to do so with everybody."

Moreover it is recorded that the *Compleat Tradesman* had a strong and beneficent influence upon the mind of Benjamin Franklin. The critic must take refuge in quoting once more *quot homines*.

Defoe's *Compleat Gentleman* was never finished, and here we enter upon a field in which the author was bound to draw almost entirely upon his imagination. The result is a dull and somewhat unconvincing sketch, though perhaps it is a necessary corrective of Addison's golden picture of Sir Roger de Coverley. It has points in common with the Norfolk reputation of Sir Robert Walpole. The grace and courtesy of the cavalier are gone; gone too is his culture. If Defoe's picture be true the heir to a great estate had little or no chance of a sound education, either at school or at the university. The private tutor, wholly inefficient, had become something of a curse. But it must be admitted that on this topic Defoe is not convincing. As usual, however, he has a proposal to make. In *Augusta Triumphans* he works out what is perhaps the first rough sketch of the University of London. " Why should a young Gentleman be sent raw from the Nursery to live on his own Hands," in the midst of the thousand temptations of Oxford and Cambridge? " Why should such a metropolis as London be without an University ? " " Knowledge will never hurt us, and whoever lives to see an University here, will find it give quite another turn to the Genius and spirit of our Youth in General." Defoe would make a university of scattered colleges, such as we know. One should be at Westminster; one at St James's ; one near Ormond Street, the centre of the homes of the nobility ; one near the Royal Exchange ; and another, quite naturally, among the Inns of Court ; Gower Street is unknown to him. He describes a college thus :

> Small Expence is required : The sole Charge being the hire of a convenient Hall or House, which if they please, they may call the College. But I see no necessity the Pupils have to lye or diet there. . . . Their only necessary Business at College being to attend their Tutors at stated Hours, and (Bed and Board excepted) to conform themselves to College Laws. . . .

Let the best of Tutors be provided, and Professors in all Faculties encouraged, this will do a double good, not only to the Instructed, but to the Instructors.

A little later he writes:

In my Scheme for an University in *London*, I proposed only a Hall or publick Room; on Recollection I find it should be a large House or Inn, in the Nature of a College, with store of convenient Rooms for Gentlemen, not only to study separately, but wherein to lodge their Books, for 'twould be most inconvenient to lug them backwards and forwards: They may indeed Breakfast, Sup, and Sleep at Home, but 'twill be highly necessary they should dine in Commons, or at least near the College ; not that I would have Cooks, Butlers, Caterers, Manciples, and the whole Train of College Cannibals retained ; but for fear they should stay too long at Home, or be hindred from returning to Study in due time, some proper Place or Person might be pitch'd upon to keep an Ordinary at a prefix'd Price and Hour, and for the Students only.

Perhaps we may pause here. Defoe's projects and inventions are unending, and as he himself said : " All men are not historians, and even many of those that are, care for but a little reading at a time."

V

This is hardly the place in which to consider Defoe's literary style, nor am I the critic to attempt the task with any seriousness. But of Defoe it is exceptionally true that *Le style, c'est l'homme*, and perhaps a word may be allowed to the mere historian.

Defoe's writing has often been described as pedestrian. True enough, yet it moves with that sense of mastery which belongs only to the pedestrian who is perfectly ' fit,' and has exactly adapted his walk to his everyday requirements. Certainly Defoe would never have been surprised to learn that he had been talking prose all his life. He was not original, and he was honest. Sooner or later every known platitude in literature must have passed through his mind. He wrote as he thought, regardless of the fact that he often thought extremely badly. He would seem to have treasured in his memory every deadening maxim ever used for " preach-

ing down a daughter's heart." Yet through the platitudes
and the maxims glows his own inimitable sympathy, and his
own ineradicable honesty. He himself attributes his mastery
of language and his love of pure English to the " Dissenting
Academy " at Newington, where he also learned not to wish
to be a minister. Some scholars, he says, " preach away all
their hearers, for want of the English tongue," while another
" jingling noisy boy " " runs away with the whole town."
English to his mind should be " easy, free, plain, unaffected,
and untainted with force, stiffness, formality, affected hard
words." He is a good divine who follows his own instructions
as thoroughly as did Defoe. Honesty and a love of clarity
inspire all his scattered critical remarks, and most of his
practice. He hates the Puritans' habit of writing *D.V.* after an
engagement, and therefore thinking themselves more religious
than others, whereas it should be assumed among Christians
that "we all know, that unless the Lord will, I cannot meet,
nor so much as live." He hates commercial jargon, and his
mockery of a current business letter is hardly yet out of date,
as the following specimen may illustrate.

SIR,
Yours receiv'd, have at present little to reply. Last post you
had bills of loading with invoyce of what had loaden for your account
in Hambro' factor bound for said port. What have further orders
for shall be dispatched with expedition. Markets slacken much on
this side, cannot sell the iron for more than 35/– wish had your
orders if shall part with it at that rate. No ships since the 11th
London fleet may be in the roads before the late storm, so hope they
are safe; if have not ensur'd, please omit the same till hear farther:
the weather proving good hope the danger is over.
My last transmitted three bills exchange, import *l.*315, please
signify if are come to hand, and accepted, and give credit in account
current to
YOUR HUMBLE SERVANT

" Our shop-rhetorick," he says elsewhere, " is a strange
kind of speech," and he greatly dislikes this " tongue-padding
flutter "; " I much wonder the shop-keepers themselves do
not leave it off, for the meer shame of its simplicity and useless-
ness." He hates swearing for much the same reasons, and

rather naïvely apologises for quoting the *ipsissima verba* of the oaths which he deprecates. How else will his readers know exactly what he means? And down go the oaths in plain print! To him belongs that " easy free plainness which is the glory and excellency of the English tongue," and which made the fortunes of *Robinson Crusoe*, or *Captain Jack*.

It is a style which owes much to his precise and accurate knowledge of the subject in hand ; although simple in his use of it, Defoe was inordinately proud of the possession of knowledge. Like most writers who have been educated outside the orthodox channels of the universities, he was immensely proud of his upbringing, still prouder of his own ability to profit by it. According to his own account, he emerged with five languages or six to his credit, an intense interest in natural science, a belief in the excellency of philosophy, and a fervent love of history. Leibnitz on comets or Spanish geographers on obscure river-courses were his typical reading. To quote his own words, " He talked of the most distant countries with an inimitable exactness " ; the reader of *Robinson Crusoe* will not be disposed to dispute it. In all his descriptive writing we find that quality of exactness ; unfortunately for the historian it may equally well be the product of his fertile imagination, or of his acute observation. It is natural to compare the author of the *Tour through Great Britain* with Cobbett, the author of *Rural Rides*. But the comparison is unfavourable to Defoe. He records the facts precisely, carefully, sometimes vividly, but he cannot *see* what is the very breath of life to Cobbett—the corn just high enough to hide a hare, the closely mown grass walks or headlands around the corn, the hedges full of the shepherd's rose, the clouds flying over the hill, the coppices changing their hue from day to day during two whole months of spring, the setting sun sending his horizontal beams through all the variety of reds and yellows of the branches, and giving a sort of silver cast to the verdure beneath them —Defoe does not know that these things exist. He is born and bred a townsman. Cobbett can tell a tale to keep old men from the chimney-corner, young women from their beds ; Defoe's *Tour* is very easily laid aside. He has not that eye for beauty nor that ear for language which might lift his writing to a higher plane. He must be ranked with Arthur

Young rather than with Cobbett—valued for the wealth of his information rather than for the beauty of his prose.

We have said that Defoe's main contribution to political thought was the power to interpret Locke to the man in the street, to make his ideas the common foundation of citizenship. How can we sum up his importance as a social reformer—his value in the world of economic and social problems? Perhaps by quoting his own words of some of the early rulers of England: " Short-sighted and ignorant in the true greatness of a nation and the true power of a prince, they did not see that the strength of a kingdom consisted in the wealth of the subjects as well as in their numbers." Wealth, it must be remembered, to Defoe meant education as well as comfort. " How unhappily and wretchedly mean does it render our poor, when added to their native misery we find them utterly untaught." And if it be objected to him that some well-educated men (such as was King Henry the Eighth) are, as he himself admits, " a little given to dogmatising and being positive," " a little impatient in temper," Defoe retorts upon us triumphantly, " The credit of a good education suffers nothing by the ill use anyone may make of it." Let these reflections, like charity, cover the multitude of sins of which Daniel Defoe has been accused. Such thoughts were none too common in his times.

A. E. Levett

BIBLIOGRAPHY

A. Primary Sources

Bibliographies of Defoe are to be found in
(a) The *Cambridge History of English Literature*, vol. ix, pp. 418–433.
(b) The *Dictionary of National Biography* (incomplete).
The works from which direct quotations are drawn in this lecture are indicated in footnotes. References to dates and precise titles are taken, whenever possible, from the bibliography in the *Cambridge History of English Literature*.

B. Biographies and Critical Essays

Aitken, George A.: Contributions to periodicals—*e.g.*, *The Contemporary Review*, February 1890; *The Athenæum*, April 1889, August 1890. Introductions to Defoe's novels.

ENGLISH THINKERS OF THE AUGUSTAN AGE

CHALMERS, GEORGE : *Life of Daniel Defoe.* 1786.

DEFOE, DANIEL : *A Tour thro' the Whole Island of Great Britain.* Introduction by G. D. H. Cole. 2 vols. 1928.

DOTTIN, PAUL : *Daniel De Foe et ses romans.* 3 vols. 1924.

LEE, W. : *Life and Recently Discovered Writings of Daniel Defoe.* 3 vols. 1869.

MINTO, W. : *Defoe* (" English Men of Letters " series). 1879.

MORLEY, HENRY : *Defoe's Earlier Life and Chief Earlier Works.* 1890.

TRENT, W. P. : " Defoe : The Newspaper and the Novel," in *Cambridge History of English Literature,* vol. ix. 1912.

WILSON, W. : *Life and Times of Daniel Defoe.* 3 vols. 1830.

WRIGHT, T. : *Life of Daniel Defoe.* 1894.

YORK POWELL, F. : *Occasional Writings.* Ed. Oliver Elton. 1906.

VIII

JONATHAN SWIFT

JONATHAN SWIFT is to many so thoroughly objectionable a person that it is difficult to discuss his social and political ideas with that judicial calm which such a subject deserves, and especially so since his critics have ranged themselves into two parties: on the one side Dr Johnson, Macaulay, and Thackeray denouncing the man; on the other those who instinctively feel that anyone attacked by Dr Johnson, Macaulay, and Thackeray must necessarily have possessed many amiable qualities. Even his greatest admirers adopt a tone of apology or rhetorical eulogy. Had he written detachedly his personal character would have been unimportant, but, as Sir Leslie Stephen puts it, " no writer has ever been more thoroughly original than Swift, for his writings are simply himself," with the result that almost every one of his actions can be interpreted in different ways. While his admirers hold that the *Drapier's Letters* are the *sæua indignatio* of an honest man who hated a job, De Quincey went so far as to say that: " Of all Swift villainies for the sake of popularity, and still more for the sake of wielding his popularity vindictively, none is so scandalous as this."

Yet from the first Swift was thwarted. Indeed, even before he was born he had a grudge against his parents: his father's marriage, as he grumbled in his brief autobiography, was

> very indiscreet; for his wife brought her husband little or no fortune, and his death happening so suddenly before he could make a sufficient establishment for his family, his son (not then born) hath been often heard to say, that he felt the consequences of that marriage not only through the whole course of his education, but during the greatest part of his life.[1]

But it was Swift's habit to regard himself as that far-off event toward which the whole divine creation had hitherto moved.

[1] Printed in Sir Henry Craik's *Life of Jonathan Swift*, vol. ii.

Moreover, thanks to the indiscreet zeal of his nurse his natural precocity was so sharpened that by the time he was three years old he could read any chapter in the Bible.

Though his father had made no provision for the education of his unborn son, Godwin Swift, his uncle, did what he could, sending the boy to Kilkenny School, then reckoned the best in Ireland, and afterward to Trinity College, Dublin. This was in 1682. At the university Swift records

> by the ill treatment of his nearest relations, he was so discouraged and sunk in his spirits that he too much neglected his academic studies; for some parts of which he had no relish by nature, and turned himself to reading history and poetry: that when the time came for taking his degree of bachelor of arts, although he had lived with great regularity and due observance of the statutes, he was stopped of his degree for dullness and insufficiency; and at last hardly admitted in a manner little to his credit, which is called in that College, *speciali gratia*.

Swift is probably a little unfair to himself in imputing this failure to dullness; the proper word is boredom, for throughout his life he had the most complete contempt for speculations, metaphysical, philosophic, or financial. Failure only confirmed his belief that academic studies were the barren pastime of fools, and it bred in him an impatience for book learning which comes out again and again in his work, as, for instance, in his *Ode to Sir William Temple*.

> But what does our proud ignorance learning call?
> We oddly Plato's paradox make good,
> Our knowledge is but mere remembrance all;
> Remembrance is our treasure and our food;
> Nature's fair table-book, our tender souls,
> We scrawl all o'er with old and empty rules,
> Stale memorandums of the schools:
> For learning's mighty treasures look
> Into that deep grave, a book;
> Think that she there does all her treasures hide,
> And that her troubled ghost still haunts there since she died;
> Confine her walks to colleges and schools;
> Her priest, her train, and followers, show,
> As if they all were spectres too!
> They purchase knowledge at th' expense
> Of common breeding, common sense,
> And grow at once scholars and fools;
> Affect ill-manner's pedantry,
> Rudeness, ill-nature, incivility.

The same sentiments are expressed more virulently in *The Battle of the Books*, and with direct personal application many years later in the third Part of *Gulliver's Travels*.

After taking his B.A. degree Swift continued at Trinity College until 1688, when the revolution in England occurred, and he with other English Protestants, deciding that Ireland was no longer safe for them, fled to England. Swift went to Leicester to stay with his mother until some employment could be found for him. The Swift family had some claims on Sir William Temple, and when application was made he offered Swift a small post in his household, and so late in 1688 he presented himself at Moor Park.

For the next eleven years Swift was for most of the time in Temple's employ, though he left his patron's service twice; on the first occasion, in 1690, his health was bad, and, being recommended a change of air, he went over to Ireland, but he soon returned.

Swift's position in Temple's household gradually improved. He was trusted with important business by his patron, on one occasion even being sent to King William III to lay before him Temple's arguments in favour of the bill for triennial Parliaments; the King was not convinced. Still, it is not surprising that Swift should have expected some substantial promotion, but nothing happened, and in 1694 he quarrelled with his employer and went over to Ireland to seek ordination. But a country living in Ireland proved little to his taste, and when in 1696 Temple warmly invited him to return Swift once more entered Temple's service, but on a very different footing. It was during these last years at Moor Park that he wrote the two books which first brought him into prominence—*The Battle of the Books* and *A Tale of a Tub*, which was not, however, published until 1704.

The period with Temple was a most valuable training in every way, for it gave Swift an insight into the actual workings of politics, so that when he turned pamphleteer he could speak as an expert, and not as the scavenger of tattle thrown out from third-rate coffee-houses. With his patron himself he had little in common. Temple's

bland, stately, patronizing manners, his refined and somewhat over-fastidious taste, his instinctive shrinking from turmoil, conflict, and controversy, denoted a man who was a little weak and a little vain, and more fitted to shine in a Court than in a Parliament. . . . He had, however, real and solid talents, a rare experience both of men and affairs, a sound and moderate judgment in politics, a kindly and placid nature, and his life, if it had not been distinguished by splendid virtues, had, at least, been transparently pure in an age when political purity was very rare.[1]

The irritation set up by contact with such a man was not the least of the advantages of Swift's education at Moor Park, for it led him to contrast theories of life and politics with realities, and he was more than ever convinced that the generalities of intellectual systems were solemn and dull humbug. He expresses this feeling strongly in the preface to *A Tale of a Tub*. He wrote:

> In England you may securely display your utmost rhetoric against mankind, in the face of the world; tell them, "That all are gone astray; that there is none that doth good, no not one; that we live in the very dregs of time; that knavery and atheism are epidemic as the pox; that honesty is fled with Astræa"; with any other commonplaces, equally new and eloquent, which are furnished by the *splendida bilis*.[2] And when you have done, the whole audience, far from being offended, shall return you thanks as a deliverer of precious and useful truths. . . .
>
> But, on the other side, whoever should mistake the nature of things so far as to drop but a single hint in public, how such a one starved half the fleet, and half poisoned the rest: how such a one, from a true principle of love and honour, pays no debts but for wenches and plays: how such a one has got a clap, and runs out of his estate: how Paris, bribed by Juno and Venus, loth to offend either party, slept out the whole cause on the bench: or, how such an orator makes long speeches in the senate, with much thought, little sense, and to no purpose; whoever, I say, should venture to be thus particular, must expect to be imprisoned for *scandalum magnatum*; to have challenges sent him; to be sued for defamation; and to be brought before the bar of the house.

In an age when no one dared be particular writers were forced to conceal their true meanings under semi-transparent allegories, to use the subtle innuendo, to fight with the cloak and stiletto.

[1] Lecky's introduction to *A Tale of a Tub*, ed. Temple Scott (Bell, 1911).
[2] Horace, "spleen."

When Temple died, in 1699, he left Swift £100 and the pious duty of seeing his collected works through the press. This task was duly carried out; but though the collection was dedicated to King William, still Swift failed to win any practical reward. He was, however, offered a chaplaincy at Dublin Castle by Lord Berkeley, and shortly afterward appointed to the country living of Laracor, where with an average congregation of fifteen worshippers he found more than sufficient leisure. He was soon back in London.

So far Swift had kept out of politics, but in February 1701 a new Parliament met, and the Commons proposed to show its zeal for Toryism by impeaching William's Whig ministers, Lord Somers, the Earl of Portland, the Earl of Oxford, and Lord Halifax. The House of Lords, however, was on the side of the late ministers, and an awkward constitutional crisis was only prevented by a prorogation of Parliament. Swift by instinct was with the Tories, who stood mainly for the Church and the county gentry against the financiers and Dissenters of the Whigs, but it was only natural that Temple's *protégé* should still have kept some sympathy for the King's party. Accordingly he wrote *A Discourse of the Contests and Dissensions between the Nobles and the Commons in Athens and Rome, with the Consequences they had upon Both those States*— a formal thesis, on familiar academic lines, applying the lessons of classical history to the immediate problem. The argument rested on the theory of a balance of power between the three forms of government, the King, or executive, the Senate of men of wealth, and the Commons; and between these " it will be an eternal rule, in politics among every free people, that there is a balance of power to be carefully held by every state within itself, as well as among several states with each other."

So long as the balance is preserved all is well, but if the balance be upset, and the Commons become uncontrolled, then they are capable " of enslaving the nation, and of acting all manner of tyranny and oppression, as it is possible for a single person to be, though we should suppose their number not only to be of four or five hundred, but above three thousand."

As for the practice of impeaching the nobility, though theoretically the inherent right of a free people, yet in practice it had the effect of driving the best men out of political life.

N

Such is Swift's argument, which gains not a little from the level sobriety of its tone. The anonymous pamphlet sold well, had a marked effect on public opinion, and was attributed to various illustrious Whigs. When it became known that he had written it the Whig Lords expressed gratitude, and promised to show it in some practical way should the country return their party to power.

Three years later, in 1704, Swift published *A Tale of a Tub*, which is usually considered his most brilliant work; indeed, Professor Saintsbury (the last of our universal epicures, albeit a lover of strong meat) declares it to be " one of the very greatest books of the world, one of those in which a great drift of universal thought receives a consummate literary form." There may perhaps be a touch of exaggeration in this judgment, but then the *Tale* is not every one's book, and those who are shocked by the audacious allegory of Peter, Jack, and Martin are not in a fit mood to appreciate the greatness of the digressions. Though the ideal critic can approach it with absolute detachment, to simpler souls who regard their religion as too sacred to be ridiculed it is a monstrous heap of ribald blasphemy. That at least was the opinion of Queen Anne, to whom Swift's enemies took care to show the book, arguing, not without some show of reason, that the man who could so anatomise the Christian religion was scarcely fitted to be one of its bishops. In the light of Swift's later career, his champions have defended the *Tale* as a fine attack on hypocrisy in religion made by a loyal son of the Church of England who sees her failings but yet remains true to her. It may be so, but it must have been difficult for the original reader, who was ignorant of the author's name, to have realised the devotion to Christianity pulsating in the veins of one who allegorises the early history of the three main sects of Christianity thus :

Being now arrived at the proper age for producing themselves they came up to town, and fell in love with the ladies, but especially three, who at that time were in chief reputation; the Duchess D'Argent, Madame de Grands Titres, and the Countess D'Orgueil. On their first appearance our three adventurers met with a very bad reception; and soon with great sagacity guessing out the reason, they quickly began to improve in the good qualities of the town; they wrote, and rallied, and rhymed, and sung, and said, and said nothing; they drank, and fought, and whored, and slept, and swore, and took snuff; they went to new plays on the first night, haunted the chocolate-houses, beat the watch, lay on bulks, and got the claps; they bilked hackney-coachmen, ran into debt with shopkeepers, and lay with their wives; they killed bailiffs, kicked fiddlers downstairs, eat at Locket's, loitered at Will's; they talked of the drawing room, and never came there; dined with lords they never saw; whispered a duchess, and never spoke a word; exposed the scrawls of their laundress for *billets-doux* of quality; ever came first from court, and were never seen in it; attended the levee *sub dio*; got a list of peers by heart in one company, and with great familiarity retailed them in another.

The answer to the charge of atheism is that Swift was strict in his observances, an exemplary and charitable dean; but then active belief in the divine origin of the Church has never been an essential part of the decanal function. The case can be argued indefinitely; but this much is barely disputable, that *A Tale of a Tub* gives more pleasure to sceptics than to believers, and that Swift was conspicuously lacking in the quality of spirituality; he was never one of those philosophers who trip into the ditch while following the stars. On the contrary, he continually fixed his attention on the gutter and delighted to paddle in the sewage on every occasion.

At the same time, it must be remembered that in the eighteenth century the orthodox Churchman regarded the Church rather as part of a divine system than as the mouth-piece of a divine revelation:

> The spacious firmament on high,
> With all the blue etherial sky,
> And spangled heavens, a shining frame,
> Their great original proclaim. . . .
>
> What though in solemn silence all
> Move round the dark terrestrial ball;
> What though nor real voice nor sound
> Amidst their radiant orbs be found?
>
> In *Reason's* ear they all rejoice,
> And utter forth a glorious voice;
> For ever singing as they shine,
> " The Hand that made us is divine."

195

Swift's next prominent appearance in print was in 1707, when Dr King, Archbishop of Dublin, sent him over to negotiate for a share of Queen Anne's bounty to be given to Ireland. During this stay in London Swift wrote three of his better-known pamphlets, *An Argument to prove the Inconvenience of abolishing Christianity*, *A Project for the Advancement of Religion*, and *The Sentiments of a Church of England Man*.

An Argument to prove that the Abolishing of Christianity in England may, as Things now stand, be attended with some Inconveniences, and perhaps not produce those Many Good Effects proposed thereby, is perhaps a deliberate attempt to show that he could use his irony as effectively on the side of Christianity as against it.

He raises a number of mock objections to Christianity, and then with complete gravity answers them, showing that the principal accusations urged against established Christianity are after all due to the natural defects of mankind; and if all causes of religious controversy were to be removed by destroying religion, then other pretexts for quarrelling would soon be found.

Admirable as is Swift's *Argument* to a Churchman, the next pamphlet on the same subject, *A Project for the Advancement of Religion and the Reformation of Manners*, must fill him with a sense of uneasiness. The argument reads simply enough; the Queen herself is renowned for piety, charity, temperance, conjugal love, and whatever virtues best adorn a private life. Princes therefore should make it " every man's interest and honour to cultivate religion and virtue; by rendering vice a disgrace and the certain ruin to preferment or pretensions; all which they should first attempt in their own courts." If effective steps were taken to purge the Court of vice, then morality and religion would soon become fashionable Court virtues.

A board of advisory censors might be created, after the old Roman pattern, to examine the moral conduct at least of all men in office, and in every institution in the country piety and virtue should be enforced by the law. In short, the universal corruption of the age was not to be reformed in

any other way than by introducing religion as much as possible to be the turn and fashion of the age, which only lies in the power of the

196

administration; the prince with utmost strictness regulating the court, the ministry, and other persons in great employment; and these, by their example and authority, reforming all who have dependence on them.

It has usually been assumed that Swift meant all this seriously; Dr Johnson, for instance, taking the pamphlet at its face value objected that, like many projects, " it is, if not generally impracticable, yet evidently hopeless, as it supposes more zeal, concord and perseverance than a view of mankind gives reason for expecting."

If Swift was indeed in earnest the pamphlet shows that by religion he meant a system of conduct enforced by the State; it reveals in him a faith in human institutions which would not be suspected from his other writings. But Dr Johnson and the rest of the critics who agree with him are deceived; this is but another example of Swift's subtle irony. The real purpose of the pamphlet was to draw attention to the licentiousness of the age, the corruption of the Government, and by implication the desirability of a change. Simplicity was never one of Swift's failings.

But of the three pamphlets the most important is *The Sentiments of a Church of England Man*, which expresses clearly and soberly Swift's attitude as a Churchman toward the State and the two political parties.

As for parties,

a Church of England man may, with prudence and a good conscience, approve the professed principles of one party more than the other, according as he thinks they best promote the good of church and state; but he will never be swayed by passion or interest to advance an opinion merely because it is that of the party he most approves; which one single principle he looks upon as the root of all our civil animosities. To enter into a party, as into an Order of friars, with so resigned an obedience to superiors, is very unsuitable both with the civil and religious liberties we so zealously assert.

But the State is supreme even when the very existence of the Church is threatened.

A Church of England man has a true veneration for the scheme established among us of ecclesiastical government; and though he will not determine whether episcopacy be of divine right, he is sure it is most agreeable to primitive institution, fittest of all others for preserving order and purity, and, under its present regulations, best calculated for our civil state; he should therefore think the abolishment of that order among us would prove a mighty scandal and corruption to our faith, and manifestly dangerous to our monarchy; nay, he would defend it by arms against all the powers on earth, except our own legislature; in which case he would submit, as to a general calamity, a dearth, or a pestilence.

These principles Swift followed, leaving the Whigs when he thought that they were too friendly with the Dissenters, though it may be that he regarded their failure to promote Jonathan Swift to be Bishop of Waterford as one of several notable signs of their open hostility to the Church of England.

In 1709 the Whig party were generally losing ground in the country. The war with Louis XIV still continued, and Marlborough tactlessly demanded the position of Captain-General for life; but the Queen refused, and when this proposal was made public there was much indignation, opponents of the Ministry suspecting, or working themselves up to suspect, that Marlborough had hoped to become a second Cromwell. Nor were the attempts of the Whigs to win over the Dissenters successful, for the clergy of the Established Church became more violent than ever in their denunciation of Nonconformity.

Matters came to a head with the impeachment of Dr Sacheverell, who had preached very abusive sermons against the Government. A solemn prosecution before the Bar of the House was decreed; the doctor became a political martyr, riots against the Dissenters followed, and though Sacheverell was condemned by a majority of the House of Lords so slight a sentence was imposed that he was considered to have triumphed. In the autumn the Whig Ministry was dismissed, and in the election which followed the Tories were returned to power with a large majority.

Swift returned to London in September 1710, and for the next four years it is possible, thanks to the *Journal to Stella*, to follow his movements from day to day. Both sides were anxious to have the support of so dangerous a writer, but his sympathies were with the Tories on matters of principle, and he owed nothing to the Whigs—except a grudge. He wrote to Stella on September 30:

> It is good to see what a lamentable confession the Whigs all make of my ill usage, but I mind them not. I am already represented to Harley as a discontented person, that was used ill for not being Whig enough; and I hope for good usage from him. The Tories drily tell me I may make my fortune if I please; but I do not understand them, or rather I *do* understand them.

The following day he was finishing off his lampoon, *Sid Hamet*, on the Earl of Godolphin, and on the next he dined with Lord Halifax.

> Lord Halifax began a health to me to-day: it was the resurrection of the Whigs, which I refused, unless he would add their reformation too: and I told him he was the only Whig in England I loved, or had any good opinion of.

Within a week Harley received him.

> I must tell you a great piece of refinement of Harley. He charged me to come to him often: I told him I was loth to trouble him in so much business as he had, and desired I might have leave to come at his levee; which he immediately refused, and said, "That was not a place for friends to come to."

Swift held no office, and was unrewarded with any sinecure, but for all that he made himself indispensable to the Tory ministers as their unofficial Director-General of propaganda at a time when the political pamphlet was the chief weapon in party warfare.

At the beginning of November he took over the *Examiner*, and for seven months contributed a weekly paper explaining the actions of the Government.

In the first of these papers (*Examiner*, No. 14) he outlined the objections to the National Debt. Three weeks later he answered the Whig argument that a change of Government at home would embarrass the Duke of Marlborough in his conduct of the campaign abroad, and was moreover a flagrant mark of the nation's ingratitude to that great commander. Swift suggested that, compared with the treatment of Roman conquerors, Marlborough could scarcely complain; and this he demonstrated by drawing up a balance-sheet of Roman gratitude and British ingratitude.

A BILL OF ROMAN GRATITUDE	£	s.	d.
Imprimis, for frankincense, and earthen pots to burn it in	4	10	0
A bull for sacrifice	8	0	0
An embroidered garment	50	0	0
A crown of laurel	0	0	2
A statue	100	0	0
A trophy	80	0	0
A thousand copper medals, value halfpence a-piece	2	1	8
A triumphal arch	500	0	0
A triumphal car, valued as a modern coach	100	0	0
Casual charges at the triumph	150	0	0
	£994	11	10

A BILL OF BRITISH INGRATITUDE	£
Imprimis, Woodstock	40,000
Blenheim	200,000
Post-office grant	100,000
Mildenheim	30,000
Pictures, jewels, etc.	60,000
Pall-mall grants, etc.	10,000
Employments	100,000
	£540,000

But in the scuffle of a trench raid general principles of strategy may sometimes be overlooked, and in the papers in the *Examiner* Swift was more concerned with hitting his immediate opponents and guarding against their counter-attacks than in displaying any philosophical system of Toryism. He gave up the *Examiner* in June 1711, when the secret of his authorship could no longer be kept.

Meanwhile the reaction against the Tories was setting in, and the Queen was known to be encouraging the Whigs about Court. The Tory party proposed to bring the war to an end; the Whigs replied that peace would be without honour or advantage, and their pamphleteers opened a hot fire. In the autumn of 1711 Swift busied himself writing the most important of his political pamphlets, *The Conduct of the Allies*.

The Conduct of the Allies was the official reply to the critics of the Government, and in writing it Swift had the help of Harley (now Earl of Oxford) and other ministers. It was a masterly piece of work, with the arguments set out with clarity and force to prove three points:

Firstly, That, against all manner of prudence or common reason, we engaged in this war as principals, when we ought to have acted only as auxiliaries.

Secondly, That we spent all our vigour in pursuing that part of the war which could least answer the end we proposed by beginning it; and made no efforts at all where we could have most weakened the common enemy, and at the same time enriched ourselves.

Lastly, That we suffered each of our allies to break every article in those treaties and agreements by which they were bound, and to lay the burden upon us.

The detailed arguments are too intricate to have much interest for any but students of history, but in the main Swift contended that there never had been any solid advantage in the war except to benefit the Dutch and to increase the fame and wealth of the Duke of Marlborough. Moreover, far from gaining by ultimate victory, England was but piling up a National Debt, conquering a noble territory for the States, where every encouragement would be given to introduce and improve manufactures, and this was the only advantage they wanted; this gain added to their skill, industry, and parsimony would enable them to undersell us in every market in the world.

The war had only been continued because of the understanding between the allies and the Duke of Marlborough for their mutual advantage, the greed of financiers who were profiting heavily, and the designs of the Whigs, who feared to lose their employment in a peace. In short, the action of the Tory ministers in seeking to end the war was a patriotic move, and directly against their private interest.

Negotiations went on, but the Peace of Utrecht was not signed until April 1713, and then Swift claimed his reward. A bishopric was out of the question, but there were other possibilities, and for some days he was kept in tantalising suspense, not knowing whether he would get a stall at Windsor, the Deanery of St Patrick's, or nothing. However, on the 27th the warrant appointing him to Dublin was passed, and he was duly installed at St Patrick's on June 13. But he was back again in London by the middle of September, for the Ministry was in a bad state: Bolingbroke and Oxford were quarrelling;

a new election was imminent, and the Whigs had more electioneering ammunition than their opponents. Swift returned to the battle, and attacked Steele in *The Importance of the Guardian*, and *The Public Spirit of the Whigs*, an answer to Steele's pamphlet *The Crisis*. Steele had tried to raise the bogey that the Tory party was flirting with the Pretender, and he also took occasion to eulogise the Union with Scotland. Swift contemptuously refuted the first, and made such bitter observations on the Scots that on the first publication of this pamphlet all the Scottish lords then in London went in a body and complained to Queen Anne of the affront put on them and their nation by the author of this treatise; whereupon a proclamation was published, offering a reward of £300 for discovering him.

Swift was still in London in the following spring, and with Gay, Pope, and Arbuthnot founded the Scriblerus Club, which had only a brief period of existence, but begat two important literary works, *The Dunciad* and the first draft of *Gulliver's Travels*.

The Tory party was now breaking up beyond repair, and Swift could endure its failure no longer. He left London, and took refuge with an old friend in a Berkshire rectory, and thence he wrote a valedictory letter to Bolingbroke, which is his own epitaph on the four years of his political supremacy.

> Will you give me leave to say how I would desire to stand in your memory? As one who was truly sensible of the honour you did him, though he was too proud to be vain upon it; as one who was neither assuming, officious, nor teasing; who never wilfully misrepresented persons or facts to you, nor consulted his passions when he gave a character; and lastly, as one whose indiscretions proceeded altogether from a weak head, and not an ill heart. I will add one thing more, which is the highest compliment I can make, that I never was afraid of offending you, nor am now in any pain for the manner I write to you in. I have said enough; and, like one at your levee, having made my bow, I shrink back into the crowd.

A noble epitaph; but not impartial.

On August 1, 1714, Queen Anne died; and that was the end of the Tory party and Swift's political career.

Swift therefore returned to his deanery, and for some years took no further part in politics, being occupied in more personal matters. For at this time occurred the tragedy of Vanessa, which was distraction enough. But in 1721 he emerged as the champion of Irish rights, though to Swift the Irish were the Protestants ; he had no sympathy for Catholics, and would have extirpated them. Ireland had indeed been scandalously treated, and the genuine grievances can best be summed up in the words of a letter which Swift sent to the Earl of Peterborough on April 28, 1726 :

> I think it manifest that whatever circumstances can possibly contribute to make a country poor and despicable are all united with respect to Ireland. The nation controlled by laws to which they do not consent, disowned by their brethren and countrymen, refused the liberty not only of trading with their own manufactures, but even their native commodities, forced to seek for justice many hundred miles by sea and land, rendered in a manner incapable of serving their king and country in any employment of honour, trust, or profit; and all this without the least demerit; while the governors sent over thither can possibly have no affection to the people further than what is instilled into them by their own justice and love of mankind, which do not always operate; and whatever they please to represent hither is never called in question.

The grievances of the Irish came to a head with the affair of Wood's halfpence. There was great shortage of small change in Ireland, and a petition had been presented that Ireland should be allowed her own Mint. This was refused by Walpole, now chief minister, and instead a patent was granted to the King's mistress to provide forty thousand pounds' worth of halfpence and farthings. The lady passed the patent on to Mr Wood for £10,000, who proceeded to mint the coins and ship them over to Ireland, to the furious indignation of the Irish.

Swift now entered the controversy with the famous *Drapier's Letters*, in which, under the guise of a certain " M. D. Drapier," he expressed and accentuated the bitterness of the Irish by an appeal to ignorance and prejudice, punctuated with all the emphasis of large capitals and copious italics. In the first letter, for instance, the Drapier declared that in England halfpence and farthings pass for very little more than they are worth, so that if you beat them to pieces and sell them to a brazier you would not lose above a penny in a shilling. But Mr Wood made his halfpence of such base metal and so much smaller than the English ones that the brazier would not give you above a penny of good money for a shilling of it. He reckoned, too, that if a farmer had £100 of rent to pay he would require six hundred pounds in weight of the new coins, that is, the load for three horses, while Squire C—— with his £16,000 a year would need two hundred and fifty horses to bring up his rent to town.

To appease the agitation a royal proclamation was issued, in which the King promised to do everything in his power for the satisfaction of his people. Wood's coins were assayed at the Mint, and found to be as good as the English copper money, and actually heavier than the weight stipulated in the patent.

In answer to this somewhat convincing test the Drapier wrote a second letter, changing the direction of his attack, accusing Wood of buying up the debased Irish copper coinage in order to cause a shortage, and roundly denouncing him for proposing that only $5\frac{1}{2}d$. in copper should be legally compulsory in any exchange. The second letter itself confutes the arguments of the first, but no matter for that. In the third he examined and disputed the points raised in the Privy Council report in more detail.

Regarded as an isolated incident, Swift's attack on Wood's halfpence in the first three of the *Drapier's Letters* appears a somewhat discreditable business. The copper coins were genuinely needed, and Wood fulfilled his contract honestly. There is much in these letters which savours of deliberate misrepresentation, if not hard lying. But Swift was not so utterly unscrupulous as his enemies pretended ; he fomented the agitation deliberately to draw attention to the scandalous way in which English politicians regarded Ireland as a mere Tom Tiddler's ground for their friends. But in the fourth letter, addressed to the whole people of Ireland, the Drapier goes beyond the immediate question of Wood's halfpence to declare that Ireland was an independent kingdom, and that the question was for the Irish to decide.

> The remedy is wholly in your own hands, and therefore I have digressed a little in order to refresh and continue that spirit so seasonably raised among you, and to let you see that, by the laws of GOD, of NATURE, of NATIONS, and of your COUNTRY, you ARE and OUGHT to be as FREE a people as your brethren in England

The *Drapier's Letters* showed that Swift had lost none of his old skill in saying exactly the right thing to appeal to the audience of the moment, but he was no longer moved by any personal ambitions, though the fact that the Whigs were still in power in England did not detract from his zest in writing them. But these and the rest of his Irish pamphlets were inspired by a genuine sympathy with the distresses of the Irish people, and imbued with a true appreciation of the causes. These feelings he expresses most clearly in his little pamphlet, *A Short View of the State of Ireland, 1727*, in which he lays down fourteen points of prosperity in a nation, none of which were enjoyed by the Irish. He drops for a moment into his old vein of irony to describe the envy and admiration which might be excited in the breasts of the Commissioners who come from England, but he finds the strain unbearable.

> My heart is too heavy to continue this irony longer, for it is manifest that whatever stranger took such a journey would be apt to think himself travelling in Lapland or Ysland rather than in a country so favoured by nature as ours, both in fruitfulness of soil and temperature of climate. The miserable dress and diet, and dwelling of the people; the general desolation in most parts of the Kingdom; the old seats of the nobility and gentry all in ruins and no new ones in their stead; the families of farmers, who pay great rents, living in filth and nastiness upon buttermilk and potatoes, without a shoe or stocking to their feet, or a house so convenient as an English hogsty to receive them. These indeed may be comfortable sights to an English spectator, who comes for a short time, only to learn the language, and returns back to his own country, whither he finds all his wealth transmitted.

As an English politician Swift effected little if anything of permanent value; but in Ireland " he first taught the Irish people to rely upon themselves." [1]

And then there is *Gulliver's Travels*, wherein Time has taken its revenges, and Fate defeated Swift at his own game of irony; turning his satire on humanity into a favourite tale for children who will misunderstand his meaning, and seldom read another word of his writing.

Gulliver's Travels was composed at two different periods.

[1] Lecky, *op. cit.*, p. lxxix.

The original version was begun in 1714 as part of the memoirs of Martinus Scriblerus; but it was unfinished when Swift returned to Ireland, and for some years the manuscript lay incomplete, though from time to time Swift took it up, altering and adding to the tales which now became a running commentary on the politics of the last twelve years. As a result, the book sometimes changes its form and becomes inconsistent. Lilliput begins as Utopia, but turns into England when Gulliver comes to describe its customs. Similarly Gulliver's fate at the hands of the Lilliputians mirrors Bolingbroke's treatment by the Whigs; he too was forced to take refuge with the enemy because his own people had decided to put him to death by judicial process.[1]

The fourth Part—Gulliver's adventures among the Houyhnhnms—has seldom found very hearty admirers, for critics and readers finding themselves included among the unpleasant horde of the Yahoos hasten to defend their species against such savage malignity. Yet it is with this fourth Part that Swift can chiefly claim to be included among the social and political thinkers of the Augustan Age.

Swift contrasts the two races: the one a debased humanity, the other an exalted equinity. The Yahoos at their worst may not seem much like ourselves, yet the race is not extinct, and should a Communist declare himself in Whitehall on Armistice Day the horde would soon swarm out to join in the chase. Nor were Swift's Yahoos very different from the real Irish who saluted his coach with stones when he first entered Dublin as Dean of St Patrick's. When Gulliver relates that the only differences between the Yahoos and himself are his clothing, his whiter skin, and his less efficient fingers he is but declaring a melancholy truth which the younger generation learned ten years ago, that civilisation is but skin deep, and the brute barely concealed behind social customs. I have myself seen men reduced by hunger to eating grass, and children fighting over camp refuse; their manners were disgusting.

Contrasted with these creatures are the horses living that blameless existence which rationalists rediscover every other generation as a new ideal. If this is Swift's New Jerusalem

---

[1] The parallels and allusions are worked out by Sir Charles Firth in *The Political Significance of " Gulliver's Travels "* (*Proceedings of the British Academy,* vol. iv).

it is some way from the happy home of the Church of England man.

The horses, for instance, are agnostics; " because reason taught us to affirm or deny only where we are certain; and beyond our knowledge, we cannot do either." They marry on eugenic principles;

> they are exactly careful to choose such colours as will not make any disagreeable mixture in the breed. Strength is chiefly valued in the male, and comeliness in the female; not upon the account of love, but to preserve the race from degenerating; for where a female happens to excel in strength, a consort is chosen with regard to comeliness.

Birth-control is practised, the allowance of young being apparently two. The institution of the family is despised :

> Friendship and benevolence are the two principal virtues among the Houyhnhnms, and these not confined to particular objects, but universal to the whole race; for a stranger from the remotest parts is equally treated with his nearest neighbour, and wherever he goes he looks upon himself as at home. They preserve decency and civility in the highest degrees, but are altogether ignorant of ceremony. They have no fondness for their colts or foals, but the care they take in educating them proceeds entirely from the dictates of reason. And I observed my master to show the same affection to his neighbour's issue that he had for his own. They will have it that nature teaches them to love the whole species, and it is reason only that makes a distinction of persons, where there is a superior degree of virtue.

In education both sexes are treated alike ; Gulliver's master

> thought it monstrous in us to give the females a different kind of education from the males, except in some articles of domestic management; whereby, as he truly observed, one half of our natives were good for nothing but bringing children into the world: and to trust the care of our children to such useless animals, he said, was yet a greater instance of brutality.

The horses too had some inkling of the evolutionary process ; some of them had evidently suggested that the Yahoos were originally produced by the heat of the sun upon corrupted mud and slime, or from the ooze and froth of the sea. Finally they never feel ill because they use a natural diet; when they die, they do it without lamentation or fuss, and

> are buried in the obscurest places that can be found, their friends and relations expressing neither joy nor grief at their departure; nor does the dying person discover the least regret that he is leaving the world, any more than if he were returning home from a visit to one of his neighbours.

The conclusion, then, is that the Yahoos are men as Swift saw them, as repulsive in their social and political morality as in their physical brutality, fundamentally incapable of reason or improvement.

Believing thus, Swift had little in common with the political theorists of his age. For political speculation needs two qualities: vision to conceive a better state and optimism to believe it possible. Swift had neither. He regarded the political philosopher as one who has reached " the sublime and refined point of felicity, called the possession of being well deceived; the serene peaceful state of being a fool amongst knaves."

Nor was he an optimist. He saw that the real obstacle to all social theories was the Yahoo in human nature, and until that is eliminated the Golden Age must remain adjourned *sine die*. Two alternatives are possible: the one is education, which is hopeless; the other is the solution put forward in the *Modest Proposal for preventing the Children of Poor People in Ireland from being a Burden to their Parents or Country*. This also is no solution, because the Yahoos exist in every class. To Swift, in short, the problem was insoluble. And being an honest pessimist, he refused to drug his reason. If there was a solution it was not to be found in Utopia or among the mystics. But he could not leave it alone; and where other men are led by their creeds and visions Swift was driven on by a despairing rage to do something to mend the public by attacking particular abuses.

He died, as he was born, thwarted; partly by circumstances, partly by physical and mental disease. His ambition was boundless, but he never knew what he wanted, and he had the critic's curse of always seeing the flaws. But with these misfortunes he committed two capital errors: the first was the writing of *A Tale of a Tub*, the second when he was ordained a priest in the Church of England. By the one he was kept from preferment in the Church; by the other from office in the State. His earlier instinct for a literary career was right, but, as it happened, in the years when he was struggling for existence he was caught in the political machine and held whirling. Twice he escaped from Temple; when he entered his service for the third time he might well have noted the day in his calendar with this epitaph : *Qualis artifex pereo.*

G. B. Harrison

BIBLIOGRAPHY

The prose works of Jonathan Swift, edited by Temple Scott, etc., with a biographical introduction by W. E. H. Lecky. London, 1894–1908.

Boyle, J., fifth Earl of Cork and Orrery: *Remarks on the Life and Writings of Jonathan Swift.* 1752.

Craik, Sir Henry : *The Life of Jonathan Swift.* 2 vols. London, 1894.

Firth, Sir Charles : *The Political Significance of "Gulliver's Travels"* (reprinted from the *Proceedings of the British Academy*). London, 1920.

Stephen, Sir Leslie : *Swift* ("English Men of Letters" series). London, 1882.

Stevens, D. H. : *Party Politics and English Journalism, 1702–42.* 1916.

o

HENRY ST JOHN, VISCOUNT BOLINGBROKE

O F all the political thinkers of the Augustan Age none was so eminent or so highly applauded during his life, none so profoundly despised or generally rejected after his death, as Henry St John, the Lord Viscount Bolingbroke. To his contemporaries, in the days of his magnificent prime, he seemed to be the embodiment of all that was splendid and effective among men. High in rank, handsome in person, stately in deportment, polished in manners, cultivated in mind, quick in wit, fascinating in conversation, unrivalled in oratorical power, a scholar, a linguist, a bold and original speculator, a capable administrator, a skilled diplomatist, a dæmonic actor, a finished courtier and man of the world—he appeared to be almost superhuman in his gifts and graces, or, at the very least, " not one, but all mankind's epitome." Jonathan Swift, who was not too well disposed toward the human race at large, said of him when he was still youthful (in a letter to Stella, November 3, 1711) that he was the greatest young man he ever knew, marked by wit, capacity, beauty, quickness of apprehension, good learning, and excellent taste ; the best orator in the House of Commons, admirable conversation, good nature and good manners, generous, and a despiser of money. A quarter of a century later Alexander Pope, also inclined to general misanthropy, writing to Swift, said (March 25, 1736) :

> I have lately seen some writings of Lord B's, since he went to France. Nothing can depress his genius. Whatever befalls him, he will still be the greatest man in the world, either in his own time, or with posterity.

Shortly afterward, in a letter to Bolingbroke himself (September 3, 1740) he exclaimed, with an amusing play upon his own name, " I would, if I were Pope, canonize you, what-

ever all the advocates for the devil could say to the contrary."
Chesterfield's eulogy is well known.   In a letter to his son he
wrote :

> I have sent you Lord Bolingbroke's *Letters on Patriotism* and
> *The Idea of a Patriot King*, which he published about a year ago.
> I desire that you will read these letters over and over again, with
> particular attention to the style, and to all those beauties of oratory
> with which they are adorned.   Till I read that book, I confess I did
> not know all the extent and powers of the English language.   Lord
> Bolingbroke has both a tongue and a pen to persuade; his manner of
> speaking in private conversation is full as elegant as his writings.
> Whatever subject he either speaks or writes upon, he adorns it with
> the most splendid eloquence; not in studied or laboured eloquence,
> but such a flowing happiness of diction as—perhaps from care at
> first—is become so habitual to him that even his most familiar con-
> versations, if taken down in writing, would bear the press, without
> the least correction either as to method or style.

After some remarks on the vicissitudes of his career he
continued :

> He has an infinite fund of various and almost universal knowledge
> which, from the clearest and quickest conception and happiest memory
> that ever man was blessed with, he always carries about him. . . .
> He engaged young, and distinguished himself in business; and his
> penetration was almost intuition.   I am old enough to have heard
> him speak in Parliament,[1] and I remember that, though prejudiced
> against him by party, I felt all the force and charms of his elo-
> quence. . . . All the internal and external advantages and talents
> of an orator are undoubtedly his.   Figure, voice, elocution, know-
> ledge, and above all the purest and most florid diction, with the
> justest metaphors and happiest images, had raised him to the post of
> Secretary-at-War at four-and-twenty years old, an age at which others
> are hardly thought fit for the smallest employments.

Bolingbroke himself deliberately and avowedly wrote for
posterity, and his editors confidently predicted for him a literary
immortality.   For instance, the anonymous author of his
Memoirs, published the year after his decease, said, " Death,
in removing him out of the reach of envy and the rage of
jealousy, has extended the utility and fixed the immortality of
his writings," adding, " His writings are the monuments which

---

[1] Bolingbroke's last speech in Parliament was delivered on March 17, 1715.

he consecrated to posterity; and, though he is now no more, these will last for ever."

II

The spell, however, which Bolingbroke cast over his contemporaries by the charm of his person, the graces of his behaviour, and the brilliance of his gifts did not long survive him. Nay, for some years before his death, when he lived retired in his ancestral home at Battersea (1744–51) he himself realised, with deep chagrin, that he was becoming isolated and impotent in an alien world. Young men, like William Pitt, who had been attracted to him by the magic of his reputation, drifted away as they found that he had no further contribution to make either to the political and social, or to the philosophical and religious, problems of their age. The spell of Bolingbroke's unquestionable genius was, in fact, broken while he was yet alive, by, first, the notorious depravity of his private conduct; secondly, his obvious lack of political principle; thirdly, the violence and factiousness of his restless and relentless antagonism to Walpole and the Whigs; fourthly, the palpable impracticability of his constitutional proposals; and, finally, his doubtful attitude toward the Christian religion. The publication of his posthumous writings, under the injudicious editorship of David Mallet, in 1754, completed the ruin of his reputation. The first two volumes showed that where he was not an unscrupulous party politician, seeking by all means to justify himself and inculpate his enemies, he was a mere empty rhetorician, propounding with pompous prolixity the emptiest platitudes. The remaining three volumes displayed him fully, for the first time, as the inveterate and envenomed foe of Christianity; as the repudiator of both revelation and immortality; as the vehement rejector of most of the articles of the creed of the Church on whose behalf he had in the days of his power persecuted and proscribed Dissenters. What the Whig bishops thought of him may best be seen in William Warburton's *View of Lord Bolingbroke's Philosophy* (1756). What even the pious Tories, who had at one time looked up to him as their champion, came to think of him is shown by Dr Johnson's severe judgment: " Sir," he said to Boswell, " he was a scoundrel and a coward: a scoundrel, for charging a blunderbuss against religion and morality; a coward, because he had not resolution to fire it off himself, but left half a crown to a beggarly Scotchman to draw the trigger after his death." Thus Bolingbroke became the shadow of an evil name, condemned for his immorality, hated for his irreligion, rejected for his political impossibility, despised for his rhetorical superficiality. Only forty years after his death, Edmund Burke asked, respecting those very works whose immortality had been so confidently predicted, "Who now reads Bolingbroke? Who ever read him through?" adding, "I do not often quote Bolingbroke, nor have his works in general left any permanent impression on my mind. He is a presumptuous and a superficial writer."

The note thus struck in the late eighteenth century by Warburton, Johnson, Burke, and their fellows, was reiterated in the nineteenth century, particularly by the Whig historians. To Macaulay Bolingbroke appeared to be merely " a brilliant knave." Carlyle described his works as " lacquered brass." Sir Leslie Stephen characterised them as " a mass of insincere platitudes," and their writer as " a showy actor." Lord Morley condemned him as " a charlatan—a bankrupt politician—a shipwrecked adventurer—a consummate posture-maker." Mr Walter Bagehot regarded insincerity and speciousness as the outstanding features of his works. Mr J. M. Robertson speaks of him as " a *condottiere*—without fixed principle or aim—unscrupulous—an adroit parliamentary swordsman, a forensic debater, but not a true thinker."

III

Such was the chorus of late Hanoverian and Victorian detraction. There can be no doubt that its note of condemnation was as much exaggerated and over-emphasised as had been the uncritical adulation of the Tories of the days of Swift, or the ' Patriots ' of the days of Pope. Bolingbroke unquestionably had the defects of his qualities; but he also had the qualities of his defects. That is to say, if he was immoral, he was also strikingly free from debilitating convention—fresh, original, emancipated: no Puritan, even when inebriated, would have run, as Bolingbroke is said to have done, naked

213

through St James's Park. Again, if he lacked political principle, he was prolific in political ideas and fruitful in political expedients.   If he was violent and factious, he was at any rate alive and active.   If he talked and wrote much mere rhetoric, he was a master of the oratorical style, with an incomparable command of the music of words. If he was vehemently anti-Christian, he was not simply destructive in the sphere of religion.   On the one hand he was a pioneer in the imperatively necessary application of historical and literary criticism to the Bible ; on the other hand he developed a positive theism, a " natural religion," based on what appeared to him to be the secure inductions of science, and on the irrefragable precepts of natural law.   That he is not universally recognised as one of the first and foremost of the rationalists—the veritable harbinger of the eighteenth-century Age of Reason—is primarily due to the fact that the publication of his philosophical and religious opinions was postponed until he was in his grave, whereas through Voltaire and other disciples they had for thirty years or more been moulding the thought of the *intelligenzia* of the West.

IV

Efforts to rehabilitate Bolingbroke have from time to time been made by those who have refused to believe that men so critical and discerning as Swift and Pope and Chesterfield were wholly mistaken in the character of the hero whom they knew and adored.   In particular Disraeli and the Young England group of the thirties and forties of the last century looked to Bolingbroke as their prophet, and took his writings as gospel.   Rarely has a more splendid and impressive appreciation of one politician by another been written than Disraeli's eulogy of Bolingbroke in his *Vindication of the English Constitution*.   He exalts him as the founder of Tory democracy—the union of Crown and nation—as against the Whig oligarchy— the corrupt coalition of feudal nobles with fraudulent financiers. He praises him to the skies because, he says, he

eradicated from Toryism all those absurd and odious doctrines that Toryism had adventitiously adopted ; clearly developed its essential and permanent character ; discarded the dogma of divine right, demolished passive obedience, threw to the winds the doctrine of non-resistance ; placed the deposition of James and the accession of George on their right basis; and in the complete reorganisation of the public mind laid the foundation for the future accession of the Tory party to power.

The same tendency to exalt Bolingbroke, extol his influence, and claim him as founder appears in the utterances of the Tory democrats of the generation of Lord Randolph Churchill.

Similarly the Young Tories of the present day, restless under the reactionary incubus of the " old gang," cry, " Back to Bolingbroke ! " For Bolingbroke, like Disraeli, like Randolph Churchill, like—but I must not mention the names of living men—stood for the curious and rare combination of Conservatism with Radicalism ; of a strenuous maintenance of old institutions with a vigorous infusion into them of a new spirit ; of a careful preservation of vital continuity with a constant modification of structure ; of a union of order with progress ; of stability with necessary change ; of antiquity with modernity. Lord Birkenhead, it is true, is critical ; but perhaps he speaks for the " old gang " : " The Whigs," he says, " went bathing, and Bolingbroke stole their clothes."[1] He, apparently, does not approve of the way in which Bolingbroke in his later writings " meets his opponents upon the pure ground of Whiggism, tries them, and finds them wanting." It certainly is a method extremely perplexing to the still-surviving Toryism of the seventeenth century. Sir Geoffrey Butler, however, perceives the greatness and importance of Bolingbroke's work in weaning the Tory party from Jacobitism and from all its implications.

> In every age Tory thinkers must perceive that the Jacobitism against which Bolingbroke fought has its counterpart in many theories dear to the Old Guard. That for the Tory, possibly for the Radical too, is the abiding lesson of Bolingbroke's career.[2]

Similarly Mr Maurice Wood, in his vivacious *History of the Tory Party*, describing Bolingbroke as " one of the two great men of practical capacity joined to intellectual genius which Toryism has produced," recognises the great and enduring

---

[1] F. E. Smith, *Toryism*, p. xxxv.
[2] G. G. Butler, *The Tory Tradition*, pp. 26–27.

influence of his ideas. They did much, he says, to determine the character and career of the elder Pitt; they were operative in the overthrow of Walpole in 1742; they inspired George III and the King's Friends to shatter the Whig oligarchy between 1760 and 1770; they guided the genius of the younger Pitt in the critical days of the Revolutionary War; they illuminated the path of Canning; above all they became the source of the prevailing power of Disraeli in his great task of educating the Victorian Tories out of Protection and into Parliamentary reform. Churton Collins says:

> To the influence of Bolingbroke's writings is to be attributed in no small degree that remarkable transformation which converted the Toryism of Rochester and Nottingham into the Toryism of Pitt and Mansfield. . . . He inaugurated a new era in the annals of Party. He made Jacobitism contemptible. He reconstructed the Tory creed.[1]

V

The education of the Tory party: that was Bolingbroke's great achievement in the eighteenth century. It strikingly resembled Disraeli's great achievement in the nineteenth century: it was indeed, as we have just remarked, the model upon which Disraeli avowedly and deliberately framed his policy and his programme. Now, few tasks can be so difficult as the education of the Tory party; perhaps the only task obviously more difficult is the education of a religious sect. For the Tory party—under whichever of its countless names it may be known—is the party that venerates antiquity, that maintains tradition, that supports old institutions just because they are old, that reverences custom, that worships ancestors, that obeys without question the authority of the dead. Its main sources of strength—the veterans and stalwarts of the 'Old Guard'—are men of emotion rather than men of reason; men of passionate devotion to causes inexpressibly dear, rather than men of intellect with minds open to new conceptions. Thus the education of the Tory party is an education in the difficult art of forgetting; it is the education of steadfast and resolute men out of convictions sincerely and strenuously held; nay,

[1] J. Churton Collins, *Bolingbroke: an Historical Study*, pp. 7, 94.

more, it is the education of zealous and consecrated devotees out of loyalties to which they cling with a passion that is stronger than love of life itself.

Just as Disraeli in the middle of the nineteenth century had to draw the followers of Lord George Bentinck away from devotion to the Corn Laws, and train the regiments of Wellington's political army to march in the direction of household suffrage, so, a hundred years earlier, had Bolingbroke to lure the Jacobites of Shippen's rout from the obsolete advocacy of divine right and passive obedience, and persuade the High Church clergy of Atterbury's way of thinking to cease from the hunting and harrying of Dissenters.

There is another resemblance, too, between Bolingbroke and Disraeli. It is this. Each of them had qualified for his post of instructor by a period of apprenticeship during which he had vigorously propounded the antiquated fallacies from which he subsequently purged his party. Just as Disraeli, before he took up his educative task, had distinguished himself by his defence of the Corn Laws in 1846, and by his destructive criticism of every Parliamentary Reform Bill introduced into the House of Commons between 1837 and 1867, so had Bolingbroke, before he assumed the work of emancipating the Tory party from Jacobitism and religious exclusiveness, rendered himself notorious by his advocacy of the Occasional Conformity and Schism Acts, and by his term of conspicuous service as Secretary of State to the Pretender. The parallel may be carried still farther. For just as Disraeli when most he defended the Corn Laws was never a Protectionist, and when most he opposed Reform Bills was always a reformer, so Bolingbroke, even when serving the Pretender, was never a Jacobite, and even when persecuting Dissenters was always a free thinker. In truth, neither Bolingbroke nor Disraeli, although each of them joined the Tory party, worked with it, and for a time led it—neither of them was ever really of it. They advocated Tory measures with perfect sincerity and with strong conviction, but for reasons wholly different from those which actuated the Tory party—reasons which the average members of the Tory party were totally incapable of comprehending. Hence they were able to abandon Tory measures—such as the eighteenth-century Penal Laws, or the nineteenth-century Corn Laws—without any abandonment of principle, or any change of policy. They were working for ends which transcended mere measures; they were labouring to realise ideals which were capable of attainment by many routes; they were educating their followers in the art of distinguishing essentials from accidents; they were moulding their reluctant and resistant pupils to the shape of their own masterful wills.

VI

It is now time to examine a little more in detail the life, the writings, the social and political ideas of Bolingbroke. Of the life not much need here be said. Those who are unfamiliar with its particulars will find them set forth with discriminating brevity in Mr Arthur Hassall's *Life of Viscount Bolingbroke* (1889, new edition 1915), and with undiscriminating fullness in Mr Walter Sichel's erudite but excessively eulogistic *Bolingbroke and his Times* (two volumes, 1901–2). Suffice it here to note a few outstanding facts. Henry St John was born at the beginning of October 1678 in the manor-house at Battersea—the house in which he was destined to die seventy-three years later.[1] His parents, Sir Henry (later Viscount) St John, a worthless reprobate, and his mother, the Lady Mary, a colourless and inert daughter of the Earl of Warwick, did not at that time own the manor. They were living as guests or dependents of the old Sir Walter St John (founder of the Free School still flourishing in Battersea) and his formidable wife, the Lady Joanna, herself a St John by birth—daughter of Oliver St John, one of the leading opponents of Charles I, and later Cromwell's Chief Justice of the Common Pleas. The ancient Joanna was the dominant personality of the household. Of Roundhead descent and of strong Puritan leanings, she controlled her grandson's early education. Hence while Sir Henry haunted taverns and gained notoriety by sanguinary brawls,[2] and while the Lady Mary sat passive with

---

[1] The relics of the old home of the St Johns are still (December 1927) to be seen, close to the Battersea Parish Church, in the yard of Messrs Mayhew's flour-mill. They are, however, in the last stages of ruin and decay, and are, I am told, soon to be swept away to make room for extensions of the mill.

[2] He killed a man in 1684, and with difficulty escaped execution.

her hands in her lap, the old lady saw to it that the infant Harry was nourished on the parables of Daniel Burgess, and was fortified by Dr Manton's hundred and nineteen sermons on the hundred-and-nineteenth Psalm.

After such a preparatory school, entry into Eton was to Harry St John what the Restoration was to the Cavaliers after the rigidities of the Commonwealth. It emancipated him from Puritanism and opened the way to that extreme reaction into scepticism and licentiousness which marked his manhood. At Eton he acquired a good working knowledge of Latin, and laid the foundation of that extensive acquaintance with Roman literature which characterises all his writings. He displayed, in particular, a marvellous memory, which enabled him to store his mind with historical precedents and illustrative passages, so that later he was able to compose without the aid of books works of considerable elaboration. On leaving Eton he travelled in France and Italy, and showed his mental alertness and natural capacity by gaining an almost perfect mastery of the two great Romance languages. In after-years Voltaire professed that Bolingbroke had been able to give him valuable lessons in French ! In France and Italy, too, it would appear, Bolingbroke learned what little his father's example had not already imparted to him of the art and craft of the debauchery then prevalent in the fashionable world. Certainly Harry St John came back to England in 1700 an accomplished *roué* and man of pleasure. London soon echoed with the report of his drunken and licentious orgies. In the hope of reforming or at any rate restraining him, his grandfather found him a wife worth £40,000, and a seat in the House of Commons for the pocket-borough of Wootton Bassett in Wiltshire. Thus auspiciously, in February 1701, Henry St John the younger entered upon his public career.

VII

It may be said at once that the immediate object at which the old Sir Walter aimed in securing for his grandson a consort and a constituency was not achieved. Henry St John remained a rake and a reprobate. There can be little doubt, indeed, that the ultimate failure which marked his career was primarily due to his personal vices. His drunkenness not only weakened his will and incapacitated him on occasions when deliberate and decisive action was necessary; it also in at least two critical junctures betrayed him into indiscretions of speech which raised up against him powerful and implacable enemies. His gross sexual excesses not only shattered his fine constitution, rendering him prematurely old when little over forty, and decrepit when he ought to have been in his prime; they also made him an object of disgust to Queen Anne, to the Anglican clergy, and to the bulk of the great party which he aspired to lead; they were indeed the main cause of his failure to secure the White Staff at the crisis of his fate (July 27–30, 1714), when to have secured it, and thereby to have become Prime Minister, would have been to alter the whole course of subsequent English history, and probably to have established for himself a political ascendancy as enduring as that actually achieved by his great rival, Sir Robert Walpole. As a contemporary observer remarked, " his character was too bad and his bottom too narrow to carry the great ensign." Nay, more, we may confidently assert that the life of lawless dissipation that he led during the period of his power—the condition of feverish and unnatural excitement in which he constantly moved and had his being—was largely responsible for the wildness of speech, the recklessness of action, the unscrupulousness of policy, the disregard of consequences, which characterised him as a Minister of the Crown.

In the matter of morals, then, the contrast between Bolingbroke and Disraeli is striking. In another respect also it is remarkable. Disraeli, beginning life with the heavy handicap of alien race, *bourgeois* rank, imperfect education, and harassing poverty, attained political power only at the end of his life, when he was too old, too weary, too forlorn, to use it to full effect. Bolingbroke, on the other hand, beginning life with every advantage of race, rank, education, and wealth, reached all but the summit of his ambition while still he was a very young man—Member of Parliament at twenty-two; War Secretary at twenty-six; chief Secretary of State at thirty-one; virtual Prime Minister (although but for three days) ere he was thirty-six. It was his (and his country's) misfortune that he was placed in high and responsible office before he was morally mature enough to perform his duties with a proper sense of their seriousness.

VIII

When he entered Parliament in 1701 he attached himself to Robert Harley, and joined the Tory party. This party, after some ten years of embittered opposition, had recently recovered power. In 1701 it was out to humiliate William of Orange; to limit the prerogative of the presumptive monarchs of the house of Hanover; to punish and proscribe the Whig leaders; to penalise Dissenters; to disband the standing army; to withdraw from Continental politics; to re-establish the ascendancy of land over money, and of country over town; and to place the Tories in permanent possession of office. It was a party large and passionate, but bucolic and inarticulate; capable of roaring and raging, but incapable of expressing its emotions in intelligible language. Henry St John gave it a voice. Without sharing, or even professing to share, its prepossessions and prejudices, he propounded with an eloquence such as the House of Commons had never before heard the extremest tenets of its most reactionary die-hards. He denounced the Partition Treaties of 1698 and 1700; he supported the impeachment of Somers and his colleagues; he assailed the Kentish petitioners; he strove to deprive the Aylesbury electors of their common law right to vote; he defended the malignant Occasional Conformity Bill. Never had there been a more conspicuous example of the mere party politician, devoid of either conscience or moderation, struggling for leadership by following the most violent section of his faction. By the almost unanimous judgment of posterity in every one of the causes which he advocated he was in the wrong.

His conspicuous abilities, however, soon procured for him place and power. Before he had been twelve months in the House of Commons he was chosen by ballot (March 1702) to be a Commissioner for taking the public accounts, with a salary of £500 a year, besides lavish allowances for expenses. Two years later he was taken into the Ministry by Godolphin and Marlborough as Secretary at War. Now, the Ministry was a mixed one, containing a good many Whigs; so that St John as a member of the Government had to modify his extreme Toryism. The War of the Spanish Succession, moreover, which in 1704 reached its climax in the decisive battle of Blenheim, was a Whig war, started by William of Orange in defence of those very Partition Treaties which St John had hitherto denounced. The Secretary at War, therefore, had to change his tone respecting foreign affairs, and had to devote such administrative abilities as he possessed to the active furtherance of the great struggle which he had hitherto condemned. He seems to have performed his official duties efficiently and well, if somewhat spasmodically. The performance of his official duties, however, while it alienated his old allies, the wildly pacific Tories, did not wholly satisfy his new associates, the belligerent Whigs. He, together with his colleague Harley, fell into suspicion of lukewarmness and intrigue, so that in 1708 he was constrained not only to resign office, but also to withdraw from Parliament for a season. He spent two years (1708–10) in retirement, watching the course of events, and spending his time in fruitful study.

The General Election of 1705, fought amid the delirious excitement caused by the victory of Blenheim and the capture of Gibraltar the preceding year, re-established the Whig party in power. The vigorous prosecution of the war became the cardinal principle of the Government's policy. The triumphs of Ramillies and Turin in 1706 gave rise to hopes that the power of France might finally be broken, and Europe freed for ever from the menace which had hung over her for nearly a century. Hence almost abject offers of peace from Louis XIV were contemptuously rejected in 1706, 1709, and again in 1710, by the allied British, Dutch, and Germans. They were resolved to be content with nothing short of the annihilation of the Bourbon power. From the British Ministry were expelled all who did not accept the full Whig programme. Thus, for the first time in our history (1708–10) a true ' Cabinet ' was brought into existence—that is to say, a body of ministers drawn entirely from one political party, and dependent for its position and power not upon the monarch, but upon a majority in the House of Commons.

Queen Anne, indeed, was notoriously hostile to her

Ministry during the two years of the Whig monopoly. She disliked Godolphin, the First Lord of the Treasury; she was jealous of the fame of Marlborough; she hated the house of Hanover with which the Whigs were in the closest alliance; she loathed the Dissenters who constituted the strength of the Whigs in the corporate towns; she longed for peace, so that she might discuss with her half-brother, the Pretender, and with Louis XIV, his patron and protector, the conditions of a new Stuart Restoration. The errors of the Whigs in flouting the Queen, in irritating the Church, in prolonging the war, in rejecting the terms offered by the French, in piling up taxation, in perpetrating jobs, and finally in impeaching Dr Sacheverell for a Tory sermon, enabled the angry Anne (under the inspiration of Harley and St John) to dismiss the Whig Ministry with ignominy, dissolve Parliament, appeal to the country, and secure an overwhelming Tory majority.

IX

Thus, in 1710, Harley (soon to be created Earl of Oxford) found himself First Lord of the Treasury, with Henry St John as his principal Secretary of State. For the four remaining years of Queen Anne's reign the Tories retained their ascendancy. Their main concern during this period was to make such arrangements as would ensure their continuance in power after the Queen's decease. To this end they desired (1) to bring the war to a close; (2) to sever England's connexion with the Dutch and the Germans; (3) to secure guarantees on the one hand from the Pretender for Protestantism and on the other hand from the Hanoverians for Toryism; (4) to break the power of the Dissenters and restore the authority of the Church of England; (5) to overthrow the might of the new moneyed magnates and re-establish the ascendancy of the old landed gentry; (6) to abolish or at any rate reduce the standing army and revive the glories of the Militia and the Navy.

It was unfortunate for the carrying out of their programme that Harley and St John soon ceased to agree concerning ways and means. Harley, in spite of certain prudent parleyings with the Pretender, was entirely devoted to the Hanoverian succession; St John, contemptuous of the Electoral Court when sober, and insolently hostile to it when inebriated, pursued a policy which inevitably led him to the Pretender. Harley was sincerely devoted to the Church of England; St John cared for it only in so far as it represented the Tory party at prayer. Harley was anxious for peace with honour; St John was resolved to secure peace at any price. Above all, Harley was willing to work with the Whigs, and was continually making overtures to them (and to Robert Walpole in particular); St John, on the other hand, was filled with an implacable rage against them (and against Robert Walpole in particular), and was determined to leave no stone unturned to accomplish their complete annihilation. These profound differences made continued co-operation between the two men impossible. Early in 1711 their old alliance was dissolved, and each began to go his several way. The Tory party became split into divergent factions, the moderates following the Treasurer, the wild men the Secretary. St John, especially when in his cups, declaimed violently and vehemently against his chief—the echoes of his declamations still reverberate through the sonorous passages of his *Letter to Sir William Wyndham*, his last *Remarks on the History of England*, and his dissertation on *The State of Parties at the Accession of George I.* Harley, for his part, intrigued against St John; told the scandalised Queen the secrets of his private life; whispered to the bishops the worst respecting his horrible infidelities; hinted to the Hanoverians that St John's ascendancy would be fatal alike to the Elector and to Protestantism. In vain did Jonathan Swift, their common friend, mediate between the two rivals; in vain did their colleagues in the Ministry seek to heal the breach; in vain did the Queen herself, alarmed at the magnitude of the brawl, command accommodation. The struggle became a mortal combat, without parallel in the annals of Parliamentary history. That St John with his violent and clear-cut measures commanded the majority of the party soon became evident: Harley, in order to retain his nominal leadership, was compelled to acquiesce in measures of which he thoroughly disapproved. St John took entire charge of the peace negotiations, and concluded the Treaties of Utrecht (1713) on terms which threw away the fruits of a

224

hundred victories, dissolved the Grand Alliance, and left in the minds of Dutch, Imperialists, and Catalans a sense of gross desertion and betrayal. He carried through Parliament a Property Qualifications Bill which made the possession of large landed estates an indispensable condition of membership of the House of Commons. He secured the passage of the Occasional Conformity Bill—a blow to the Dissenters and therefore to the Whigs—which had been a matter of furious conflict in Parliament for ten years. He added an incredible Schism Act, intended to exclude Dissenters from the teaching profession, which went beyond the extremest expectations of the High Anglican clergy. He attacked his quondam colleagues of the Godolphin Ministry on the ground of peculation, and got his enemy Walpole condemned, expelled from the House of Commons, and sent to the Tower. He began to clear Whigs out of offices in the Army, out of lord-lieutenancies in the counties, out of all administrative posts where their influence might jeopardise the complete Tory control of the machinery of government. Never had party fury raged so ferociously as it did during these four hectic years; never had a party politician shown a more complete disregard of all save party considerations than did Henry St John.

But though St John thus, as he expressed it, " gave the view-halloo " to the pack that followed him, " showed the Tories game," and established a masterly ascendancy over the majority in both Houses of Parliament, his position was insecure and his triumph incomplete so long as he was out of favour at Court. The English monarch still ruled as well as reigned; still presided at Councils; still determined policies; still appointed and dismissed ministers; still vetoed legislation. In order to oust Harley and obtain supreme power it was necessary to win Anne. This was no easy matter; for Anne had been thoroughly poisoned against St John by well-authenticated reports of his evil life and his heterodox opinions. The difficult task, however, was achieved by the instrumentality of the dominant serving-woman, Abigail Hill (Mrs Masham).[1] Hence on July 27, 1714, Harley (since 1711 Earl of Oxford) was dismissed, and St John (who in 1712 had been made

[1] She persuaded the Queen not so much to like St John as to dislike Harley more.

Viscount Bolingbroke) found himself in undisputed headship
of the Tory party, and virtually Prime Minister.

X

Bolingbroke's triumph was short-lived. It rested on an
extremely insecure basis, viz., the life of Queen Anne. Now
Anne had been in failing health for many months. The
agitations incident to the expulsion of Oxford (who did not
retire gracefully) were more than her constitution could stand.
She had an apoplectic fit on July 30, and on August 1 she died.
If Anne had really liked and trusted Bolingbroke she would
on July 27 have made him Lord Treasurer in succession to
Oxford, and he would then have controlled the administration
during the crisis of the next five days and after the Queen's decease. She steadily refused, however, to confer this command-
ing office upon him; his character was too bad, his principles
were too loose, his partisanship was too violent and unscrupulous, to render it possible to place the kingdom in his charge.
Above all, she felt that the Church would be unsafe in his
keeping. If Bolingbroke had during the four years of his
power shown himself less reckless in his pursuit of the Whigs,
less outrageous in his persecution of Dissenters, less perfidious
in his diplomacy, less malignant in his hostility to Harley, less
devoid of all the qualities required for statesmanship except
brilliance and audacity, he still might have controlled the
situation through his leadership of the Tory party. But not
even the Tory party could trust him. For if he had always
subordinated the interests of his country to the interests of his
party, he had, equally obviously, invariably subordinated the
interests of his party to his own ambitions, and even to his own
lusts. The Tory party, therefore, in the crisis of the summer
of 1714 was paralysed by dissension and distrust. Finally, if
Bolingbroke had even been sure of himself he might have
seized the reins of power and have prevailed. For three days,
indeed, the reins were actually in his hands. But at the crucial
moment his nerve and his courage failed him. The brilliance
and the audacity which had been his outstanding characteristics
deserted him: he fumbled for a policy, hesitating between
George and James; he played for safety, groping for lines of

retreat. Through sheer ineptness, indecision, cowardice, and incompetence he let the Whigs secure control of affairs. George was proclaimed ; a Council of Regency was established ; the seals of office were taken from him, and he was relegated to private life.

Rarely has there been a more sudden change of fortune than that which befell Bolingbroke in 1714, between July 27, when he secured the dismissal of Oxford at the hands of Anne, and August 28, when he received his own formal and emphatic expulsion from George I. He, of course, like most ambitious men who have spectacularly failed, attributed his disaster to circumstances : if only Anne had lived another six weeks, he said, all would have been well both for himself and for the Tories. But no amount of specious argument could conceal from himself, from his disillusioned followers, or from the world at large, the fact that his failure and the ruin in which he involved his party were attributable to himself alone. His vices had alienated Anne ; his impiety had alarmed the Church ; his violence and fierce invective had turned the Earl of Oxford from friendship to embittered antagonism, and had split the Tory party in hopeless schism ; his malignant persecution of Whigs and Dissenters had roused against him the disapproval of most moderate and reasonable men ; his unscrupulous and short-sighted conduct of foreign affairs had left Britain without a friend in Europe. Finally, his resourcelessness, nervelessness, feebleness, and inefficiency in the cardinal week of Queen Anne's illness and death showed alike to Whigs and Tories, Jacobites and Hanoverians, Britons and interested peoples on the Continent, that clever as Bolingbroke might be in debate, and crafty as he undoubtedly was in diplomacy, he was but a broken reed in the day when decisive and courageous action was called for. His reputation never recovered from the shock of the fiasco of August 1714.

If any things remained to be done to complete his political damnation, these things he proceeded incontinently to do. In March 1715, at a threat of impeachment, he fled to France ; in July he joined the Pretender at Commercy, accepted office as Secretary of State in his shadow Ministry, and helped to organise the Jacobite rebellion in England and Scotland which marked the autumn of that fateful year. Quite naturally and properly, therefore, he was, in September 1715, attainted of high treason, deprived of his property, degraded from the peerage, and condemned to death. Comedy followed tragedy. He soon mortally offended his new master, the Pretender, by what he said in his cups concerning him and his tinsel Court; he outraged the Catholic priesthood which surrounded and sustained the Pretender by his contemptuous attitude toward their religion and by his frank insistence that they were the main obstacles to the Pretender's restoration to his ancestors' throne; he exasperated the Irish and the Scottish Jacobites by his refusal to approve of the rash and ridiculous schemes with which their imaginations teemed. The failure of the '15 was attributed to him. In February 1716 he was summarily and ignominiously dismissed by the Pretender, and his dismissal was followed by an impeachment on the alleged grounds of treachery, incapacity, and neglect. By Jacobite writers in France he was attacked with a ferocity not less intense than that with which he was attacked by Whig writers in England.

XI

Thus in 1716 Bolingbroke's political damnation was complete. He was regarded both by the Tories in England and by the Jacobites in France as the main cause of the disasters which had overwhelmed them. By the dominant Whigs, headed by George I himself and by Robert Walpole, he was looked upon as a malicious and unscrupulous arch-enemy to be kept at all costs from any restoration to place or power. His official career was, in fact, at an end. He was but thirty-eight years old, and he had thirty-five more years to live. In vain, however, did he toil, intrigue, and bribe with a view to securing the removal of his attainder and his readmission to Parliament. In 1723, it is true, he obtained a cancellation of the sentence of death and permission to return to England. Two years later, by Act of Parliament, his property was restored to him. But that was all. He remained till the end of his days a peer merely by courtesy, an exile from the House of Lords, and an alien ineligible for office under the Crown. Such was the Nemesis of Bolingbroke's application of the principles of Machiavelli to British politics.

The thirty-five years of his outlawry were, however—precisely because he was shut out from public life—the all-fruitful years of his literary and philosophical activity. The written remains of the earlier portion of his career are negligible. We have a few worthless poems ; an anonymous attack on Marlborough and Godolphin contributed to the *Examiner* in 1710 ; numbers of diplomatic dispatches in English and in French penned during the peace negotiations of 1711–13 ; and a mass of private correspondence, much of which lies yet unpublished in the archives of Petworth and Hemel Hempstead. After 1716, however, Bolingbroke's literary output was extensive : in the first collected edition of his works, issued by David Mallet in .1754, it fills five large folio volumes. Four periods in his later career can be distinguished : (1) from 1716 to 1723 he was a proscribed exile in France ; (2) from 1723 to 1735 he was mainly in England working with the energy of mortal hatred to overthrow the Ministry of his implacable enemy, Sir Robert Walpole ; (3) from 1735 to 1744, disappointed by his complete failure either to destroy the Whig ascendancy or to recover his own position, he was for the most part back in France ; (4) from 1744 to his death in 1751, having inherited the family manor of Battersea (on the removal of that " monument of extinct profligacy," his aged and disreputable father, in 1742), he returned finally to England, and there in failing health, gathering obscurity, and depressing impotence, finished his distressful career.

Each of these four periods has its own peculiar literary memorials. During the first of them, viz., 1716–23, Bolingbroke, in order to distract his mind from contemplation of the appalling mess which he had made of things, dabbled in philosophy and theology. He compiled some vapid and platitudinous *Reflections upon Exile*, in which he plagiarised from Seneca a number of inane truisms which one virtuous fool might think capable of consoling another virtuous fool under the buffetings of inexorable fate, but which can assuredly have afforded no solace to a highly intelligent knave suffering the consequences of his own moral delinquencies. He composed, in French, a series of brilliant letters to the philosophic M. de Pouilly, arguing for a theistic, as against an atheistic, interpretation of the universe. He indited, also in French, a vehement and powerful criticism of one of Archbishop Tillotson's sermons, in which he assailed with merciless logic and much asperity the Mosaic cosmogony. In these two theological works he took up the religious position which he occupied for the remainder of his life. That is to say, he maintained the cause of Deism against materialistic philosophy on the one side and against Christian divinity on the other. If these works had been published when they were written—about 1720—they would have created a sensation. They would have established Bolingbroke's reputation as a pioneer of free thought, or more exactly anti-Christian thought; for he was much more passionate and much more effective in his attacks upon the Anglican divines and the Old Testament patriarchs than he was in his defence of theism against atheism. But in establishing his reputation as a free thinker they would have seriously impeded his chances of restoration to the leadership of the Tory party in England. And that leadership he was at this time eager to recover. Hence his theological dissertations of 1720 remained unpublished—although known in manuscript to the elect—until they were printed posthumously by David Mallet in 1754, by which time they were obsolete. Their substance had been made known to the world by Voltaire and others who had sat at Bolingbroke's feet in his French house at La Source, near Orleans. A corrective to such serious argument as they contained had been provided by Butler's *Analogy* and kindred works.

Bolingbroke, however, as we have just noted, while he employed his excessive leisure at La Source in privately pleading with atheists and in pounding divines, was primarily concerned in his working hours with laborious endeavours, on the one hand, to secure from the Hanoverian Government of England a reversal of his attainder, and, on the other hand, to rehabilitate his reputation with the English Tories, who now regarded the noble and disinterested Sir William Wyndham as their chief. In order to achieve the reversal of his attainder, he condescended to abject petitions to George I; he made futile attempts to conciliate his inveterate enemy Sir Robert Walpole; he tried to win the favour of the dominant Duchess of Kendal; he finally secured the effective advocacy of the influential lords Stanhope, Sunderland, and Stair, and by their aid gained in 1723 a partial pardon under the Great Seal. To rehabilitate his reputation with the deserted, disillusioned, and desperate Tories was a less easy task. In fact, we may say that he never fully achieved it. The Tories as a party, in spite of Wyndham's whole-hearted endeavours to persuade them, were never able either to forgive or again to trust the man who, by identifying the reigning house of Hanover with Whiggism and the impossible house of the exiled Stuarts with Toryism, had condemned his misguided followers to half a century of impotence and contumely. Bolingbroke's famous *Letter to Sir William Wyndham* (1717) is his *apologia pro vita sua*. It is, on the whole, the ablest, the best written, the most powerful of all his works. It contains a masterly survey from his own point of view of the events of the critical six years 1710 to 1716. It attempts to justify and defend every one of his important measures and significant acts during that fateful period, including his persecution of the Dissenters, his desertion of the Allies at Utrecht, his behaviour at the death of Anne, his flight, his adherence to the Pretender, his support of the '15 rebellion, his procedure subsequent to his dismissal from the Pretender's service. He tries to show that from first to last he was actuated by one motive, and one alone, viz., zeal for the Tory cause. On the one hand he protests that he was never moved by personal ambition, personal fear, or personal resentment. On the other hand he confesses that the interests of his country were entirely subordinated to the interests of his party. His vivid description of the Pretender's Court and his lurid story of the Jacobite proceedings in 1715–16 are magnificent as literature. In the world of affairs they sufficed to sweep Jacobitism out of the sphere of practical politics. The concluding sections of this inimitable pamphlet are devoted to a passionate appeal to the Tories to free themselves from all thought of recalling the exiled Stuarts. The Pretender little dreamed when in sudden fury he insolently dismissed Bolingbroke from his service in 1716 that he was doing a deed which would render the restoration of himself and his house for ever impossible. Yet so it was. The one great and successful task accomplished by Bolingbroke during the course of his long and generally unsuccessful life was to purge Toryism of Jacobitism with its concomitant superstitions of divine right and passive obedience. He re-established Toryism on the surer foundation of the Revolutionary Settlement of 1688–89.

XII

In 1723, as we have seen, Bolingbroke received a pardon under the Great Seal, and in 1725 he definitely came back to England to reside, soon taking up his abode on a fine estate which he bought at Dawley near Uxbridge. He brought with him his second wife, the French Marquise de Villette, whom he had formally married in 1722, four years after the death of his unhappy first wife, whom he had treated with unpardonable faithlessness and neglect. The years 1723–25 had been primarily occupied in efforts to obtain the complete reversal of the attainder of 1715, and complete readmission into English public life—on the one side humiliating, rather discreditable, and wholly unsuccessful efforts to win the favour of Walpole and the Whigs; on the other side extremely expensive, most disreputable, but partially successful efforts to win the favour of the King, by means of his German mistress, the recently exalted Duchess of Kendal. The Duchess detested Walpole, and naturally fostered any influence opposed to his; the King was dissatisfied with Walpole's foreign policy (which paid no regard to the interests of Hanover), and was wishful to draw upon Bolingbroke's unique knowledge of Continental politics. Walpole became seriously alarmed for his ascendancy. In 1725 he was strong enough to prevent the Act of Parliament which restored Bolingbroke's private rights as a citizen from being extended to include his public rights. In 1727, however, it appeared probable that the King and the Duchess would insist on complete rehabilitation, and that Bolingbroke would at last triumph over his arch-antagonist. But just as in 1714 Bolingbroke's Tory hopes were shattered by the death of Anne, and just as in 1715 his Jacobite designs were ruined by the death of Louis XIV, so in 1727 the sudden demise of George I at Osnabrück destroyed his dreams of restoration, and left him for ever excluded from Parliament and office. It is true that he tried to win the favour of George II by means of his mistress, Mrs Howard (later Countess of Suffolk); but in doing so he 'put his money on the wrong horse.' His intrigues with Mrs Howard merely won for him the mortal enmity of Queen Caroline, the real controller of the King's policy, who threw the whole weight of her influence on to the side of Walpole. It is also true that when Frederick, Prince of Wales, quarrelled violently and publicly with his parents and was excluded from the Court, Bolingbroke cultivated his company, and hoped that when he should become King he might come back in his train as 'patriotic' minister. But Frederick—well described by Mr J. M. Robertson as "the one thorough fool and rascal in the Hanoverian line"—died before his father, and Bolingbroke's last illusive vision of his rehabilitation and his earldom was dispelled. Bolingbroke's 'patriotic' ideas of government were left to be realised by George III with not Bolingbroke, but Bute as his minister. This, however, was all in the far future.

In 1725 Bolingbroke, seeing that Walpole and the Whig magnates were his implacable enemies, determined to do what in him lay to secure their overthrow. For ten years he toiled enormously at this engrossing task—and toiled in vain. Nevertheless he made much stir in the world, and he left a permanent impress upon British politics. He organised the first persistent and avowed 'opposition' to the King's Government; he inspired it with the conviction that the one and only function of an opposition is to oppose; he conducted, in the Press and through his allies in Parliament, a virulent and sustained attack both upon the men who constituted the Ministry and upon their measures; he did much to rouse the power of that latent public opinion in England which under Chatham and Pitt was destined to assert its claim to sovereignty in the State. He found three groups of men hostile to Walpole, viz., the Jacobites led by Shippen, the Hanoverian Tories led by his friend Wyndham, and a number of Dissentient Whigs led by the two Pulteneys and Carteret. He tried to weld these disparate factions into a coherent whole, and soon found that the only thing on which they were all agreed was desire for the degradation of Walpole. Hence he started an organ for his crazy coalition, the single and simple theme of which was the iniquities of the Prime Minister and his fellow-conspirators. It first appeared as *The Country Gentleman* in

July 1726; in December of that year it changed its name to
The Craftsman, and under that name continued to appear—
at first twice a week, later once a week—until April 1736.
Much of the writing was done by Bolingbroke himself; no
one loathed Walpole so much as he, and no one had so rich
a vocabulary of virulent abuse. He poured forth without
restraint the vials of his detestation upon his hated foe. He
found able coadjutors, however, in Swift and Pope, Arbuthnot
and Gay, the two Pulteneys, Chesterfield and Lyttelton,
Amherst and Akenside. Never had a periodical excited so
much interest in the political world; it was read and discussed
in every club and *salon*; the secret of the authorship of
its anonymous tirades was eagerly debated. Bolingbroke's
superior style and fiercer malignity made the identification of
his articles easy. Even the pachydermatous Prime Minister
writhed under some of his lashes. Once—unless, as some
critics think, the composition has been fathered upon him—
he was goaded to reply. The following extracts will give
some conception of the tone of the political controversy of this
Golden Age of peace and prosperity.

> Though you have not signed your name, I know you. Because
> a man who is without all principle of honesty ; who in no one thing
> can be relied upon; a betrayer of his friend [Oxford]; a traitor to
> his prince; an enemy to his country; a perjured, ungrateful, un-
> faithful rascal, must be you. . . . You are an infamous fellow who
> makes a reputation of doing mischief. . . . You are of so profligate
> a character that in your prosperity nobody envied you, and in your
> disgrace nobody pities you. . . . You are a fellow who has no
> conscience at all. . . . You have no abilities. You are an emanci-
> pated slave, a proscribed criminal, and an insolvent debtor. . . . You
> have been a traitor and should be used like one. . . . I do not value
> what you or your company say of me. . . . You rail at me because
> you envy me, and I despise all that a man in the impotence of dis-
> grace can do against me, who could never terrify me in the zenith of
> his power. . . . I would rather have you my enemy than my friend.
> Change your names, and be as scurrilous as you please. I shall find
> you out. I am Aristæus; you are Proteus. You may change to a
> flame, a lion, a bull, or a bear, I shall know you, baffle you, conquer
> you, and contemn you.[1]

[1] *The Occasional Writer*, Article No. III.

This style of controversy lacks delicacy, and it tends speedily to exhaust its freshness. Bolingbroke's retorts were much more skilful, sustained, and artistic productions. They were rapier-thrusts, not bludgeon-blows. Many of them dealt with topics of current concern, the interest of which has wholly vanished away—such, for example, as the fortification of Dunkirk, the restoration of Gibraltar to Spain, the levying of an excise, the terms of the Treaty of Hanover, the hiring of Hessian troops. Other subjects of discussion were of more enduring importance—such, for example, as the repeal of the Septennial Act, or the exclusion of placemen from Parliament. But first and foremost were the personal attacks upon Walpole, for his greed of power, his degradation of the monarchy, his supersession of the 'patriotic' Privy Council by the party Cabinet of submissive Whigs, his dictatorship over Parliament, his corruption of the constituencies, his tyranny over local administrators, his bribery, his jobbery, his sordid mercantilism, his peculation and dishonesty.

The most sustained, most brilliant, and most damaging of Bolingbroke's attacks upon his elephantine enemy were those which he delivered in the two series of articles entitled respectively *Remarks on the History of England* (twenty-four letters, published in *The Craftsman*, 1730–31) and *A Dissertation upon Parties* (nineteen letters prefaced by a mock-dedication to Walpole, published in *The Craftsman*, 1733–34). The *Remarks on the History of England* are extremely clever and infinitely diverting, but of course entirely valueless as contributions to knowledge. The only thing that Bolingbroke is out to do is to find plausible parallels in English history to the political circumstances of his own time. He wants to strike Walpole—and to give an occasional poke at George II and Queen Caroline—without incurring the risk of prosecution for libel or sedition. He clearly hints at George in his account of every weak and woman-ridden king; he draws readily recognisable portraits of Queen Caroline in Isabella, wife of Edward II, Margaret of Anjou, wife of Henry VI, and Elizabeth Woodville, wife of Edward IV. But he reserves his richest *répertoire* of rascals to illustrate Walpole. It is suggested with the subtlest innuendo that he combines in his portly person all the qualities which rendered infamous the whole series of bad ministers from the Norman Conquest to the days of Anne. Mortimer in Edward II's day, Vere in Richard II's, Warwick the King-maker in Henry VI's, Empson and Dudley in Henry VII's, Wolsey in Henry VIII's, Leicester in Elizabeth's, Buckingham in James I's, all are denounced for doing precisely those things that Walpole was popularly supposed to be doing in George II's day. Walpole, goaded out of his usual complacency by the deadliness of this veiled assault, meditated prosecution. But recollections of Sacheverell, and knowledge of Bolingbroke's dialectic skill, prudently restrained him. As to the substance of Bolingbroke's *Remarks*, apart from a number of political and social ideas to which I shall revert later, most noteworthy are his exaltation of Elizabeth and his unmitigated condemnation of the whole house of Stuart. He commends Elizabeth for her patriotism ; her popularity ; her maintenance of her prerogative ; her superiority to parties and factions ; her freedom from foreign entanglements ; her development of England's sea-power. He blames the Stuarts, and James I in particular, for their absurd doctrines, for their injudicious treatment of their Parliaments, for their inflammation of religious passions, for their foolish fumblings in foreign affairs. It was strong medicine for Tories—descendants and representatives of the old Cavaliers—to be told by their great champion that the breach between monarch and people in the seventeenth century, and the Civil War in which it culminated, were wholly due to the follies and errors of James I and Charles I. Yet that is what Bolingbroke emphatically and with frequent iteration told them in these disquisitions. It would appear that the education of Tories consists in the simple if laborious process of converting them into Whigs.

The *Dissertation upon Parties* may be regarded as the sequel to the *Remarks on the History of England*. It deals in detail with the Revolution of 1688 and with the constitutional changes that flowed from it. Its Whiggism is even more pronounced than that of its predecessor. " The revolution," says the revolutionised Bolingbroke,

> is looked upon by all sides as a new era. . . . On this foundation all the reasonable, independent Whigs and Tories unite. . . . If this creed [viz., the civil faith of the old Whigs] were made a test of

236

political orthodoxy, there would appear at this time but very few heretics amongst us.

He condemns James II; considers that the policy of the Exclusion Bill was justified; applauds the deposition of James, which he says was effected by the whole nation, Tories as well as Whigs. He proceeds to argue that since 1689 the terms Whig and Tory had lost all intelligible meaning; that all had accepted the new kingship based on popular will and constitutional contract, and that the only serious peril which the country had now to face was the peril that the new monarchy, the unreformed Parliament, and the sovereign people should be degraded and corrupted by an unscrupulous and crafty Prime Minister. He called upon the "Country" party of his allies to overthrow the pernicious "Court" party of the evil minister and the weak King. Walpole is alluded to as "a little statue placed on a mighty pedestal," as a "stock-jobber," as "one of those saucy creatures of fortune whom she raises in the extravagance of her caprice," as "a clumsy, busy, bungling child of fortune," as one of "those wooden images which princes gild and then worship," as one of "those upstarts in power who owe their elevation to the favour of weak princes," as one of those "wretches whose crimes would have been punished, and whose talents would scarce have recommended them to the meanest offices, in the virtuous and prosperous ages of the Commonwealth," as a "veteran sharper," as one of "the meanest grubs on earth," and so on.

At the time when Bolingbroke launched this furious tirade against his enemy, viz., the autumn of 1733 and the spring of 1734, it seemed that the hour of Walpole's doom had struck. His Excise Bill—an eminently wise and politic measure—had roused throughout the country a wild fury of opposition based on ignorance and prejudice. Bolingbroke and his colleagues of *The Craftsman*, with a total disregard of either political principle or national interest, fomented the outcry against the harassed minister, and hoped, in spite of the Court, to effect his ruin. At the same time they stirred up a considerable agitation against the Septennial Act, demanding, in the interests of popular control, a return to triennial elections. All their assaults, however, were vain. Walpole withdrew his

Excise Bill, vindicated the Septennial Act, stuck to his post, and secured a new lease of office by his success in the General Election of 1734.

Bolingbroke was bitterly disappointed at the failure of all his plans and the frustration of all his labours. Walpole, who seems to have got on the track of some doubtful correspondence of Bolingbroke with foreigners, threatened prosecution ; Pulteney hinted that the non-success of the anti-Walpole coalition was due to the unpopularity of Bolingbroke himself; Bolingbroke's health was breaking ; his finances were in a tangle ; he thought it best to depart. Hence in 1735 he vacated Dawley, said farewell to his fellow-craftsmen, and returned to France.

XIII

During the years 1735 to 1744 Bolingbroke was mainly abroad. He settled first at Chanteloup in Touraine, but soon moved to Argeville near Fontainebleau, where he had the privilege of hunting in the royal forest. During these nine years he visited England three times. The first visit was a long one, viz., June 1738 to May 1739. The death of Queen Caroline and the serious illness of George II caused him to hope that the day of Whig and Walpole supremacy was ending, and that the day of Frederick and ' patriotism ' was dawning. It was during this visit that he wrote his famous *Patriot King*, a work which was intended to exalt its author in the eyes of Frederick ; to make Walpole's Government odious in the eyes of the nation ; and to furnish the ' patriots ' with a programme. As a party pamphlet it is of supreme excellence ; as a contribution to political thought or constitutional practice worse than worthless. George II recovered ; Frederick lapsed into imbecility and vice ; Bolingbroke returned to France and philosophy. His second visit, in 1742, was occasioned by the death of his father, and his succession to the ancestral manor of Battersea. The fall of Walpole which occurred the same year caused him to linger in England in the hope that ' patriotism ' might get the better of party. But the Dissentient Whigs—Pulteney, Carteret, and company—who pulled down Walpole soon showed that all they desired was to succeed to his office and his power, and that they had not the

238

slightest wish to obliterate party government, increase the royal prerogative, or purify Parliament. Bolingbroke's last hope of his own generation was dispelled. He could only look to posterity for the realisation of his ideals. His third visit, occasioned by the care of his estates, was paid in 1743. On this visit it became so clear that business matters would require his frequent presence in England that, after much hesitation, he decided finally to return. Accordingly in June 1744 he took up his abode in his first and last home, the old manor-house of Battersea, on the south bank of the Thames.

His main activity during the nine years 1735 to 1744 was literary. His health was very bad: gout, rheumatism, low fever, haunted and harassed him, and he was able to keep going only by frequent pilgrimages to the waters of Aix, and by regular exercise in the forest of Fontainebleau and elsewhere. He was troubled, too, by the steady decline in the strength of his wife, the Marquise de Villette, to whom he had become devotedly attached. Nevertheless, in spite of anguish and anxiety, his intellect remained vigorous, and he produced some of his most important writings. He planned, and began to collect materials for, two large and impressive works, viz., a *History of Europe from 1659 to 1713*, which was to vindicate his official career, and a *Treatise on Metaphysics*, which was to define the limits of knowledge and extinguish the theologians. He was, however, incapable of the steady application required for the production of large and systematic works. Neither of these *magna opera* was ever achieved. He could labour only by jerks and in spasms. He could compose nothing which could not be expressed in the form of a series of articles, a collection of letters, or a congeries of notes. He was essentially a journalist and a jotter.

He began his second sojourn in France as he had begun his first, twenty years earlier, by seeking to drown his chagrin in a flood of platitudes let loose from the inexhaustible reservoir of Seneca's inanity. In the form of a letter to Lord Bathurst he treated of *The True Use of Retirement and Study*. Churton Collins justly remarks of this production that in it " all that is new is false, and all that is true is trite." But Mr Macknight points out that, worthless as it is, it does serve to indicate the everlasting conflict which went on in Bolingbroke between his intellect and his emotions. By passion and by prejudice he was a thorough reactionary : in mind and soul he was a pronounced revolutionary. In this letter he insists that " we ought always to be unbelieving," and that " in religion, government and philosophy we ought to distrust everything that is established." [1]   Strange doctrine, this, for a Tory !

More important and interesting was the series of eight letters addressed to Lord Cornbury on *The Study and Use of History* (1735–36). The first seven merely lead up to the eighth, which is a vindication of Bolingbroke's conduct of the peace negotiations of 1713 ; he could never get far away from politics or from himself. The earlier letters, however, incidentally contain a number of arresting observations. First, as to the true end and object of the study of history : it is ethical, viz., the training of citizens in private and public virtue. Secondly, as to the scope of historical study : ancient history both sacred and profane is valueless as a civic educator ; modern history, since the Renaissance and the Reformation, is alone useful. Finally, as to the content of this modern history : three periods can be distinguished—viz., 1500–1600, 1600–59, and from 1659 onward, of which there follows a summary account, culminating in a detailed study of the Utrecht negotiations.

This series of letters on history was followed by another long epistle, also addressed to Lord Cornbury, on *The Spirit of Patriotism* (1736). This brilliant disquisition is significant as marking a change in Bolingbroke's political programme. He was, throughout his career, always against the Whigs, even when he was attempting to destroy them by the appropriation and application of their own principles. He attacked them first (1701–15) as a Tory ; secondly (1715–16) as a Jacobite ; thirdly (1716–35) as a Coalitionist ; finally (1735–51) as a ' Patriot,' the enemy of all parties, the prophet calling for, and predicting, the advent of a monarch who should sweep away the corrupt Whig oligarchy, appoint his own ministers, and rule an emancipated people by his own beneficent will. *The Spirit of Patriotism* is instinct with indignation at the defection of the malcontent Whigs in the crisis of 1734, and quick with the consciousness of the impotence of coalitions.

[1] T. Macknight, *Life of Bolingbroke*, p. 630.

LORD BOLINGBROKE

The Idea of a Patriot King (1738) was intended to be a study supplementary to that of *The Spirit of Patriotism*. The two were issued together in 1749 by Bolingbroke himself, when it seemed to him that, with the advent of Frederick, the day of the realisation of his dream was at hand. *The Spirit of Patriotism*, he tells us, was written to set forth " the duties which men owe to their country " ; the *Patriot King* to delineate " the duties of a king to his country, of those kings particularly who are appointed by the people ; for," he adds, " I know of none who are anointed by God to rule in limited monarchies." The duties of a " Patriot King," it appears, are, first, to admit that the monarch derives his authority from his people, and to abandon all nonsensical theories of divine right ; secondly, to recognise that this authority is not absolute, but limited— limited by natural law, by the rights of his subjects, and by the customs of his realm ; thirdly, to realise that his supreme task as monarch is to establish and maintain the " free Constitution " of his kingdom, that is to say, a Constitution marked by the two outstanding features of personal liberty and national unity ; hence, fourthly, to suppress parties and factions, to reconcile antagonistic classes, and to make patriotism the dominant virtue throughout the land ; fifthly, to expel from his councils corrupt partisans (such as Walpole) and call to his side pure patriots (such as Bolingbroke) ; sixthly, to reclaim the royal prerogatives, wrongly appropriated by the Whigs, and weakly yielded by " silly kings " (such as George II) ; and, finally, to rule Britannia with the help of a subjugated Parliament and a grateful people, on sound patriotic lines, by which is implied the fostering of sea-power, the reduction of the standing army, the avoidance of foreign entanglements, and the general reversal of the policy of the Whigs. The fundamental conception of the *Patriot King* may be said to be " Back to Elizabeth." The realisation of Bolingbroke's ideal would have meant the undoing of the Revolution Settlement, the repeal of the verdict of the Civil War, and the return to the Tudor autocracy. It might be attractive to antiquarians and sentimentalists, but in the middle of the eighteenth century it was not practical politics. To the *Patriot King* he added an appendix on " The State of Parties at the Accession of King George the First," in which he defended his own conduct during the closing years of Anne's

reign; made another ferocious attack on his old *bête noire*
Harley; and blamed the fury of the Whigs in 1714–15 for
driving the Tories, including himself, into Jacobitism.

XIV

The closing years of Bolingbroke's life, 1744–51, spent
in the old manor-house at Battersea, were marked by little
activity. The health both of himself and his wife rapidly
declined. The friends of his earlier days passed away, and he
made few new ones. He found himself isolated and forlorn.
He employed himself in preparing his writings for posthumous
publication, devoting much time to the revision of some of
them, especially his *Letter to Sir William Wyndham*. He
secured the services of a certain David Mallet who commended
himself to Bolingbroke as a Deist, as an under-secretary to the
Prince of Wales, as the prospective biographer of Marlborough,
and as an enemy of Bishop Warburton—which eminent
ecclesiastic was the successor of Harley and of Walpole as
Bolingbroke's enemy-in-chief. Only two new works—neither
of them of any importance—distinguished these closing years.
One was a *Familiar Epistle* to Warburton, full of violence and
abuse, occasioned by a controversy concerning some shady
proceedings of Alexander Pope, revealed after his death in
1744. The other was entitled *Some Reflections on the Present
State of the Nation*, written after the Peace of Aix-la-Chapelle,
and left unfinished in 1749. It is an attack upon the Whig
foreign policy. It takes a very gloomy view of the situation
of Britain; expresses profound alarm at the magnitude of the
National Debt, which has reached the enormous sum of
£80,000,000; deplores the dominance of the moneyed over
the landed interest in the country; and predicts catastrophe
unless there is a reversion to peace, retrenchment, and reform.
Bolingbroke was without an inkling of the fact that Britain
was actually at the moment entering upon the most remarkable
period of prosperity—colonial expansion, commercial advance,
industrial supremacy, agricultural revival, military and naval
victory—ever known in the whole course of her long annals.
It is not amazing, however, that to one situated as Bolingbroke was the whole world should seem to be going to the bad.

He had no prospect of health or happiness in this life, and he had no belief in any life beyond the grave. His domestic felicity perished with his beloved wife in March 1750; his last political hope vanished with the death of Frederick, Prince of Wales, in March 1751; he himself was seized by virulent cancer in the summer of the same year, and he died after six months of agony on December 12, 1751.

XV

We have noted cursorily most of Bolingbroke's leading social and political ideas. It remains now merely to summarise and systematise them.

To social and political theory Bolingbroke contributed nothing. He had not the profound philosophic mind of his great disciple Burke, who was never content until he had based the practical expedient of the moment upon the solid foundation of eternal principle. Bolingbroke invented his principles to suit the exigencies of the passing day. Hence they lack consistency, homogeneity, authority. As a Tory he should have had an organic conception of the State, and on one occasion at least he seems to have gained an inkling of it. In his short paper on *The Constitution of Great Britain* he says :

> Our constitution may, in some sense, be said to be a fleeting thing, which at different times hath differed from itself, as men differ from themselves in age and youth, or in sickness and health; but still it is the same, and it is our duty to preserve it, as far as we are able, in its full strength and vigour.

Burke might well have taken this as the text of his *Reflections*. As a rule, however, Bolingbroke accepted the contractual view of the State set forth by Locke and exemplified by the Revolution of 1688–89. Thus in his *Dissertation upon Parties* (Letter XIII) he emphasises the artificial origin of political institutions, and in particular maintains that " our Constitution is in the strictest sense a bargain, a conditional contract between the prince and the people, as it always hath been, and still is, between the representative and collective bodies of the nation." Again, he accepts Hobbes's doctrine of sovereignty in one passage of his *Patriot King*: " There must be an absolute, unlimited, and uncontrollable power lodged somewhere in every government "; but usually he is concerned to dissipate sovereignty among a group of co-ordinate powers so that individual liberty may remain unimpaired.

It is not then in the region of pure theory, but in the region of applied politics, that we must look for Bolingbroke's operative ideas. In his opposition to the Whigs he passed through four phases : he was successively Tory, Jacobite, Coalitionist, and 'Patriot.' Each phase, except perhaps the second, had its own conceptions and principles of action.

Of his Tory phase (1701–15) we have but scanty literary remains. It is remarkable that, although he was admitted to have been the most superb Parliamentary orator of his day, no report of a single one of his speeches has come down to posterity. William Pitt, once commenting upon this extraordinary circumstance, proclaimed that he would rather recover one of Bolingbroke's famous orations than all the lost works of Livy or of Tacitus. We have, however, the record of his deeds, and they are eloquent of the extremest partisanship. He provided Walpole with the model upon which he framed that purely party administration which Bolingbroke attacked with such ferocious vehemence during the third and fourth phases of his career. He sought to reassert the ascendancy of the landed interest over the moneyed interest; of the country over the city; of the Church of England over Dissent ; of the navy over the army ; of the policy of splendid isolation over that of interference in Continental politics ; of the old England of the Tudors over the new England of Oliver Cromwell and William of Orange. With Machiavellian violence and unscrupulousness he did everything in his power to destroy the Whigs and to establish Toryism in perpetual possession of office.

His Jacobite phase (1715–16) was a mere aberration which—as his letter to Wyndham and all his later writings abundantly show—he never ceased to regret. His adherence to the Pretender was a false move due to the impulse of ungovernable passion—disgust at his failure and folly in 1714, resentment at his treatment by George I and the Whigs, fury at the triumph of Walpole and Townshend, Stanhope and Sunderland. The central doctrine of Jacobitism was the divine hereditary right of kings, with its corollary, the doctrine of the duty of passive obedience on the part of subjects. This doctrine Bolingbroke never so much as pretended to believe. Hence he was always an alien at the Court of the exiled Stuarts. As little did he sympathise with the mediæval theories of the relation between Church and State which were maintained by the ultramontane priests who dominated the Pretender's *entourage*. He was, in fact, wholly out of harmony with both the politics and the religion—to say nothing of the manners and the intellectual interests—of his motley associates during the tragic year 1715–16. It was a profound relief to him when the Pretender saved him from the odium of resignation by dismissing him.

The third phase of his career (1716–35) was that in which he made his appearance as a paper-politician. He had now two sets of virulent enemies to contend against—viz., Whigs and Jacobites—and he had no means of fighting them except his pen. With his pen, then, he waged a wordy battle on two fronts. As against the Jacobites he denounced the dogma of the divine right of kings, arguing that monarchs are mere magistrates deriving their authority from their subjects and having only a conditional claim to their allegiance and obedience; against them, too, he proclaimed (at the end of his letter to Wyndham) the impossibility of allowing a Catholic king to ascend the English throne. On the other hand, as against the Whigs, he maintained that the party distinctions of the days of Charles II and James II had become obsolete in 1688; that the Glorious Revolution had been effected by a coalition of Whigs and Tories; that the great object of the Revolution had been the vindication of English liberty; and that since 1714 the main peril to English liberty had come not from the royal prerogative, but from ministerial corruption. He therefore appealed for the formation of a new "Country" party, inspired by Elizabethan traditions, whose object should be to reunite the nation, emancipate the monarch, purify Parliament, dispossess placemen, purge the constituencies, and free the electorate from the spell of faction and the lure of lucre. In accordance with his appeal, he tried, as we have seen, to weld together Tories, Jacobites, and Dissentient Whigs into a coalition capable of overthrowing Walpole. By 1735 his failure was patent.

From 1735 to his death in 1751 'patriotism' was his watchword. Under cover of that term (of which Dr Johnson in his Dictionary spoke with great disrespect) he developed a theory of the English Constitution which had a profound influence upon George III and the King's friends in the late eighteenth century, and upon Benjamin Disraeli and the Young England group in the mid-nineteenth century. On the Continent it inspired the political writings of Montesquieu and Voltaire, and through them it helped to fix the principles of the American Constitution in 1789. The supreme good of man, said Bolingbroke, is personal liberty. Liberty can be retained and secured only under a Constitution in which the legislative, executive, and judiciary powers are separated from one another, and in which an accurate balance between them is established. In England, according to the spirit of its ancient polity, the supreme executive power should reside in the King in council, the supreme legislative power should be the function of the King in Parliament, and the supreme judicial power should be exercised by the King in his royal Court. The centre and bond of the Constitution is, or should be, the King. The King, too, is the head of the Church, and the Church (even though what it teaches is false) is the indispensable support of the State, and as such should be respected and maintained. In England since 1714 the balance of the Constitution has been destroyed, and consequently liberty endangered, by the decline of the royal authority. In the interest then of liberty it is necessary to revive the royal prerogative. Let the " Patriot King " once more choose his own ministers irrespective of party ; let him determine the policy of the Government ; let him nominate bishops ; let him issue royal warrants ; let him summon and dissolve Parliament at his will ; let him freely dispose of the money voted for the conduct of the administration. The strength of Bolingbroke's 'patriotism' is its plea for personal freedom ; for loyalty to the Crown ; for reverence for the Church ; for national unity ; for the subordination of the interests of party, class, and *clique* to the interest of the people as a whole. Hence, haughty and exclusive as Bolingbroke was, he is rightly regarded as the founder of the modern Tory democracy.

THE EDITOR

BIBLIOGRAPHY

A. Primary Sources

Bolingbroke : *Works,* edited by David Mallet. 5 vols. 1754. In particular: *Letter to Sir William Wyndham* (1717); *Remarks on the History of England* (1730–31); *Dissertation upon Parties* (1733–34); *Study and Use of History* (1735–36); *The Spirit of Patriotism* (1738); *The Idea of a Patriot King* (1739).

B. Secondary Sources

Butler, G. G.: *The Tory Tradition.* 1914.
Collins, J. Churton: *Bolingbroke and Voltaire.* 1886.
Cooke, G. W.: *Memoirs of Lord Bolingbroke.* 2 vols. 1835.
Harrop, R.: *Bolingbroke: a Political Study.* 1884.
Hassall, A.: *Life of Viscount Bolingbroke.* 1889; revised edition 1915.
Macknight, T.: *Life of Henry St John, Viscount Bolingbroke.* 1863.
Robertson, J. M.: *Bolingbroke and Walpole.* 1919.
Sichel, W.: *Bolingbroke and his Times.* 2 vols. 1901–2.
Stephen, L.: *History of English Thought,* vol. ii. 1881.

6647